An Introduction to Modern CBT

D1354019

DATE DUE

16/7/14	

Praise for An Introduction to Modern CBT

An Introduction to Modern CBT by internationally known researcher and clinical psychologist Stefan Hofmann is exactly the right book for the busy clinician who wants to know the latest research, how it is relevant to clinical practice, and what to do with patients who need help now. Written in a clear, compelling, and caring style, this book will be invaluable for graduate students interested in the application of empirically supported approaches—and for experienced clinicians who need to know the latest innovative CBT treatments.

Robert L. Leahy, *Director, American Institute of Cognitive Therapy, New York*

A world leader in the treatment of social phobia, Stefan Hofmann has written the ideal introductory guide to 21st century cognitive-behavior therapy. Lucid and accessible, *An Introduction to Modern CBT* will be especially valuable for students and for seasoned therapists keen to learn the latest evidence-based interventions for the most common problems therapists see today.

Richard J. McNally, *Professor of Psychology, Harvard University, and author of "What is Mental Illness?"*

An Introduction to Modern CBT

Psychological Solutions to Mental
Health Problems

Stefan G. Hofmann, Ph.D.

WILEY-BLACKWELL

A John Wiley & Sons, Ltd., Publication

This edition first published 2012
© 2012 Stefan G. Hofmann

Wiley-Blackwell is an imprint of John Wiley & Sons, formed by the merger of Wiley's global Scientific, Technical and Medical business with Blackwell Publishing.

Registered Office
John Wiley & Sons Ltd, The Atrium, Southern Gate, Chichester, West Sussex, PO19 8SQ, United Kingdom

Editorial Offices
350 Main Street, Malden, MA 02148-5020, USA
9600 Garsington Road, Oxford, OX4 2DQ, UK
The Atrium, Southern Gate, Chichester, West Sussex, PO19 8SQ, UK

For details of our global editorial offices, for customer services, and for information about how to apply for permission to reuse the copyright material in this book please see our website at www.wiley.com/wiley-blackwell.

The right of Stefan G. Hofmann to be identified as the author of this work has been asserted in accordance with the UK Copyright, Designs and Patents Act 1988.

Library of Congress Cataloging-in-Publication Data

Hofmann, Stefan G.
  An introduction to modern CBT : psychological solutions to mental health problems / Stefan G. Hofmann.
      p. cm.
  Includes bibliographical references and index.
  ISBN 978-0-470-97176-5 (cloth) – ISBN 978-0-470-97175-8 (pbk.)
 1. Cognitive therapy.   I. Title.
  RC489.C63H64 2011
  616.89′1425–dc22
                                             2011001670

A catalogue record for this book is available from the British Library.

This book is published in the following electronic formats: ePDFs 9781119973218; ePub 9781119951414; eMobi 9781119951421
Set in 11.5 on 14 pt Minion by Toppan Best-set Premedia Limited
Printed and bound in Singapore by Ho Printing Singapore Pte Ltd

1 2012

To Aaron T. Beck for his ground-breaking work that has changed the field of psychotherapy forever. His therapy has helped countless of patients with debilitating mental disorders, and his theory has been an inspiration for generations of clinicians and researchers.

Contents

About the Author

Stefan G. Hofmann, Ph.D., is Professor of Psychology at the Department of Psychology at Boston University where he directs the Psychotherapy and Emotion Research Laboratory. His main research focuses on the mechanism of treatment change, translating discoveries from neuroscience into clinical applications, emotion regulation strategies, and cultural expressions of psychopathology. His primary area of research is on cognitive behavioral therapy and anxiety disorders. His research has been supported by the National Institute of Mental Health, the National Alliance for Research on Schizophrenia and Depression, pharmaceutical companies, and other private foundations. He has written more than 200 scientific publications and nine books. He is currently an associate editor of the *Journal of Consulting and Clinical Psychology,* the former editor of *Cognitive and Behavioral Practice*, a Board member of the Academy of Cognitive Therapy, and an advisor to the DSM-V Development Process. He also works as a psychotherapist using cognitive behavioral therapy. For more information, visit http://www.bostonanxiety.org/.

Foreword

Cognitive therapy is an evolving field. After an initially stormy adolescent period, it has now moved into the stage of maturity. Although pharmacotherapy has proven beneficial, it may have reached its limits, making it clearer that there will likely never be a "magic pill" for every psychiatric condition. Consequently, it has become apparent that psychotherapeutic interventions are needed to effectively treat the range of mental disorders.

A number of disorder-specific cognitive therapy protocols have been developed over the years. These treatments target many different problems, including pain, sleep disorders, sexual dysfunctions, depression, anxiety, and substance use, to name only a few. Despite the various specific symptom focus of these cognitive therapy protocols, they all share features that ground them within the same conceptual framework. The basic approach of cognitive therapy, which applies to virtually all mental disorders, can be separated into three parts: first, there are external triggers that activate maladaptive beliefs that subsequently lead to automatic, maladaptive thoughts; second, there is an attentional focus on these beliefs and thoughts; and third, there are maladaptive control mechanisms. For example, in the case of panic disorder, the external trigger may be feelings of heart palpitations. The person's belief may be that the bodily symptoms are harmful and uncontrollable. In an attempt to control these feelings, the person may engage in avoidance behaviors that serve as maladaptive control mechanisms. These control mechanisms worsen the problem. As a result, the person is compelled to focus even more on the feared symptoms and engage in more avoidance behaviors that lead to the further maintenance of the problem.

A number of treatment techniques arise from the adoption of this triad in the conceptualization of mental dysfunction. For instance, the therapist can identify and evaluate maladaptive beliefs, target maladaptive control mechanisms, and address attentional focus by, for example, encouraging the person to focus his or her attention on to other, nonthreatening stimuli.

The present book has adapted these fundamental principles of cognitive therapy to a wide range of mental disorders. Although the specific treatment techniques are very specific and tailored to a particular problem and patient, all techniques are grounded on the same basic treatment model. I believe this text will be a valuable resource for therapists in training and a handy reference tool for the practicing clinician.

Aaron T. Beck, M.D.
Professor of Psychiatry
Department of Psychiatry
University of Pennsylvania

Acknowledgment

It is impossible to thank everybody who has helped me develop this book. Therefore, the list of people that follows is necessarily incomplete and arbitrary. First and foremost, I would like to thank my wife Dr. Rosemary Toomey and my sons Benjamin and Lukas for their support and love. Next, I want to thank my patients for their courage, trust, insight, and willingness to share their personal suffering, and for making me part of the healing experience. Personally witnessing the power of healing teaches more than any lecture or textbook can do, including this one. I also want to thank my teachers, friends, and collaborators who are the giants upon whose shoulders I have been standing while writing this book. These include Drs. Aaron T. Beck, Leslie Sokol, Anke Ehlers, Walton T. Roth, C. Barr Taylor, David H. Barlow, Michael W. Otto, and Richard J. McNally. Your ideas have made this world a better place. Finally, I want to thank my current students and collaborators for proofreading parts of this book, including (in alphabetical order) Dr. Idan Aderka, Anu Asnaani, Hans-Jakob Boer, Jacqueline Bullis, Michelle Capozzoli, Angela Fang, Cassidy Gutner, Dr. Angela Nickerson, and Alice (Ty) Sawyer. I am fully aware of how lucky I am for having had the privilege to work with these wonderful friends, superb mentors, excellent students, and remarkable patients.

Preface

Mind over Matter: If you don't have a mind, what does it matter?
        —Benjamin Franklin Impersonator, Boston, Massachusetts

Psychiatric disorders are common and cause a high degree of personal suffering and financial burden on society. Psychotropic drugs are common treatments for these problems. These medications are among the most successful products of a highly profitable industry.

Psychological treatments, and in particular cognitive behavioral therapy (CBT), are highly effective alternatives to drug treatments. CBT is a very simple, intuitive, and transparent treatment. It encompasses a family of interventions that share the same basic idea, namely that cognitions profoundly and causally influence emotions and behaviors and, thereby, contribute to the maintenance of psychiatric problems. The specific model and treatment techniques depend on the disorder that is targeted, and the techniques change as more is known about the targeted problem. This book will give an introduction to the modern CBT approach for some common psychiatric problems. Although CBT has become well known, there are still many misconceptions and "cognitive errors" (no pun intended) regarding this treatment, which is well on its way to becoming the dominant treatment for psychiatric disorders. My intention is to summarize the established empirically supported and efficacious CBT strategies, as well as modern and developing CBT approaches that still require validation from well-controlled clinical trials and laboratory tests.

The main message of this text is simple: CBT is a coherent model, but it is not one single approach. Because CBT is evolving and changing as more knowledge is accumulating, it is more accurate to view it as a maturing scientific discipline rather than as an assembly of specific treatment techniques. The reason for this is the strong commitment to the scientific enterprise and openness to translating and integrating new empirical findings about the psychopathology of a disorder into a working CBT model of the disorder.

This is an ongoing and iterative process; for example, CBT for anxiety disorders 10 years ago looked very different from CBT for such disorders today. Although the core assumption of CBT remains the same—changes in cognitions causally predict changes in psychopathology—the specific treatment techniques have certainly changed and will continue to change as basic research on psychopathology progresses.

My hope is that this book will facilitate dissemination of CBT. Studies comparing CBT and pharmacotherapy consistently demonstrate that CBT is at least as effective as pharmacotherapy, and in many instances, CBT proves even better than the most effective medications, especially when considering the long-term effects. In addition, CBT is much better tolerated, less expensive, and associated with fewer complications than pharmacotherapy. Nevertheless, pharmacotherapy remains the standard treatment for common psychiatric problems.

There are many reasons why CBT is still struggling to be the first-line treatment, or at least the first-line alternative, for a variety of psychiatric problems. Drug companies have a vested interest in promoting and selling their medication, because a great deal of money can be made by treating people with medication, and a large number of people earn a great deal of money by developing and selling drugs: researchers who develop the drugs, researchers and sales people who work for the pharmaceutical industry, and the doctors and nurses who prescribe the drugs. In contrast, CBT is considerably less lucrative. These treatments are typically developed by psychologists as part of their research projects. If the researcher is lucky, he or she may receive a grant from the National Institute of Mental Health to test the effectiveness of the treatment. However, these grants are scarce and extremely difficult to obtain. Furthermore, the funding that is provided for those trials is a far cry from the profits of the billion dollar drug industry. My hope is that this book can help to disseminate CBT to an educated public.

Pharmacological treatments are often preferred over psychological interventions due to the stigma associated with psychotherapy. Taking a pill for a problem implies that the problem is linked to a medical condition. This also shifts the presumed reason for a problem from the patient's behavior or maladaptive thinking to the biochemical imbalance and thereby relieves the patient from responsibility. Tying psychiatric problems to biochemical dysregulations is also consistent with the general medical model of human suffering and gives the appearance that the medication treats the root cause of the problem. Mental health care specialists know that this is far from the truth, as psychological models provide an equally (and sometimes more) plausible and scientifically validated explanation for psychiatric problems.

This book will provide the readers with these contemporary psychological models.

Finally, the preference for pharmacotherapy over psychological treatments appears to be related to the erroneous assumption that pharmacotherapy has a superior scientific foundation compared with psychological treatments. Psychiatric medications undergo years and sometimes decades of research to establish safety and efficacy. These tests typically begin with animal research and later examine the effects of the drug in humans. In contrast, the process of psychological treatment development is largely unknown to the public. In this book, I aim to clarify this process and to summarize the empirical basis of psychological treatment development.

This book is primarily for the students and clinicians in training, as well as the policymakers and consumers who want to learn about effective psychological treatment options. My intention was not to write yet another self-help book. Instead, my goal was to provide a one-step practical treatment guide for some of the most common and debilitating psychiatric conditions to those who wish to learn about psychological treatment alternatives for common mental disorders. The choice of disorders covered in this text was arbitrary and many important disorders were not included, such as eating disorders, personality disorders, and psychotic disorders. Moreover, I have not compiled an exhaustive review of the CBT literature, but rather, provide the reader with snapshots of some established and developing CBT models and approaches. The book is intended to present a coherent introduction that is practically oriented and that captures some of the established as well as newer, evolving techniques of CBT. Personally, I will use this text when training and supervising clinicians and as a way to refresh my own knowledge of CBT for a particular disorder. I hope you, the reader, will do the same.

Stefan G. Hofmann, Ph.D.
Boston, Massachusetts

1 The Basic Idea

Joe

Joe is a 45-year-old car salesman. He and his wife Mary live in a suburban home just outside Boston. They have two children, ages 9 and 12. The family had been doing well financially until Joe was laid off 3 months ago. Mary had been working part-time as a receptionist for a dentist and was able to upgrade this to a full-time job once her husband was out of work. Her income is enough to make ends meet, at least for now.

Since Joe was laid off, he has been staying home. He helps to get the kids ready for school, but then goes back to bed and stays there until 1 or sometimes 2 in the afternoon. He watches TV until his kids and wife come home. Sometimes, he doesn't even have the energy to do that. He feels worthless and believes he will never find a job again. Mary cares deeply for Joe. Although his lack of motivation has created some conflict around doing household chores and cooking, she does whatever she can to make him feel better. However, the added responsibilities are at times burdensome for Mary.

Joe is depressed. He often struggles with his mood, motivation, and energy. But this time, his depression is more severe than usual. Getting laid off from his job apparently triggered the onset of a major depression. Anyone would be upset and sad after being laid off. But in Joe's case, the level and duration of the sadness are clearly outside the normal range. This is not the first time Joe has felt like this. Shortly after the birth of his second son, he slipped into a period of severe depression that lasted for almost a year. There was no clear trigger, aside from having a second

---

An Introduction to Modern CBT: Psychological Solutions to Mental Health Problems, First Edition.
S. G. Hofmann. © 2012 S. G. Hofmann. Published 2012 by John Wiley & Sons, Ltd.

child. He was so depressed that he even thought about suicide by hanging himself. Fortunately, he did not act on these thoughts. He has tried various medications for his depression, but he did not find them to be helpful and did not like the side effects they caused.

Mary recently read about a form of talk therapy in a magazine. The therapy is called *cognitive behavioral therapy* (CBT). She was very excited and decided that Joe should try it. When she came home that day, she asked Joe to read the article in the magazine. Joe did not think that it could help him. The couple got into an unusually heated argument, and Mary made Joe promise that he would try this treatment. Mary arranged for an appointment with a psychologist in Boston who specializes in CBT.

During the course of sixteen 1-hour CBT sessions, Joe's depression lifted. By the end of treatment, it had virtually disappeared. He developed a positive outlook on his life and a positive attitude toward himself. His relationship with his wife and children improved dramatically, and he started a new job as a car salesman within weeks after starting therapy.

Joe's recovery after treatment is not at all unusual. The treatment that he received, cognitive behavioral therapy (CBT), is a highly effective, short-term form of psychotherapy for a wide range of serious psychological problems, including depression, anxiety disorders, alcohol problems, pain, and sleep problems, among many other conditions. The CBT strategies that target some of these common disorders are described in detail in the following chapters. The current chapter will review the guiding principles on which these disorder-specific strategies are based.

The Founding Fathers

Aaron T. Beck and Albert Ellis independently developed the therapy that later became known as CBT. Beck was trained in Freudian psychoanalysis and became dissatisfied with the lack of empirical support for Freudian ideas. In his work with depressed patients, Beck found that people who were depressed reported streams of negative thoughts that seemed to appear spontaneously. Beck called these cognitions *automatic thoughts*. These thoughts are based on general, overarching core beliefs, called *schemas* (or *schemata*) that the person has about oneself, the world, and the future. These schemas determine how a person may interpret a specific situation and thereby give rise to specific automatic thoughts. These specific automatic thoughts contribute to the maladaptive cognitive appraisal of the situation or event, leading to an emotional response. Based on this general model, Beck developed a treatment method to help patients identify and evaluate these thoughts and higher-order beliefs in order to encourage patients to think more realistically, to behave more functionally, and to feel better psychologically.

Like Beck, Ellis was trained in Freudian psychoanalysis, but later became influenced by the neo-Freudian Karen Horney. Similarly to Beck's, Ellis's treatment approach emphasizes the importance of cognitive processes and is an active and directive form of psychotherapy. Therapists help patients realize that their own beliefs contribute greatly to, maintain, and even cause their psychological problems. This approach leads patients to realize the irrationality and rigidity of their thinking and encourages them to actively change self-defeating beliefs and behaviors. Ellis initially named the treatment Rational Therapy, then Rational-Emotive Therapy, and finally Rational-Emotive Behavior Therapy to stress the interrelated importance of cognition, behavior, and emotion. Beck prefers the term *maladaptive* or *dysfunctional,* rather than *irrational,* to describe the nature of the distorted cognitions, since thoughts do not have to be irrational in order to be maladaptive. For example, some people with depression might have a more realistic assessment of the potential danger in life. However, this "depressive realism" is maladaptive because it interferes with normal life.

Sadly, Dr. Ellis passed away on July 24, 2007. Dr. Beck, now well into his 90s, is still an active practitioner and scientist with an insatiable thirst for knowledge. Beck and Ellis, who developed their two therapy approaches in the 1960s, have had an enormous influence on contemporary clinical psychology and psychiatry. In the face of the overwhelming dominance of psychoanalytic thinking, these two pioneers began to question some fundamental assumptions of psychiatry. Driven by their intuition that human problems are best solved by human solutions, Beck and Ellis began to use empirical methods to treat psychological problems and to critically study uncomfortable questions in psychiatry. Ellis, a practicing psychologist, set up his clinic in downtown Manhattan. Like many other places at that time, New York was heavily dominated by psychoanalysis. Similarly, Beck, an academic psychiatrist at the University of Pennsylvania, continued to pursue his quest in the face of strong resistance by the general psychiatric community, which was dominated by Freudian ideas. When he applied for research grants to test his ideas and was rejected, he assembled friends and colleagues to conduct his studies without financial support from the government or other funding agencies. When his papers were rejected by academic journals, he convinced open-minded editors to publish his writing in the form of books.

In recognition of his influence, Beck received the Lasker Award in 2006, a highly prestigious medical prize that is often bestowed on individuals who later win the Nobel Prize. The chairman of the Lasker jury noted that "cognitive therapy is one of the most important advances—if not the most important advance—in the treatment of mental diseases in the last 50 years" (Altman, 2006).

Despite the clear influence of the approach and the effectiveness of the treatment, the majority of people with psychological problems do not have easy access to CBT services. Unlike that involved with psychiatric medications, there is no sizable industry promoting CBT. In an attempt to increase the availability of CBT, politicians in some countries have decided to not let the fate of mental health care be ruled by the financial interest of drug companies and have taken matters into their own hands. In October 2007, the Health Secretary of the United Kingdom announced a plan to spend £300 million ($600 million) to initiate a six-year program with the goal of training an army of therapists to provide the British people with CBT for psychological problems. This change in health care delivery was based on economic data showing that provision of CBT for common mental disorders is overall less expensive than pharmacotherapy or psychoanalysis. Similarly, in 1996 the Australian government recommended the provision of CBT and introduced a plan to provide better access to these services.

A Simple and Powerful Idea

Although Beck and Ellis are rightly credited for their pioneering work, the basic idea that gave rise to the new approach to psychotherapy is certainly not new. It could even be argued that it is simply common sense turned into practice. Perhaps the earliest expression of the CBT idea dates back to Epictetus, a Greek stoic philosopher who lived from AD 55 to 134. He has been credited with saying, "Men are not moved by things, but by the view they take of them." Later, Marcus Aurelius (AD 121–180) wrote in his Meditations, "If thou are pained by any external thing, it is not this thing that disturbs thee, but thine own judgment about it. And it is in thy power to wipe out this judgment now." And William Shakespeare wrote in Hamlet, "There is nothing either good or bad, but thinking makes it so." Other philosophers, artists, and poets have expressed similar ideas throughout history.

The central notion of CBT is simple. It is the idea that our behavioral and emotional responses are strongly influenced by our cognitions (i.e., thoughts), which determine how we perceive things. That is, we are only anxious, angry, or sad if we think that we have reason to be anxious, angry, or sad. In other words, it is not the situation per se, but rather our perceptions, expectations, and interpretations (i.e., the cognitive appraisal) of events that are responsible for our emotions. This might be best explained by the following example provided by Beck (1976):

The housewife (Beck, 1976, pp. 234–235)

A housewife hears a door slam. Several hypotheses occur to her: "It may be Sally returning from school." "It might be a burglar." "It might be the wind that blew the door shut." The favored hypothesis should depend on her taking into account all the relevant circumstances. The logical process of hypothesis testing may be disrupted, however, by the housewife's psychological set. If her thinking is dominated by the concept of danger, she might jump to the conclusion that it is a burglar. She makes an arbitrary inference. Although such an inference is not necessarily incorrect, it is based primarily on internal cognitive processes rather than actual information. If she then runs and hides, she postpones or forfeits the opportunity to disprove (or confirm) the hypothesis.

Thus, the same initial event (hearing the slamming of the door) elicits very different emotions, depending on how she interprets the situational context. The door slam itself does not elicit any emotions one way or the other. But when the housewife believes that the door slam suggests that there is a burglar in the house, she experiences fear. She might jump to this conclusion more readily if she is somehow primed after having read about burglaries in the paper, or if she has the core belief (schema) that the world is a dangerous place and that it is only a matter of time until a burglar will enter her house. Her behavior, of course, would be very different if she felt fear than if she thought that the event had no significant meaning. This is what Epictetus meant when he said that "men are not moved by things, but by the view they take of them." Using more modern terminology, we can say that it is the cognitive appraisal of the situation or event which determines our response to it, including behaviors, physiological symptoms, and subjective experience.

Beck calls these assumptions about events and situations *automatic thoughts,* because the thoughts arise without much prior reflection or reasoning (1976). Ellis refers to these assumptions as *self-statements,* because they are ideas that the person tells him- or herself (1962). These self-statements interpret the events in the external world and trigger the emotional and behavioral responses to these events. This relationship is illustrated in Ellis's ABC model, in which A stands for the antecedent event (the door slam), B stands for belief ("it must be a burglar"), and C stands for consequence (fear). B may also stand for *blank* because the thought can occur so quickly and automatically that the person acts almost reflexively to the activating event, without critical reflection. If the cognition is not in the center of the person's awareness, it can be difficult to identify it, which is the reason why Beck refers to this as an *automatic* thought. In this case, the person has to carefully observe the sequence of events and the response to them, and then explore the underlying belief system. Therefore, CBT often requires the patient to act as a detective or a scientist who is trying to find the missing pieces of the puzzle (i.e., to fill in the blanks).

Despite differences in the terminology they used, Beck and Ellis independently developed very similar treatment approaches. The idea underlying their methods is that distorted cognitions are at the center of psychological problems. These cognitions are considered distorted because they are misperceptions and misinterpretations of situations and events, typically do not reflect reality, are maladaptive, and lead to emotional distress, behavior problems, and physiological arousal. The specific patterns of physiological symptoms, emotional distress, and dysfunctional behaviors that result from this process are interpreted as syndromes of mental disorders.

Initiating versus Maintaining Factors

The reason a psychological problem develops in the first place is usually not the same as the reason the problem is maintained. It may be interesting to know why a problem developed in the first place, but this information is relatively unimportant for treatment in the context of CBT. Knowing the initiating factors provides neither necessary nor sufficient information for treatment. A simple medical example may illustrate this point: there are many ways to break an arm. One may fall down the stairs in one's house, get into a skiing accident, or get hit by a car. When we see a doctor, he or she may ask how it happened out of curiosity, but the information is rather unimportant for selecting the appropriate treatment—putting the arm in a cast.

Obviously, psychological problems are considerably more complex than a broken arm. In Joe's case, for example, more than one single reason led to his depression. He apparently had a tendency to be depressed. When he got laid off from work, he was unable to deal with the stress. However, many people get laid off from work, but only a minority develops depression. Others do not develop depression, but experience substance use problems, anxiety disorders, or sexual problems. In other words, the same stressor can have vastly different effects on different people. Most people cope with it without experiencing any long-lasting consequences. In only a minority of people does the stressor lead to psychological problems, and when it does, the same stressor is rarely associated with a specific psychological problem. A notable exception is post-traumatic stress disorder (PTSD), in which case a horrific event outside of everyday human experiences—such as a psychological trauma caused by a rape, war experience, or an accident—is specifically linked to the development of a characteristic syndrome of psychological problems. However, even in those extreme cases, only a minority of people will experience PTSD. In most cases, stressors have rather unspecific effects on psychological disturbances, if they have any effect at all.

Whether a stressor leads to a particular psychological problem is determined by the vulnerability of the person to developing this problem. This vulnerability, in turn, is primarily determined by one's genetic predisposition for developing a specific problem. This so-called diathesis-stress model of psychopathology is a generally recognized theory of how psychological problems develop in the first place. However, determining which of the more than 20,000 protein-coding genes predispose some individuals to psychological problems is a task for future generations of researchers. Even if we knew the identity and combinations of those genes, it would be very difficult to predict who will and will not develop a psychological problem; in addition to the person's genetic makeup, we would need to know if or when the person will be exposed to certain stressors and whether or not the individual will be able to deal with the stressors. To complicate the matter even further, the evolving field of epigenetics suggests that environmental experiences can lead to the expression or deactivation of certain genes, and these changes not only lead to long-term changes in traits within an individual, but it might also be transmitted to later generations. This highlights the importance of learning and experience, the process that occurs in CBT, for psychopathology within and between generations.

In most cases of psychological problems, initiating and maintaining factors are very different, because the reason a problem developed in the first place is often unrelated, or only tangentially related, to the reason the problem persists. In Joe's case, for example, the depression was to a great extent maintained by his self-deprecating thoughts, his inactivity, and his excessive sleeping. Note that psychiatrists generally consider self-deprecating thoughts, inactivity, and excessive sleeping to be symptoms of his depression, whereas CBT therapists believe that these factors are partly responsible for his depression, and that Joe has the power to change them.

CBT in Psychiatry

CBT is a highly effective strategy for dealing with many psychological problems. In fact, CBT is at least as effective as medication for the problems that will be discussed in this book. Furthermore, CBT is not associated with any side effects, and can be practiced without any risks for an unlimited period of time. The goal of CBT is to change maladaptive ways of thinking and acting in order to improve psychological well-being. In this context, it is important to explain the term *maladaptive*. This goes to the heart of the definition of mental disorders. Psychiatrists and psychologists alike have been engaged in a long, heated, and still ongoing battle over the way to best define a mental disorder. Jerome Wakefield (1992) offered a popular contemporary definition of mental disorder. He defines it as a *harmful dysfunction*. It is harmful because the problem has negative consequences for the person and also because the dysfunction is negatively viewed by society. It is a dysfunction because having the problem means that the person cannot perform a natural function as designed by evolution (for a critical discussion, see McNally, 2011).

Some of the most extreme positions in this debate question whether mental disorders even exist. One of the earliest and most vocal proponents of this position was Thomas Szasz (1961). Szasz views psychiatric disorders as essentially arbitrary and manmade constructions formed by society with no clear empirical basis. He argues that psychological problems, such as depression, panic disorder, and schizophrenia, are simply labels attached to normal human experiences by society. The same experiences that are labeled as a disease in one culture or at one point in history may be considered normal or even desirable in another culture or at another point in history.

Proponents of CBT acknowledge that culture contributes to the expression of a disorder, but they disagree with the view that human suffering is simply a made-up construction by society. Instead, CBT conceptualizes psychiatric disorders as real human problems that can be treated with real human solutions. At the same time, CBT is critical of the excessive medicalization of human experiences. In CBT, it is not important whether or not a psychological problem that interferes with normal functioning is labeled as a psychiatric disease. The names of mental disorders come and go, and the criteria used to define a specific mental disorder are arbitrary and manmade. But human suffering, emotional distress, behavioral problems, and cognitive distortions are real. Regardless of what the name for the human suffering is—or whether there is even a name for it—CBT helps the affected person to understand and alleviate the suffering.

On the other extreme is the view that mental disorders are distinct medical entities. Psychoanalytically oriented clinicians believe that these disorders are rooted in deep-seated conflicts. Based on Freudian thinking, these conflicts are typically considered to result from repression (e.g., suppression) of unwanted thoughts, desires, impulses, feelings, or wishes. For example, the conflict in Joe might be considered to be rooted in his relationships with his mother or father, and his depressed mood might be seen as a result of anger toward them that is turned inward toward himself. More modern psychoanalysts, who often identify themselves as insight-oriented or psychodynamic psychotherapists, might place a greater emphasis on existing or unresolved interpersonal conflicts, compared to Freudian therapists, who focus on experiences during early childhood. For example, modern psychodynamic therapists might see Joe's depression as a result of unresolved grief from a lost relationship to a significant person, such as his father or mother. The problem with these ideas is that even after more than 100 years of psychoanalysis, there is almost no scientific support for them.

Instead of delving into the past to uncover any early parent-child relationship conflicts that might have caused the problem, CBT primarily focuses on the here and now, unless the past is clearly causing the present. For example, Joe's recent layoff, his previous attempts to deal with depression, and any events that happened in the past and that might have contributed to the present are important. However, unlike psychodynamic therapy, CBT is not based on a preconceived notion that Joe's current depression must be related to unresolved conflicts with his father, mother, or any other attachment figure, or that Joe's depression is an expression of an elusive energy that is turned against himself. Instead, CBT takes a scientific and exploratory approach in trying to understand human suffering. In doing so, the patient is seen as an expert who has the ability to change the problem, not as a helpless victim.

Biologically oriented psychiatrists believe that psychological disorders are biological entities. Proponents of this perspective believe that mental disorders are causally linked to particular biological factors, such as dysfunctions in certain brain regions and an imbalance of neurotransmitters.

Neurotransmitters are molecules that transmit signals from one nerve cell to another. For example, serotonin is a neurotransmitter that is involved in feelings of anxiety and depression. Many biologically oriented psychiatrists today believe that a deficiency of serotonin is the cause of many emotional disorders. The specific brain area that has received the most research attention is the amygdala, a small, almond-shaped structure located inside the brain. With advancements in genetic technology, some researchers are trying to locate specific genes that contributed to psychological problems. CBT acknowledges the importance of biology in psychological problems and human suffering. However, finding the biological substrate of a feeling does not explain the feeling. We are simply shifting the question of what causes an emotion from a psychological level to a biological level. The actual reason for the emotional distress remains unknown. This fact is often difficult to accept. To illustrate this issue, let us consider another, perhaps more obvious example. We can develop headaches for many different reasons. Examples may include hangovers, sleep deprivation, and caffeine withdrawal, to name only a few. Aspirin is an analgesic drug that can help in all of these cases. One could argue that aspirin works because our body needs it; that the headache pain is caused by some sort of aspirin deficiency syndrome, and that if our body does not get enough aspirin, it will give us a headache (no pun intended). Alternatively, it could be argued that aspirin acts by blocking the production of prostaglandins, leading to a general analgesic effect (which appears to be the mechanism of action). Alternative methods to treat the same headache may include drinking a Bloody Mary (in the hangover case), taking a nap (in the case of sleep deprivation), or getting a double espresso (in the case of caffeine withdrawal).

Similarly, some people feel less depressed when taking drugs that prolong the action of the naturally released serotonin. An example is the popular drug Prozac, which is a part of a drug class called selective serotonin reuptake inhibitors (SSRIs). As in the case of aspirin for headaches, we cannot conclude that depression is *caused* by a deficit of serotonin. But it is fair to say that depression and serotonin levels are related, and that taking an SSRI can help lift the depression. However, other methods for treating depression are also possible because taking an SSRI for depression is not the only way to lift depression, and Prozac does not work for everybody with depression. As in Joe's case in the vignette, some people dislike the side effects of the medication, or they want to stop taking the medication for other reasons. The literature on combining traditional pharmacotherapy and CBT has been rather disappointing in that adding traditional pharmacotherapy only adds very little, if anything, to CBT. Some studies even report that adding a sugar pill to CBT is more effective than a combination treatment of CBT and a standard antianxiety medication (Barlow *et al.,* 2000). The reason for these curious results is not completely clear. It is possible that state-dependent learning plays a role because the learning that occurs during CBT while under the influence of a psychogeneic agent is of a different state when the patient is asked to retrieve this information as compared to that which happens when the patient is no longer under the influence of the medication. Another possible reason is an attribution effect, in which the patient is likely to attribute the gains to an active medication and discontinuing this medication may thereby increase his expectation and subsequently also his risk of relapse. In contrast, placebo pills are often correctly identified as such by patients, leading the patient to attribute the gains to CBT. Another more recent strategy that my colleagues and I have investigated in recent years is to augment CBT with a cognitive enhancer (d-cycloserine), which appears to facilitate the learning that occurs during CBT. Since the first positive trial that was conducted in patients with height phobia (Ressler *et al.,* 2004), a considerable body of evidence has accumulated, telling a remarkably consistent and highly promising story (for a review, see Hofmann, 2007b; Norberg *et al.,* 2008). The purpose of this text, however, is to present contemporary CBT approaches for a variety of disorders. Combination strategies will only be mentioned peripherally.

Focus on Emotions

For the past two decades, the entire field of psychology has clearly been experiencing a shift into research on emotions and affect. The formation of the discipline *affective neuroscience* is certainly a telling example. It is a relatively new subdiscipline of psychology that examines the biological correlates of affective states and emotions. Other signs for the popularity of this topic area include the creation of the journal *Emotion* and the publication of *The Emotional Brain* by Joseph LeDoux (1996). This book was written by a frontline neuroscientist and became a very popular text even among the general public. The theories and studies in affective neuroscience were particularly eye-opening to many CBT theorists, including myself, because it provided a biological framework to explain why CBT strategies are effective for regulating emotions—and how to further improve them.

Emotions have always occupied a central element of CBT. Contrary to a common misconception, CBT is not at all limited to changes in thinking and behaviors. Instead, the central notion of CBT is the idea that our emotional responses are strongly moderated and influenced by our cognitions and the way in which we perceive the world, ourselves, other people, and the future. Therefore, changing the appraisal of an object, event, or situation can also change the associated emotional response. Since the first patients were treated by Beck and Ellis, CBT has evolved into a scientific enterprise which has had an unprecedented impact on the field of psychotherapy. In contrast to other psychotherapeutic approaches, CBT has embraced the scientific method and opened itself up to empirical scrutiny. Basic assumptions about the treatment model have been taken into the laboratory and empirically tested. Moreover, as laboratory research has accumulated new knowledge about specific disorders, CBT-oriented therapists have developed more tailored techniques to treat specific psychological problems. Very early on in its development, CBT was rigorously tested in clinical trials, which were previously the domain of pharmaceutical research. Initially, specific CBT approaches for clearly identified problems (depression, social anxiety disorder, etc.) were compared to waitlist control groups (i.e., patients who did not receive the treatment and simply waited for the same period of time that the treatment lasted) and to psychological placebo conditions (i.e., general psychotherapy that does not include the specific CBT techniques or a sugar pill that looks like a real medication). Later, CBT was compared to the most effective psychiatric medications in randomized placebo-controlled studies. These studies are the most rigorous way to study the effectiveness of a treatment because participants are randomly assigned to either the active treatment (CBT or pharmacotherapy) or a placebo condition. The placebo effect in psychiatry is remarkably strong. Between 30 and 40% of patients suffering from psychological disorders recover from their problems after taking an inactive sugar pill. Even when using highly rigorous standards, the results are remarkably reliable. Time and again, CBT has been shown to be clearly more effective than placebo therapy and as effective, and sometimes even more effective, than the most effective forms of pharmacotherapy.

Today, CBT is an umbrella term that includes many different empirically supported therapies that share the basic CBT principles. However, CBT is not a one-size-fits-all treatment. There are clear differences in the specific strategies for targeting specific problems. But despite the differences in the CBT conceptualizations of and approach to treating these different psychological problems, the strategies are firmly rooted within the basic CBT approach—namely, that maladaptive cognitions are causally linked to emotions, behaviors, and physiology, and that correcting maladaptive cognitions results in the elimination of psychological problems and greater general well-being. Strong scientific evidence for this general model has come from the field of affective neuroscience and emotion regulation research.

Neurobiology of Emotions

Recent neuroscience research has been able to link these cognitive processes with specific brain activities. Based on experimental research with animals, LeDoux and others have argued that the amygdala in particular, a small, almond-shaped structure in the center of the brain, is crucially important for processing and expressing emotions. LeDoux's model assumes that emotional cues are processed in two different ways, which differ in the speed and depth of processing. For example, let's assume you are hiking somewhere and you see an object that looks like a large snake. LeDoux's model states that this information is processed in two different ways. First, the visual information of this object goes to the visual thalamus, which is the central relay station of the visual sensory input and then directly to the amygdala, which has close connections to the autonomic nervous system. Because the information resembles a snake, the amygdala becomes activated, leading to an immediate fight-or-flight response with little conscious awareness. LeDoux named this process the *low road* to the amygdala. He referred to this as the low road because the process happens without higher cortical involvement. In addition to this subcortical process, it is assumed that the information is also sent from the thalamus to the visual cortex that then further processes the information. If the object only looks like a live snake, but it is in fact a stick or a dead snake, higher cortical processes then inhibit the activation of the amygdala, suppressing the initial fight-or-flight response. Because this path to the amygdala involves higher cortical centers, LeDoux referred to it as the *high road* to the amygdala. This model is compatible with CBT, because the cognitive processes, which require higher cortical functions, may inhibit subcortical brain areas that are evolutionarily more primitive.

One can imagine that it is not easy to study the biological mechanisms or even correlates of CBT, because many factors influence the treatment process, including but not limited to the patient's motivation, the empathy by the therapist, and the relationship between the therapist and the patient. However, it is possible to isolate and study specific components of CBT, such as cognitive reappraisal. Those studies are beginning to appear and they provide general support for this notion. For example, Ochsner and colleagues (2002) presented neutral pictures (e.g., a lamp) or negatively valenced pictures (e.g., a mutilated body) to some healthy women while they were lying in an fMRI scanner that measured subjects' brain activation. The women were instructed to view the picture and fully experience any emotional response it might elicit. The picture remained on the screen for an additional period of time with the instructions either to simply look at it or to reappraise the stimulus. As part of the reappraisal instructions, the women were asked to reinterpret the negative picture so that it no longer generated the negative emotional response (e.g., the picture of the mutilated body is part of a horror movie that is not real). As predicted by LeDoux's model, reappraisal of the negative pictures reduced their negative affect and was associated with increased activity in higher cortical structures (including the dorsal and ventral regions of the left lateral prefrontal cortex and the dorsal medial prefrontal cortex) and decreased activity in the amygdala. Furthermore, increased activation in the ventrolateral prefrontal cortex was correlated with decreased activation in the amygdala, suggesting that this part of the prefrontal cortex may play an important role in conscious and voluntary regulation of emotional processes.

Emotion Regulation Strategies

Emotion regulation is the process by which people influence which emotions they have, when they have them, and how they experience and express these emotions. Gross and colleagues (Gross, 2002; Gross and Levenson, 1997) have conducted a number of well-designed experiments which demonstrated that it is possible to willfully change one's emotional response, including the physiological response, depending on the approach one takes to deal with the emotional material. In a typical experiment, healthy subjects are asked to view different pictures. Some of these pictures (e.g., that of an amputated human hand) might elicit very strong negative reactions in all people, such as feelings of disgust. During the experiment, we might measure subjects' psychophysiological response before, during and some time after viewing these pictures. When using such a paradigm, Gross and colleagues observed that simply giving participants different instructions on what to do when viewing these pictures can have a dramatic effect on their subjective and physiological response. A very effective strategy is reappraisal. For example, if we can find alternative, less distressing explanations, the information (picture, event, etc.) results in less negative emotions. In contrast, when subjects are asked to suppress their emotions when viewing the pictures by behaving in a way in which nobody would be able to tell how they are feeling, it increases the subjective distress and raises psychophysiological arousal as compared to people who do not attempt to suppress their emotions.

This may appear to be counterintuitive, but it is consistent with a large number of studies demonstrating the paradoxical effects of suppression: the harder we try not to be bothered by something, the more this something is bothering us, whether they are feelings, thoughts, images, or events in our surrounding environment (such as a dripping water faucet or the ticking of a clock). This phenomenon has been studied by Daniel Wegner who has developed the White Bear experiment to illustrate this point (Wegner, 1994). The experiment is very simple and reliably effective: Picture a fluffy, white bear. Now think for 1 minute about anything you like, except the fluffy white bear. Every time the white bear pops into your mind, count it. How many white bears popped up? A white bear typically does not create an intrusive image, unless there was a personal experience with a white bear in the person's life, especially if this experience was emotional. Obviously, this experiment works even better if we choose personally meaningful or emotionally valenced thoughts or images. In this small experiment, the reason why a neutral image of a white bear became an intrusive image was simply because of the attempt to suppress it. The reason for this paradoxical effect is obviously related to the cognitive activity that is required in order to suppress it. In order to not think about something, we have to monitor our cognitive processes. As part of this monitoring process, we focus on this very thing that we are trying not to focus on, which leads to the paradox and, when done regularly, could potentially lead to emotional disorders. Wegner further demonstrated that attempts to suppress thoughts about a white bear paradoxically increased the frequency of such thoughts during a post-suppression period in which participants were free to think about any topic (Wegner, 1994). Subsequent research has shown links between this rebound effect as a laboratory phenomenon and clinical disorders. For example, thought suppression leads to increased electrodermal responses to emotional thoughts (Wegner, 1994), suggesting that it elevates sympathetic arousal. Similarly, ruminating about unpleasant events prolongs both angry and depressed moods (Nolen-Hoeksema and Morrow, 1993; Rusting and Nolen-Hoeksema, 1998), and attempts to suppress pain are similarly unproductive (Cioffi and Holloway, 1993).

Generally speaking, many psychiatric problems are related to ineffective attempts to regulate unwanted experiences, such as feelings, thoughts, and images. Effective psychological treatments focus on promoting beneficial regulation strategies and discouraging the use of ineffective strategies. Depending on the treatment target, CBT strategies include a variety of different techniques. Some strategies target *experiential avoidance* and the attempts to manage unpleasant emotions through suppression and other dysfunctional emotion regulation strategies, whereas other strategies focus on the emotion-eliciting stimulus itself—the situation or event that generates the emotional experience.

Gross's process model of emotions emphasizes the evaluation of external or internal emotional cues (Gross, 2002; Gross and John, 2003; Gross and Levenson, 1997). Once these cues have been processed, a set of experiential, physiological, and behavioral responses are activated and influenced by emotion regulation tendencies. The point in time at which individuals engage in emotion regulation influences the efficacy of their regulatory efforts. Accordingly, based on their timing during the emotion-generative process, emotion regulation strategies can be divided into antecedent-focused and response-focused strategies. Antecedent-focused emotion regulation strategies occur before the emotional response has been fully activated. Examples include cognitive reappraisal, situation modification, and attention deployment. In contrast, response-focused emotion regulation strategies are attempts to alter the expression or experience of an emotion after the response tendency has been initiated. Examples include strategies to suppress or tolerate the activated emotional response. Results of empirical investigations have so far converged to suggest that antecedent-focused strategies are relatively effective methods of regulating emotion in the short term, whereas response-focused strategies tend to be counterproductive (Gross, 1998; Gross and Levenson, 1997).

Another effective strategy to regulate emotions is to encourage the person to separate him- or herself from his or her thoughts. This may be achieved through mindfulness and meditation practices that encourage a present-focused, nonjudgmental stance in regard to thoughts and feelings. In the more recent literature, this is often referred to as *decentering*. This concept is closely related to *distancing* in traditional CBT (Beck, 1970). Although similar in the practical implications, there are subtle differences between these two constructs, especially in their respective theoretical foundations. Distancing refers to the process of gaining objectivity toward thoughts by learning to distinguish between thoughts and reality. Therefore, distancing assumes that true knowledge can be achieved by evaluating one's thoughts, which are often expressed in the form of predictive statements (i.e., hypotheses). In contrast, distancing, as it is used by some authors (e.g., Hayes, 2004), assume a theoretical model that does not make a distinction between thoughts and behaviors on a conceptual level (i.e., thoughts are seen as verbal behaviors).

The inability to engage in decentering and distancing can result in *thought-action fusion* (TAF). This refers to the difficulty of separating cognitions from behaviors. It has been proposed that TAF is comprised of two discrete components (Shafran *et al.*, 1996). The first component refers to the belief that experiencing a particular thought increases the chance that the event will actually occur (likelihood), whereas the second component (morality) refers to the belief that thinking about an action is practically identical to actually performing the action. For example, the thought of killing another person may be considered morally equivalent to performing the act. This moral component is assumed to be the result of the erroneous conclusion that experiencing "bad" thoughts is indicative of one's "true" nature and intentions.

General Approach of CBT

Although CBT is a popular treatment method, there are a number of false beliefs (cognitive errors, if you will) concerning what (modern) CBT is all about. Contrary to popular belief, CBT does not mean that therapy is limited to cognitive modification. It simply means that identifying and modifying cognitive distortions are important goals of treatment, because CBT rests on the principle that cognitions are causally linked to emotional distress and behavioral problems. CBT also targets emotional experiences, physiological symptoms, and behaviors. Depending on the nature of the treatment strategy, Beck distinguishes between intellectual, experiential, and behavioral approaches, all of which are important aspects of CBT. As part of the intellectual approach, patients learn to identify their misconceptions, test the validity of their thoughts, and substitute them with more adaptive ideas. The experiential approach helps patients to expose themselves to experiences in order to change these misconceptions. In Joe's case, the CBT therapist explored the reasons for his feelings of worthlessness and for his previous suicide attempts. An important treatment goal was to raise Joe's level of energy and motivation. This was initially accomplished by assigning Joe some simple and then more complex tasks to do during the day, ranging from mild physical exercise, household chores, and shopping, to sending out job applications, going to job interviews, and pursuing a hobby. The central element of the behavioral approach is to encourage the development of specific forms of behaviors to improve the patient's well-being. This assignment is often referred to as *behavioral activation*. It can break the cycle of negative thinking and low energy and motivation. Behavioral activation lifted Joe's energy, changed his self-perception, and improved his mood. Because of the strong emphasis on the behavioral aspects of many psychological problems, the term CBT appears to be more appropriate than only *cognitive therapy* or *rational therapy,* as it was initially referred to by the two founding fathers.

CBT is primarily focused on the here and now. The patient is an active collaborator who is considered to be an expert on his or her psychological problems. The relationship between the therapist and patient is warm and genuine and the communication is direct but mutually respectful. The patient is not seen as deficient and the therapist is not seen as an omnipotent healer. Instead, the therapist and patient form a collaborative relationship in order to solve a problem. The initial role of a CBT therapist is typically very active as he or she educates the patient about the underlying principles of this treatment approach. However, as treatment progresses, patients are expected to become increasingly active in their own treatment, more proactive, and more independent.

Usually, patients seek help for a variety of different problems. A careful analysis often shows that the different problems are directly related to one another or that different sub-problems can be subsumed under one larger problem. For example, Joe's lack of motivation, low energy, and tendency to oversleep are clearly related to his overarching problem of depression and feelings of low self-worth. If CBT were to primarily target Joe's sleep problems, it would obviously miss the main point of Joe's psychological problems. It appears that Joe's feelings of low self-worth are the main problem that should be targeted in treatment. Some of Joe's core beliefs (schemas) were: "I am worthless unless I can support my family," and "I am incompetent." These core beliefs are typically more overt at a later stage in the treatment process, when it becomes apparent that the various automatic thoughts share certain commonalities. This process requires careful self-exploration by the patient and guided questioning (or guided discovery) by the therapist (which has been referred to as a Socratic questioning style in Beckian CBT). As therapy progresses, the goals of CBT become more focused and oriented toward the patient's core beliefs. However, these goals are not determined by one person alone. Throughout the treatment process, the therapist and patient frequently revisit the goals of therapy, including identifying the types of interventions that will be most effective for reaching these goals and delineating concrete observable outcomes that will indicate that each goal has been achieved. Patients are fully involved in these decision-making processes.

There is a common misconception that CBT replaces negative thinking with positive thinking, which will then miraculously solve all psychological problems. This is incorrect on several levels. CBT cannot and should not attempt to make a bad situation good. CBT does not encourage patients to think positively about realistically distressing events or to ignore a tragedy that has happened to them. Rather, the CBT therapist helps the patient to critically examine whether his or her response to a situation is justified. If there is good reason to have a negative emotional response, then CBT encourages the patient to mobilize his or her own resources in order to deal with the negative event and to live a meaningful life.

A grieving mother in Missouri who has lost both of her sons in the Iraq war has good reason to be grief-stricken. There is absolutely nothing positive about losing your sons, and the mother has very good reason to go through a period of immense grief. Bad things happen, and they happen to good people. Yet, most of us are able to cope with life's adversities and somehow find ways to move on with our lives. Losing children in war is an extreme example, and most people are fortunate enough to be spared of those tragedies. In Joe's case, the trigger for his depression was being laid off. Although getting laid off is not a pleasant event, it is not a catastrophe, and most people can cope with this challenge. However, triggers for depression are not necessarily present. In fact, many people do not even recall a triggering event for their depression. The same is true for other psychological problems. Patients often report that their psychological problem simply happened. CBT therapists encourage patients to identify the reasons for which the problem persists, and help to motivate patients to change these reasons.

By treating thoughts as hypotheses, patients are put into the role of observers or scientists rather than the victims of their psychological problems. In order to challenge these thoughts, therapist and patient discuss the evidence for and against a particular assumption. This can be achieved by using information from patients' past experiences (e.g., what is the probability based on your past experience?), by delivering more accurate information (e.g., what do we know about the event?), by re-evaluating the outcome of a situation (e.g., what is the worst thing that could happen?), and by giving patients the opportunity to test their hypotheses by exposing them to feared and avoided activities and situations.

Many automatic thoughts reported by patients with emotional problems are associated with thinking patterns that lead to *probability overestimation*. This term refers to the cognitive error that occurs when a person believes that an unlikely event is likely to happen. For example, people with panic disorder or health anxiety might interpret harmless heart palpitations as a sign of an impending heart attack, and a woman with generalized anxiety disorder might conclude that her husband must have gotten into a car accident because he did not get home at the usual time. Although these events (heart attack, car accident) are not impossible, the likelihood of occurrence is very low. However, the likelihood that such an event has occurred might be higher, meaning that the woman would have some reason to worry about her husband, if he is a poor driver who often gets into car accidents, if he is always on time, or if he promised he would be home on time.

Another typical thinking pattern is called *catastrophic thinking*. Catastrophic thinking means "blowing things out of proportion," or "making a big deal out of something," even if it is not a big deal. In other words, a person who makes this cognitive error perceives an outcome as catastrophic, even if it is not. An example is a man with social anxiety disorder who, after being rejected by a woman whom he had asked out on a date, believes that he will never find a partner in life because no woman will ever be interested in him.

Once maladaptive thoughts are identified and challenged, patients must put their old beliefs to the test. For example, in the case of anxiety disorders, patients will be confronted with events and situations (which may also include images and activities) that they have typically interpreted in a dysfunctional way. Patients are further given the opportunity to conduct field experiments to examine the validity of their assumptions. For example, the person with social anxiety disorder may be asked to strike up a conversation with ten random women in a book store. In later practices, he might be asked to deliberately set himself up for rejection by women in order to deal with his concerns about the consequences of getting rejected. In addition to these general forms of cognitive errors, the following chapters will discuss other, disorder-specific cognitive dysfunctions and interventions for these cognitive dysfunctions. In all of these chapters, the cognitive dysfunctions are explored and modified in the context of behavioral experiments in which patients are confronted with situations that allow them to test the validity of their beliefs. The majority of these experiments typically occur outside the therapist's office, in a less safe environment.

One of the most difficult steps in cognitive-behavior therapy is substituting maladaptive thoughts for adaptive ones. In order to come up with alternative thoughts, patients must ask themselves "What are alternative ways of interpreting this particular event?" or "How would other people interpret this event?" With repeated practice, patients learn to change their perspective, moving from passive victim of their psychological problems to active observer. Self-monitoring forms are often used to guide this process.

Like any bad habit, the way we interpret things tends to be very resistant to change. The first step toward change is to realize that there are many different ways an event can be interpreted. In order to interpret an event, we need to formulate hypotheses, which ultimately determine our emotional response to the event. As discussed, the goal of treatment is to test patients' hypotheses and, if these hypotheses are invalid, to modify them in order to develop a more realistic perspective of the real world. The assumption of the cognitive approach is that predictions and self-statements have a powerful influence over behavior and experience. Thus, in order to ensure that a practice session will provide the maximal ability to challenge patients'

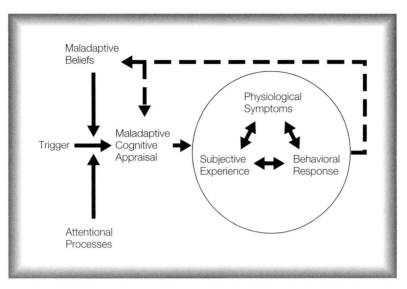

Figure 1.1 CBT model.

dysfunctional thoughts, preparation for the practice is essential. In addition, processing of experiences following an exposure is equally important.

The general model of CBT, as it will be used in this book, is depicted in Figure 1.1. This model shows that maladaptive beliefs (schemas) can lead to maladaptive specific (and often automatic) cognitions when attention is allocated to aspects of certain triggers, such as situations, events, sensations, or even other thoughts. These attention processes often show a high degree of automaticity and can happen on a subconscious level. Once the process reaches the level of consciousness, the triggers are evaluated and interpreted. This appraisal then leads to a subjective experience, physiological symptoms, and behavioral response. For example, a person who holds the view "I am socially incompetent" is more likely to interpret an event (e.g., an audience member yawning) in way that is consistent with this belief or schema. This interpretation of the situation leads to physiological symptoms (heart racing), behavioral responses (stuttering), and a subjective experience (fear and embarrassment). Physiology, behaviors, and the subjective experience of the emotion distract from the actual task performance, feeding onto each other and further supporting the maladaptive cognitive appraisal of the situation and the schema of the person as being incompetent, establishing a positive feedback loop and vicious cycle. This positive feedback loop can further be established by a process that has been referred to as emotional reasoning, which is a maladaptive cognitive process that uses one's emotional experience as evidence for the validity of a thought.

An example of emotional reasoning is a child who is afraid of dogs who then uses this fear as evidence for the belief that dogs must, therefore, be dangerous. Emotional reasoning is a crucial process because it establishes a positive feedback loop by turning a consequence of a thought (e.g., fear of dogs) into an antecedent of the same thought (e.g., dogs are dangerous). We encounter this positive feedback loop in all emotional disorders.

The distinction between physiology, subjective experience, and behaviors is based on a general tripartite model of emotions. Separating the emotional response into these three components may seem artificial and some schools of psychology believe that it is unnecessary to make such a division. For example, a proponent of a theoretical approach that is referred to as behavior analysis may argue that every response to an event or a situation is a behavioral response and that it is not useful to even assume that cognitive appraisal precedes the response and that subjective and physiological responses are uniquely different from overt behavior response. However, the empirical literature provides sufficient evidence to support such a model, and it is useful to derive treatment targets and when formulating specific intervention strategies. The three components, behaviors, physiology, and subjective experience, form a system together, but can be targeted separately. The behavioral component may be expressed in the form of overt signs of the emotional experience. In the case of anxiety, these behaviors may be avoidance strategies with the goal of improving or eliminating the unpleasant state the person experiences. Other avoidance strategies can be experiential by, for example, avoiding the subjective experience or physiological sensations of an emotional response. These strategies, however, maintain the maladaptive approach toward external experiences because the positive feedback loop does not allow the system to change by considering any disconfirming evidence. A positive feedback may further be established as a result of emotional reasoning and self-perception, physiological symptoms, behaviors, and subjective experiences are both determined by and determine the cognitive appraisal of the situation, an observation with a long research tradition (Bem, 1967; Festinger and Carlsmith, 1959; Schachter and Singer, 1962).

2 Empowering the Mind

Readiness for Change

Psychiatric disorders are unpleasant and undesirable. They cause subjective distress to the affected individual and his or her friends and family members, and can severely restrict a person's personal life, career, and overall happiness. Despite all these negative consequences, people often engage in activities that maintain these undesirable states. They often have awareness about this, but still engage in these activities, similar to a lung cancer patient who can't stop smoking. Other, perhaps less dramatic examples, may be the person with depression who sleeps 12 hours a night and is inactive during the day or the person with social anxiety who avoids parties. Although people often realize that many behaviors worsen their condition, it is very difficult to change them. There are many reasons for this. For example, lack of motivation and inactivity in the case of depression or avoidance behaviors in the case of anxieties is not only a maintaining factor, but also an expression of these disorders.

Stages of Change

An influential theory that describes these change processes is the *transtheoretical model* of change. This model identifies different stages of change that differ in the readiness for change (Prochaska *et al.,* 1992). Although this model has been developed for addictive behaviors, it is not limited to any

An Introduction to Modern CBT: Psychological Solutions to Mental Health Problems, First Edition.
S. G. Hofmann. © 2012 S. G. Hofmann. Published 2012 by John Wiley & Sons, Ltd.

specific psychological problem or therapeutic change process (therefore the term "transtheoretical" model). Moreover, the problem does not need to be limited to changes in overt behaviors but also applies to changes in cognitions and perceptions.

More specifically, the model posits that the change process involves the progression through six stages: *precontemplation, contemplation, preparation, action, maintenance,* and *termination.* In the precontemplation phase, a person is not intending to initiate any change in the foreseeable future. People in the contemplation phase are contemplating to take action in the foreseeable future (in the case of addictive behaviors, within the next 6 months). They start weighing the cost and benefits of the maladaptive behaviors or cognitions. In the preparation stage, people intend to change their behaviors or cognitions in the immediate future (usually within the next month). They may start experimenting with small changes, but are not yet ready to undertake any major changes. Only when people reach the action phase will they take definite action to change their maladaptive behaviors or cognitions. Maintenance is the phase in which people make a continuous effort to continue with the change strategies. Finally, the termination phase is reached when the person has no temptation and is very confident that he or she will not fall back to the old and maladaptive behavioral or cognitive patterns.

Initiating a change requires enormous motivation and courage, because the strategies to overcome the problems are typically difficult, painful, or distressing. In addition, the person cannot be certain whether the therapeutic strategies will, in fact, result in the desired consequences. Therefore, the treatment goal has to be desirable and achievable in order for the patient to be ready for change and to fully engage in treatment. This readiness for change can be enhanced by conducting a cost-benefit analysis of having the problem and comparing it with a cost-benefit analysis of being free from the problem. In the case of behavioral change, the person is likely going to change if the cost-benefit ratio for continuing the behavior is greater than the cost-benefit ratio for changing the behavior (i.e., if it is more costly and less beneficial to continue than to change the behavior). Important factors considered in this cost-benefit analysis are personal values, happiness, life decisions, and future plans.

Motivational Enhancement

A specific intervention strategy that can aid patients in this cost/benefit analysis of their behaviors is motivational enhancement or motivational interviewing. Motivational enhancement techniques were first developed and tested in individuals with alcohol and substance use disorders (Miller and Rollnick, 2002). However, they can be also applied in principle to any distressing psychological problem and are most effective for people in the contemplation phase, but also have the potential to motivate people who are in other stages of the transtheoretical model. These techniques are based on four general therapeutic principles: (1) expression of empathy, (2) developing discrepancy, (3) rolling with resistance, and (4) supporting self-efficacy.

Expression of empathy

It is normal that the patient will be ambivalent about changing his or her behaviors. The therapist responds to such ambivalence with empathy for the patient's struggle and without judgment. Some of the strategies for achieving this include asking open-ended questions, using reflective listening techniques, and creating a respectful and collaborative therapeutic relationship.

Developing discrepancy

Patients with emotional disorders will typically have some degree of ambivalence toward changing their behaviors that contribute to the psychopathology. For example, patients with obsessive-compulsive disorder might recognize that their compulsive behavior is excessive and maladaptive. However, they may also feel that not engaging in the compulsion makes it more likely for a feared outcome or catastrophic consequence (the content of the obsession) to occur. Similarly, patients with generalized anxiety disorder (GAD) might feel distressed when they worry, but may also perceive worrying as a way to control their anxiety. The therapist can help patients push the balance of the scales toward behavior change by helping the patient realize that there is more to gain by replacing old, maladaptive behaviors with new, more adaptive behaviors and by creating and amplifying a dissonance between the patient's current situation and his or her desired situation. If a person views his or her current behavior as conflicting with important personal goals or values, it is more likely to be changed. The therapist can enhance the extent to which a given behavior is perceived as discrepant with one's goals or values. This then increases the likelihood that the behavior will be changed. Some of the important therapeutic skills for implementing this principle include identification and selective reflection of statements or sentiments supporting behavior change.

Rolling with resistance

The goal of motivational interviewing is to encourage patients to resolve their ambivalence by choosing to adopt more adaptive behaviors. In order to achieve this goal, the therapist does not argue for behavior change, because it may result in the patient presenting arguments against behavior change. Treatment can then become a struggle between therapist and patient, rather than a collaborative process. In order to avoid this, the therapist responds to resistance or ambivalence expressed by the patient not with confrontation, but with understanding and empathy with the goal to explore alternative perspectives from the patient. The change strategies have to be initiated by the patient, not the therapist. Resistance from the patient is to be expected. As a response to this resistance, the therapist typically engages patients in discussion to explore ways to resolve this ambivalence by discussing problem solving strategies while at the same time validating the patient's concerns, using open-ended questions to invite new perspectives and facilitate problem-solving strategies.

Support self-efficacy

Bandura's (1977) research has convincingly shown that belief in one's ability to successfully change a behavior predicts actual behavior change above and beyond the intention to change a behavior. Therefore, a patient's belief in his or her ability to successfully change the behavior in question (i.e., his or her self-efficacy) is critically important for initiating behavior change. The therapist can encourage self-efficacy by reinforcing positive behavior change and by pointing patients to successful steps made or attempted toward behavior change. In general, behavior change during motivational interviewing is believed to proceed in two separate phases (Miller and Rollnick, 1991). The first phase focuses on building motivation for behavior change and consists of techniques designed to identify important personal goals or values. It also highlights the discrepancy between current behavior and personal goals and explores the costs and benefits associated with behavior change. The second phase focuses on enhancing the patient's belief in his or her ability to successfully change the maladaptive behavior. This phase capitalizes on the shifting decisional balance by enhancing the patient's self-efficacy for successfully changing the maladaptive behaviors. Useful techniques for this phase include setting concrete behavior change goals, generating and exploring different plans for changing behavior, and committing to a finalized behavior change plan. At this stage, CBT strategies that are tailored to the individual should be considered. These strategies are outlined in the following chapters. All of these strategies are conducted in the context of the general CBT process.

Patients fluctuate considerably in their motivation, going in and out of different stages and even jumping between stages of the transtheoretical model. Nevertheless, it is useful to consider this model to generate a working hypothesis when conducting treatment with patients, in order to apply motivational interviewing methods to motivate the patients to continue treatment, if necessary.

Assessment

Once the patient is motivated and committed to treatment, the first step of any treatment should be a careful diagnostic evaluation. Ideally, this can be done with semi-structured interviews, such as the Structured Clinical Interview for DSM-IV (SCID-IV) (First *et al.*, 1995). Alternatively, a trained and skilled clinician can directly use the DSM criteria to determine the presence or absence of specific disorders. It is important not only to assess the disorders the clinician assumes to be present but also to rule out the presence of other, seemingly unrelated disorders. Experienced clinicians keep an open mind and are willing to revise their initial clinical assessment about the patient's problem. This means that the clinician should not only try to find evidence supporting his or her hypothesis, but also to gather information that would contradict and falsify one's initial assumptions. In addition to a thorough diagnostic assessment, it is useful to ask patients to keep a diary that lists, at the minimum, the day and time, situation, and a description of the problem that is the target of the treatment (e.g., level of mood, anxiety, etc). In addition to serving as an indicator for change, these diaries can also identify any conditions or triggers of the problem. At the minimum, an assessment should answer the following basic questions:

What are the primary complaints? Patients frequently come in with a number of different, somewhat related problems. Identifying the primary problem is an important step toward recovery.

Why did the patient decide to search for help at this point? Psychiatric conditions are chronic illnesses. Patients typically report having psychological problems for many years before consulting mental health professionals. The reason why the patient decides to look for help at this particular point in time often provides important treatment-relevant information. For example, a new job might mean that somebody with social anxiety disorder will have to deal with more social interactions, or the husband of the woman with depression is at his wit's end and threatened to divorce her unless she can overcome her illness.

What is the history of the problem? Although psychiatric problems are chronic illnesses, specific symptoms wax and wane. A detailed assessment of the history of the problem can give the clinician important clues about any contributing factors. For example, a patient's depression might correlate with changes in jobs or family environment. If changes in symptoms are directly linked to specific external changes, it is advisable to explore whether there are any benefits that come of having the problem. For example, the depression might result in more lost days at work but also less stress associated with a particular activity at work. Such *secondary gain* of the disorder is an important factor that can contribute to the maintenance of the problem.

What is the patient's psychiatric history? In addition to the history of the presenting problem, the clinician should gather detailed information of the patient's psychiatric history, even if this is apparently unrelated to the presenting problem. It is not unlikely that other psychological problems are directly related to the primary concern, even if the patient does not believe that there is such a connection. For example, a patient's extreme shyness might contribute to the depression, because the patient avoids social contact and leads an isolated life without much positive interactions.

What is the important family and social history? Knowing the patient's family and social history can give the clinician an idea about the contribution of genetic and other environmental factors. However, even if the family reports a lot of psychological problems, including some of the same presenting problems of the patient, it does not mean that the problem cannot be targeted with effective psychological intervention. The reason why a problem develops in the first place is usually not the same as the reason why a problem is being maintained.

General Process of CBT

Once a thorough assessment is completed and the patient is motivated, the treatment can begin. The specific strategies depend on the primary problem, and these strategies are described below. Although these strategies are directed toward specific disorders, they also show a number of commonalities with regard to the general process. These commonalities are as follows:

Establishing a good therapeutic relationship

Positive therapist-patient interactions flow from a collaborative relationship. In general, therapists' behavior should be honest and warm. Patients are not considered to be helpless and passive but, rather, experts of their own problems. Therefore, patients are actively involved in treatment. For example, they are encouraged to formulate and test certain hypotheses in order to gain a better understanding of the real world and their own problems. The emphasis during therapy is placed on solving problems. The therapist's role is to work with the patient to find adaptive solutions to solvable problems. Every step in therapy is transparent and clearly reasoned. Patients are encouraged to ask questions to ensure that they understand and agree with the treatment approach.

   The initial role of the CBT therapist is very active. Therapists should educate patients about the underlying principles of this treatment approach. In addition, therapists often find that patients need a great deal of guidance in the beginning stages of therapy in order to help them successfully identify their misconceptions and the associated automatic thoughts. As treatment progresses, patients are expected to become increasingly active in their own treatment. A masterful CBT therapist reinforces his or her patient's independence while at the same time being aware of the need for continued support and education as patients first begin to apply the concepts of CBT to their difficulties.

Problem focus

CBT is a problem-solving process. This process includes clarifying the status of the presenting problem, defining the desired goal, and finding the means to reach that goal. Therefore, the therapist and patient discuss the goals of therapy at the beginning of treatment, including identifying the type of interventions that are to be used to reach these goals and delineating concrete, observable outcomes that indicate that each goal has been achieved. CBT case formulation can facilitate this step. The goal of a formulation-based assessment is to identify core beliefs that underlie misconceptions and associ-ated automatic thoughts in order to intervene effectively during treatment. Through the process of problem reduction, therapist and patient then iden-tify problems with similar causes and group them together. Once the major problem is identified, the therapist typically breaks it up into component problems to be attacked in a given case. Therapists frequently elicit feedback from the patient throughout treatment to ensure that problem-solving efforts are on target with identified goals.

Identifying maladaptive cognitions

Once patients define their problems and goals for treatment, CBT therapists encourage them to become aware of their thoughts and thought processes. As discussed in Chapter 1, cognitions are generally classified into negative automatic thoughts and maladaptive (sometimes also referred to as dysfunc-tional or irrational) beliefs. Negative automatic thoughts are thoughts or images which occur in specific situations when an individual feels threatened in some way. Maladaptive core beliefs, on the other hand, are assumptions that individuals have about the world, the future, and themselves. These more global, overarching core beliefs provide a schema that determines how a person may interpret a specific situation. Just as with automatic thoughts, therapists can identify maladaptive core beliefs through the process of guided questioning.

Challenging maladaptive cognitions

By treating maladaptive cognitions as hypotheses, patients are put into the role of observers—scientists or detectives—rather than victims of their con-cerns. In order to challenge these thoughts, therapist and patient discuss the evidence for and against a particular assumption in a debate, engaging in what Beck calls *Socratic dialogue*. This can be done in a variety of ways, typi-cally by using information from patients' past experiences, empirically evaluating a situation, evaluating the outcome of a situation, and giving patients the opportunity to test their hypothesis by exposing them to feared and/or avoided activities or situations.

At first, patients are often asked to generate rational alternatives to their irrational responses to a challenging situation. As this skill is polished, patients are encouraged to use their skills both before and during difficult situations. In addition, given the presumed automatic and habitual nature of their negative thoughts, continued and repeated restructuring may be required before a thought is fully challenged. It is assumed that, with consistent practice, more accurate thinking becomes the automatic mode of response.

Testing the validity of thoughts

Once irrational thoughts are identified and challenged, patients are asked to put the previously held and maladaptive core beliefs to the test. By confronting stimuli (e.g., situations, bodily sensations, images, activities) that provoke negative emotions (e.g., anxiety, embarrassment, guilt), patients have the opportunity to conduct field experiments to examine the validity of their assumptions.

Substituting maladaptive with adaptive cognitions and eliciting feedback

One of the most difficult steps in CBT is substituting maladaptive cognitions with adaptive ones. This is because habits, such as automatic thoughts, can be very resistant to change. The goal of CBT is neither to demonstrate to patients how ridiculous their thoughts are nor to teach them positive thinking techniques. Instead, the goal is to test the patient's hypotheses and, if these hypotheses are invalid, to modify them in order to get a more realistic perspective about the real world. Direct tests through behavioral experiments provide the feedback that is necessary to substitute irrational with rational thoughts.

Categories of Maladaptive Cognitions

Maladaptive cognitions can easily lead to distortion of reality because they lead to misperception or exaggeration of a situation. In Chapter 1, we identified two general types of maladaptive thinking patterns: probability overestimation (overestimating the probability of an unlikely and unpleasant event) and catastrophic thinking (catastrophizing an event that is unpleasant, but not catastrophic). These two thought patterns often lead to a number of specific and typical automatic thoughts (adapted from Burns, 1980). This list is not complete and it is not essential to discuss each of the categories with the patient in therapy, although some earlier treatment protocols do this. Rather, this list is intended to provide the reader with examples of some typical maladaptive thoughts that might be encountered in therapy. To illustrate each error, a simple example is given of a person with public speaking-related anxiety.

Black-and-white thinking

This maladaptive cognition divides reality into two discrete categories. Everything is viewed as either black (bad) or white (good) with no shades of gray. For example, if a person's social performance is not completely perfect, the situation is interpreted as a total failure.

Personalization

Negative events are taken personally. For example, if one person in the audience yawns, the speaker might conclude that everybody is bored to death. Alternatively, the person might be yawning because she didn't get enough sleep last night.

Focusing on the negatives

The person focuses on one single negative detail and ignores any positive aspect of a situation or event. As a result, the perception of reality becomes darkened, like the drop of ink that discolors an entire bucket of water. For example, the speaker focuses excessively on the one person in the audience who was yawning, in addition to any other negative aspects of the situation that would confirm the belief that everybody was bored.

Disqualifying the positives

The person dismisses the positive aspects of the situation. For example, even if many people in the audience apparently liked the speech performance, the speaker still focuses on the one person in the audience who was yawning.

Jumping to conclusions

The person derives a negative interpretation from an event, even though there is no good evidence to support it. For example, the speaker might anticipate that the presentation will be a disaster, and is convinced that this predication is an already-established fact. This is also referred to as a "fortune teller error." Another expression of this error occurs in the case when the speaker believes that an audience member reacted negatively toward the speaker even though there is no clear evidence to make this assumption. This is also referred to as the "mind reading error."

Overgeneralization

The speaker sees a single negative event as a never-ending pattern. For example, she may believe that one bad presentation means that she is a bad speaker and should choose a different career.

Catastrophizing

Similarly, catastrophizing occurs when a person blows things out of proportion. For example, the speaker may believe that just because she performed poorly once at work, her boss is going to fire her and that that this would mean that her career is over.

Emotional reasoning

This error is of particular importance in understanding why maladaptive cognitions and psychological disorders are so persistent and resistant to change. This error is made when the person interprets an emotional response to a thought as evidence for the validity of this thought. Therefore, if a particular thought (e.g., worrying about being unemployed) causes distress, then a person who engages in emotional reasoning uses the distress as evidence that she should have good reason to worry about losing his or her job.

These categories serve as general descriptors. Discussing examples with the patient helps to illustrate that the patient's specific maladaptive cognitions are not unique and are often experienced by many other people.

General CBT Strategies

CBT uses various strategies to target the different components of the CBT model. A summary of the general strategies is depicted in Figure 2.1. The specific strategies depend on the particular problems that are targeted and will be covered in the following chapters.

The strategies include attention modification and modification of the situation to change the triggering stimuli. Cognitive restructuring is one of the core strategies used to modify maladaptive thoughts and schema. Meditation strategies, including loving-kindness meditation, can be helpful emotion regulation strategies and thereby aid cognitive restructuring. Behavioral activation and behavioral modification procedures more directly

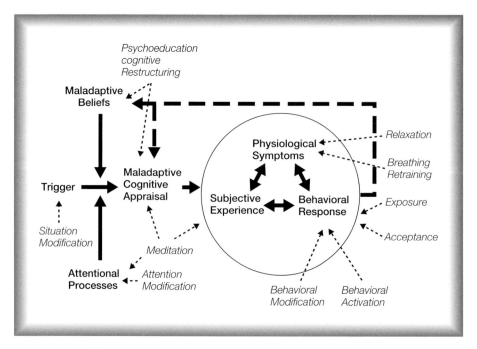

Figure 2.1   CBT strategies.

target the behavioral components of the emotional response. Similarly, relaxation and breathing retraining exercises can be applied to modify physiological symptoms associated with psychiatric problems. Avoidance tendencies play a critical role in the maintenance of a psychiatric disorder. Acceptance and exposure strategies can directly target experiential or overt avoidance behaviors, thus breaking or interrupting the positive feedback loop that leads to the maintenance of the disorder. While Figure 2.1 shows a schematic depiction of all of these strategies, a more detailed description of the techniques is provided below.

Attention and situation modification

A response to an event or situation can be dealt with by modifying the event or situation that is responsible for causing the distress. For example, stress at work can be reduced or eliminated by restructuring the work or by quitting the job altogether. Similarly, marital problems can be resolved by improving the relationship or filing for a divorce. It is also possible to focus on less distressing aspects of an event or situation and instead focus on pleasant and enjoyable aspects, thus changing the general experience of the event or situation.

Cognitive restructuring

A core element of CBT is cognitive restructuring of schemas. Schemas are core beliefs about the world, the self, and the future. These cognitive schemas determine the specific cognitive appraisal of a situation or event. For example, a person who encountered many unstable and hurtful interpersonal relationships in the past may be more likely to think that her new boyfriend fell out of love with her because he decided to stay late at work rather than spend time with her. Repeated experiences such as this can strain the relationship, leading to a self-fulfilling prophecy.

In CBT, maladaptive appraisals are treated as hypotheses that may or may not be true. In order to explore the validity of these thoughts, patients are put into the role of observers—scientists or detectives—rather than victims of these thoughts. In order to examine the validity of maladaptive cognitions, different sources of information will be used. For example, the therapist and patient may discuss the evidence for and against a particular assumption in a debate, engaging in what Beck calls *Socratic dialogue*. This is typically done using information from patients' past experiences, empirically evaluating a situation and its outcome. Another way of examining the validity of a thought may be accomplished by encouraging patients to directly test their hypotheses through behavioral experiments, in conjunction with exposure techniques. As discussed in Chapter 1, the types of maladaptive cognitions show considerable differences between the disorders and can generally be classified into misconceptions due to *probability overestimation,* a cognitive error that occurs when a person believes that an unlikely event is likely to happen, and *catastrophic thinking,* a cognitive error that occurs when one exaggerates the negative outcome of a situation.

Schemas are overarching beliefs that give rise to the specific maladaptive thoughts. For example, people with depression may hold the schema "I am worthless," and people with anxiety disorders may view the world as a dangerous place. Schemas can also be expressed in the form of cognitions about cognitions. A case in point is generalized anxiety disorder. Patients with generalized anxiety disorder typically worry excessively about a number of things, such as their finances, future and health. Maladaptive meta-cognitions may be beliefs about the possible function of these worries. For example, some people may believe that worrying about an undesirable situation makes this situation less likely to happen in the future. These meta-cognitions can be handled similarly to the way we deal with worry and other maladaptive thinking patterns.

An effective strategy for identifying maladaptive schemas is the downward arrow technique (Greenberger and Padesky, 1995). This approach begins by identifying an automatic thought. However, instead of disputing this thought, the patient is encouraged to deepen his or her level of affect and explore the thought with questions such as "what would it mean if this thought were true?" This typically leads to the emergence of an underlying conditional assumption, a level of cognition that typically takes the form of "if . . . then" statements. These "rules" typically specify a circumstance and an emotional consequence that is dysfunctional.

Generally, these rules exist at a lower level of awareness such that the patient has rarely been able to reflect on them. In these instances, it is often the therapist who detects a kind of emotional rule that seems to reoccur in the patient's difficulties. A number of situations may share some features and cause similar emotional responses. Often, this means that similar rules are in operation across these situations. The therapist might initially verbalize this rule, and a collaborative effort is then made to modify the specific wording of the conditional assumption. Other times patients may be aware of their conditional beliefs and will be able to state the rules that seem to govern their emotional and behavioral responses to situations.

In contrast to conditional rules, core beliefs represent extreme, one-sided views of self, other, and the world that give rise both to conditional assumptions and automatic thoughts. Core beliefs are assumed to be primitive, extreme views that are formed as a result of early experiences. Content for these beliefs varies for each individual, but it is important to emphasize that core beliefs are ways of understanding the world and were rational in the circumstances under which they originally formed. The most important precursor to identifying core beliefs is to explain these concepts in therapy. Patients are encouraged to view their automatic thoughts as outgrowths of something that deeply and profoundly impacts their interpretations of events over time. The rationale (early learning) should also be provided, as it is important for the patient to understand that his or her negative core beliefs are not accidental or random, but rather understandable outcomes of previous experiences (e.g., that which was functional and rational early in life may no longer serve the same purpose or be grounded in evidence given different circumstances). Core beliefs often take on the form of an absolute statement such as "I'm a failure," "I am unlovable," or "I am in constant danger." Patients usually experience considerable affect when exposed to their core beliefs and often become tearful, sad, or very anxious. This is usually a sign that a highly salient type of processing has been tapped.

Many of the techniques used for changing automatic thoughts (e.g., examining distortions, evidence-gathering) can be applied to deeper levels of cognition, although changing beliefs will take longer and requires more effort than altering a negative automatic thought. In addition to these techniques, there are three other processes that help to change core beliefs. First, patients need to have a narrative concerning the development of these beliefs. Second, patients need to view these experiences more objectively and sympathetically, acknowledging that they learned something negative and potentially damaging. Third, it is important to engender hope that these kinds of beliefs can be "relearned" with the help of the strategies learned in therapy. Once patients have acknowledged the need to change core beliefs, they can be encouraged to create an alternative core belief, just as they worked on alternatives to their automatic thoughts and conditional assumptions. Once the alternative belief is identified, the patient is encouraged to gather evidence for the old core belief and the more adaptive alternative core belief. This encourages the patient to view subsequent experiences through a new filter and assess which of the two beliefs is a better fit to his or her current reality.

Sessions focused on deep cognitions are typically less structured than earlier sessions, in part because they cover more areas of the lifespan and do not have the thought record as a unifying theme. Discussions may involve reflections on early life events, focusing on the rigidity of certain conditional assumptions, or exploring a core belief, but can also move fluidly between these points. At the same time, therapists need to attend to opportunities to implement various worksheets and exercises such as the downward arrow, a positive events log, and core belief worksheet (see Beck, 1979).

Meditation

Derived from Buddhist practices, mindfulness-based therapy (MBT), such as mindfulness-based CBT (Segal *et al.*, 2002) and mindfulness-based stress reduction (Kabat-Zinn, 1994) have become very popular forms of treatment in contemporary psychotherapy (for review, see Baer, 2003; Hayes, 2004; Hofmann *et al.*, 2010; Kabat-Zinn, 1994). Mindfulness, as it has been used in the contemporary literature, refers to a process that leads to a mental state characterized by nonjudgmental awareness of the present moment experience, including one's sensations, thoughts, bodily states, consciousness, and the environment, while encouraging openness, curiosity, and acceptance (Bishop *et al.*, 2004; Kabat-Zinn, 2003; Melbourne Academic Mindfulness Interest Group, 2006). Bishop and colleagues (2004) distinguish two components of mindfulness—one that involves self-regulation of attention and one that involves an orientation toward the present moment characterized by curiosity, openness, and acceptance.

A recent review of the literature suggests that MBT is a beneficial intervention to reduce negative psychological states, such as stress, anxiety, and depression (Hofmann *et al.*, 2010). This review identified 39 studies totaling 1,140 participants receiving MBT for a range of conditions, including cancer, generalized anxiety disorder, depression, and other psychiatric or medical conditions. Effect size estimates suggest that MBT is associated with strong effects for improving anxiety and mood symptoms in patients with anxiety and mood disorders. In other patients, this intervention was moderately effective for improving anxiety and mood symptoms. These effect sizes were robust and unrelated to number of treatment sessions or publication year. Moreover, the treatment effects were maintained over follow-up periods. These findings suggest that mindfulness-based therapy is a promising intervention for treating anxiety and mood problems in clinical populations. Another form of meditation practice with a high potential value as a therapeutic tool is loving-kindness meditation. In this meditation practice, people cultivate the intention to experience positive emotions during the meditation itself, as well as in their life in general. The goal is to learn about the nature of one's mind and dispel false assumptions about the sources of one's happiness (Dalai Lama and Cutler, 1998). These experiences can, in turn, shift a person's basic view of the self in relation to others, increasing general empathy. This particular meditation technique appears to be particularly helpful for treating anger, aggression, and interpersonal conflict.

Acceptance

Acceptance techniques are important strategies of acceptance and commitment therapy (ACT; Hayes 2004), a newer form of treatment that is rooted in behavioral analysis. Although ACT opposes the cognitive model, acceptance strategies are certainly compatible with CBT (Hofmann and Asmundson, 2008). The general goals of ACT are to foster acceptance of unwanted thoughts and feelings, and to stimulate action tendencies that contribute to an improvement in circumstances of living. More specifically, the goal of ACT is to discourage *experiential avoidance*, which is the unwillingness to experience negatively evaluated feelings, physical sensations, and thoughts. Acceptance strategies can be viewed as techniques used to counteract maladaptive response-focused emotion regulation strategies, such as suppression. Patients are encouraged to embrace unwanted thoughts and feelings—such as anxiety, pain, and guilt—as an alternative to experiential avoidance. The goal is to end the struggle with unwanted thoughts and feelings without attempting to change or eliminate them.

Breathing retraining

Hyperventilation has been linked to a number of psychiatric disorders. For example, in 1929 hyperventilation was used to explain DaCosta's syndrome, or "irritable heart syndrome," which incapacitated soldiers in the American Civil War. Similarly, hyperventilation was assumed to explain "neurocirculatory asthenia" or "effort syndrome" in 1938 (Roth *et al.*, 2005). Since then, breathing exercises have become common components of many psychological interventions, especially for treating anxiety disorders such as panic disorder.

Behavioral modification

As depicted in Figure 2.1, subjective feelings, behaviors, and physiological symptoms bi-directionally influence each other. For example, the subjective experience not only influences physiological arousal and behaviors, but behaviors and physiological arousal also influence the subjective experience. Therefore, changing behaviors leads to changes in physiological arousal and subjective experience.

Modifying behaviors is at the heart of psychology, which is why many psychologists identify themselves as behavioral scientists. Unlike subjective experience and physiological symptoms, it is relatively easy to control behaviors directly. In addition, all psychiatric disorders covered in this text are significantly influenced by associated maladaptive behaviors. Reinforcing adaptive and discouraging maladaptive behaviors has a direct and significant effect on the problem.

The effect of behavior on physiological arousal is evident. Less evident might be the influence of behaviors on the subjective experience. However, a powerful method to change depression, for example, is behavioral activation. In other words, instructing patients with depression to be active, to engage in pleasant activities or exercise and to resist their tendency to stay in bed and isolate themselves is a powerful method of countering depression by stopping the vicious cycle between behavioral inactivation and subjective and physiological symptoms of depression. Similarly, other psychological problems can be effectively treated by behaving as if the psychological problem was not present.

Relaxation

Relaxation strategies used to be the common intervention for a range of psychological problems, including anxiety and stress-related disorders. Carefully executed experimental studies and treatment outcome trials, however, have demonstrated that relaxation therapy is generally not an overly effective strategy for treating psychiatric disorders, with some notable exceptions (sleep disorders and generalized anxiety disorder). For some psychiatric problems, it may even be counter-therapeutic. For example, patients with panic disorder may be more likely develop panic attacks as a result of the relaxation practice because some patients focus on their bodily symptoms, which can unintentionally trigger an attack. Such relaxation-induced panic attacks could be used in treatment as a challenge procedure if other strategies have been developed to cope and manage the bodily symptoms in a more adaptive way. Without such strategies in place, however, relaxation as a sole intervention method is counter-productive for panic disorder and ineffective for many other problems. This may be surprising given the efficacy of breathing retraining for panic disorder, which includes a relaxation component. The crucial difference is the breathing retraining component, which is not present in simple relaxation techniques, and which might encourage patients to focus on a pleasant image or to progressively tense and relax muscle groups.

It is important to note that, on average, any plausible treatments that have been developed with the intention to benefit the patient are likely to help a small number of patients, primarily because of the placebo effect. In other words, some patients improve only because they receive an intervention that they believe will help them. Similar to drug trials that often use a sugar pill as a placebo control condition, some clinical trials that examine the efficacy of a psychological treatment use relaxation strategies as a control condition which produces robust and moderately strong effects (Smits and Hofmann, 2009).

Exposure

In the treatment of fear and anxiety disorders, exposure is an essential, if not the single most important component of CBT. The precise mechanism through which exposure works remains unknown. Exposure refers to the repeated and continuous presentation of the feared and previously avoided stimulus in the absence of all manner of avoidance strategies (e.g., safety signals and behavior). These changes are more likely to occur if internal fear cues and other significant contexts are systematically produced, and if the outcome of the social situation is unexpectedly positive, because it forces the person to re-evaluate the actual threat of the situation. This process shares many similarities with extinction learning in animals and humans and has, therefore, been regarded as primarily responsible for exposure therapy from the early beginnings of experimental studies in psychology (Watson and Rayner, 1920) to the contemporary field of neuroscience (e.g., Myers and Davis, 2002).

Modern learning theories of extinction assume that conditioning takes place as participants form representations of the relevant cues (conditioned stimulus and unconditioned stimulus) and situational contexts, and as they acquire information about the association between these cues and the situations (Myers and Davis, 2002). These associations can be either excitatory (i.e., activation of one representation activates another) or inhibitory (i.e., activation of one representation inhibits activation of another). Acquisition of conditioned responses is explained by the formation of an excitatory association between representations of the conditioned stimulus (CS) and unconditioned stimulus (US). The US representation is activated indirectly through its association with the CS representation which, in turn, triggers the conditioned response. Extinction is assumed to proceed through multiple mechanisms (Myers and Davis, 2002) which also includes new learning that inhibits the excitatory association between CS and US. As part of this new form of learning, the participant changes the CS-US contingency in such a way that the CS no longer signals an aversive event and thereby inhibits the expression of the fear response (Myers and Davis, 2002). Exposure in humans is beneficial for at least the following reasons:

Exposure allows for the identification and testing of maldaptive cognitions. Exposure provides people with opportunities to identify maladaptive cognitions and to test their accuracy.

Exposure changes the emotional experience. Repeated and prolonged exposure while resisting the urge to engage in any behaviors that modify the experience will result in a decrease of the unpleasant emotion.

Exposure enhances the sense of control. A lack of control leads to distress. In contrast, exposure provides the person with control over the situation and the emotional response to it. As the person starts learning new ways of coping with the situation or event and the associated emotion, the sense of control over the emotion and the triggering stimuli will also increase. Related to self-control is self-efficacy, which refers to one's sense of competence in mastering a situation (Bandura, 1977).

Monitoring Treatment Changes

In order to track a patient's progress during the course of treatment, it is important to monitor the symptoms that are primarily targeted. It would be impossible to provide a comprehensive list of assessment instruments for the various psychiatric problems that are discussed in this book. Therefore, the recommendation of instruments is necessarily arbitrary and limited. The selection was primarily based on ease of administration and popularity. Table 2.1 gives some recommendations for some short and sound assessment instruments that are commonly used in clinical practice.

Table 2.1 Recommended measures for tracking treatment progress

Disorder	Measure Name	Authors	Description
Panic Disorder	Panic Disorder Severity Scale	Shear et al. (1997)	This seven-item clinician-administered scale measures panic attack frequency, distress during panic attacks, severity of anticipatory anxiety fear and avoidance of agoraphobic situations, fear and avoidance of panic-related sensations, and impairment in work and social functioning. The scale could be easily modified into a self-report scale.
Agoraphobia	Mobility Inventory	Chambless et al. (1985)	This 26-item scale asks respondents to rate different situations that are commonly avoided by people with agoraphobia. Each item is rated twice: once to measure avoidance when accompanied and the second time when alone.
Social Anxiety Disorder	Liebowitz Social Anxiety Scale	Liebowitz (1987)	This 24-tem scale asks respondents to rate their fear and avoidance of different social situations. The original scale is clinician-rated, but it can also be used as a self-report measure (Baker et al., 2002).
Phobias	Fear Survey Schedule-III	Wolpe and Lang (1964)	This 72-item scale measures the fear of a number of objects and situations. Alternatives to this rather lengthy measure are a variety of self-report instruments for specific fears and phobias (see Antony et al., 2001).
Obsessive Compulsive Disorder	Maudsley Obsessional Compulsive Inventory	Hodgson and Rachman (1977)	This 30-item scale measures common rituals. The scale includes a total score, and subscales for checking, cleaning, slowness, and doubting.

Table 2.1 Recommended measures for tracking treatment progress (*Continued*)

Disorder	Measure Name	Authors	Description
Generalized Anxiety Disorder	Penn State Worry Questionnaire	Meyer *et al.* (1990)	This 16-item questionnaire measures the general tendency to worry excessively.
Unipolar Depression	Beck Depression Inventory	Beck *et al.* (1979)	This is a 21-item self-report inventory that measures the severity of symptoms of depression. A revised version is available for purchase.
Alcohol Problems	Timeline Followback Calendar	Breslin *et al.* (2001)	The Timeline Followback Calendar asks respondents to indicate the amount of alcohol they consumed each day during the course of a certain time period. It can be used to monitor the patient's alcohol consumption during treatment.
Erectile Dysfunction	International Index of Erectile Function	Rosen *et al.* (1997)	This is a 15-item self-report questionnaire used to measure erectile function.
Chronic Pain	Pain Catastrophizing Scale	Thorn (2004)	This is a 13-item self-report instrument used to measure catastrophic beliefs associated with experiencing chronic pain.
Insomnia	Sleep Log	Edinger and Carney (2008)	The sleep log includes 11 questions about general sleep hygiene, daytime naps, sleep time, wake-up time, and sleep quality.

In addition to these instruments, it is highly recommended that the clinician generates a monitoring sheet for the patient to record specific problems, behaviors, or symptoms on a regular basis. Monitoring progress provides important feedback to the therapist, but it should not be overwhelming and overly time-consuming. If monitoring symptoms exceeds 15 minutes a day, the burden is probably too great and the patient is more likely to discontinue from treatment prematurely or is forced to complete the monitoring forms and questionnaires in a fast and unreliable way.

3 Confronting Phobias

Stewart's Spider Phobia

Stewart is a 25-year-old graduate student in international affairs at a large private university in the Northeast. He is engaged to one of his classmates, Alice. Both live off campus in a single family house they share with two other students. Stewart is a generally healthy person with no serious chronic disease, except for prehypertensive blood pressure and slightly elevated levels of cholesterol. Although he does not do any exercise, his weight is within the normal range for his height. He has not been taking any medication. Stewart's only health problem is a severe fear of spiders. He has been afraid of spiders for as long as he can remember. He avoids going to places where he expects spiders to be, especially basements, attics, old barns, and certain outdoor places, especially wooded areas. He is even uncomfortable looking at spider pictures, toy spiders, or movies and documentaries with spiders in them. To make sure that there are no spiders in his bedroom, he vacuums his room and the closet every night before going to bed. He further leaves a nightlight on, assuming that spiders avoid light and has to keep the door and windows closed throughout the night. He is afraid that spiders would crawl or jump at him and bite him. He reported that he believes that he was once bitten by spiders during a camping trip with his parents when he was around 10 years old. He realizes that his fear of spiders is more extreme than necessary and that it interferes with his life. His fiancée, Alice, urged him to do something about this issue, which she initially found cute, but which now puts increasing strain on the relationship.

An Introduction to Modern CBT: Psychological Solutions to Mental Health Problems, First Edition.
S. G. Hofmann. © 2012 S. G. Hofmann. Published 2012 by John Wiley & Sons, Ltd.

Definition of the Disorder

Specific phobia is characterized by excessive fear that is experienced in response to particular feared objects or situations. Stewart has an excessive fear of spiders. Exposure to spiders results in an immediate fear response that Stewart recognizes as being in excess of what is reasonable. Aside from fear, Stewart also experiences a strong sense of disgust that motivates him to avoid spiders. Other people may be concerned about panicking, experiencing anxious arousal, losing control, or fainting when encountering the phobic object or situation. Therefore, it is not at all uncommon for people with specific phobias to report panic attacks upon confronting the phobic stimulus. Fainting is a common concern among people with phobias of blood or injections.

As a result of his fear of spiders, Stewart avoids places where he might be confronted with spiders, such as basements, attics, old barns, wooded areas, and certain outdoor places. His fear of spiders causes him a significant degree of distress and significantly interferes with his normal functioning.

The DSM-IV distinguishes five types of specific phobias, namely *animal type* (e.g., fears of dogs, spiders, snakes), *natural environment type* (e.g., fears of heights, storms, being near water), *blood-injection-injury type* (e.g., fears of receiving an injection, seeing blood, undergoing surgery), *situational type* (e.g., fears of flying, closed spaces, driving), and *other type* (e.g., vomiting, costumed characters such as clowns). Stewart's specific phobia can obviously be described as animal type. As is common for specific phobia, Stewart's fear began when he was a child.

Specific phobias are the most common form of anxiety disorder in the population, with a lifetime prevalence rate of 12.5% (Kessler *et al.*, 2005). Without treatment, they follow a chronic course. Some of the specific phobia types (e.g., animals, lightning, enclosed spaces) are more commonly reported by women than by men, possibly because men underreport their degree of fear. Fewer sex differences are found in the case of heights, flying, and blood-injection-injury phobias (Stinson *et al.*, 2007). Furthermore, specific phobias appear to be less common among Asian and Hispanic adults than among white adults, the reasons for which have not yet been determined (Stinson *et al.*, 2007).

It has been suggested that humans are predisposed to acquire fears of objects or situations that were relevant to the survival of the species from an evolutionary perspective, such as poisonous spiders or snakes, more readily than other dangerous objects, such as cars, outlets, or fire arms (Seligman,

1971). Consistent with this notion is, for example, an experiment showing that that rhesus monkeys developed a fear of biologically relevant stimuli (a toy snake) but not of biologically irrelevant stimuli (flowers) after watching spliced video footage of monkeys appearing to respond fearfully to both kinds of stimuli (Cook and Mineka, 1989). However, a number of other studies suggest that the biological relevance of stimuli may not have as profound an influence on the ease with which a fear is acquired as was initially hypothesized (for a review, see Koerner *et al.*, 2010).

The development of specific phobias is often linked to Mowrer's (1939) two-stage theory of fear development. According to this model, specific phobias develop when a previously neutral stimulus (e.g., a dog) becomes associated with an aversive stimulus (pain after getting bitten by a dog) through the process of classical conditioning. This association is then maintained through avoidance of the feared stimulus (dog). However, despite its simplicity, Mowrer's theory cannot account for all, or even the majority, of cases of specific phobia in humans (e.g., Field, 2006). Similarly, Rachman (1991) argued that classical conditioning is not a sufficient explanation for the development of specific phobias because many individuals with this problem cannot recall a specific conditioning event that led to the onset of their fear, and conversely, many individuals who have had traumatic experiences do not develop a phobia. Instead, Rachman hypothesized that phobias can be acquired through an information pathway (e.g., by learning about the danger of dogs) and vicarious learning (e.g., by observing the mother being fearful of dogs). This explanation is consistent with the previously cited animal studies (e.g., Cook and Mineka, 1989). In addition to these learning pathways, it is possible that other fears are part of an inborn repertoire and phobias are acquired through "nonassociative pathways" (Poulton and Menzies, 2002a). However, this is an issue of current controversy (Davey, 2002; Mineka and Öhman, 2002; Poulton and Menzies, 2002b). For example, the nonassociative pathway hypothesis does not consider the important role of interoceptive cues (e.g., bodily symptoms) in conditioning events (Mineka and Öhman, 2002), and relies too heavily on explanations that are based in evolution, that by necessity are constructed *post hoc* (Davey, 2002).

The Treatment Model

Based on a review of the literature on both animals and humans, it can be concluded that cognitive processes are essential aspects in the acquisition and extinction of fears and phobias (Hofmann, 2008a). More specifically, it appears that two higher-order cognitive processes are important in fear acquisition: *harm expectancy* and *perceptions of predictability and controllability*. These cognitive processes appear to play a critical role in all forms of fear learning, even basic Pavlovian conditioning. For example, Stewart reported that he once was bitten by a spider when he was around 10. Although it is difficult to test the accuracy of this report, he still believes that spiders are dangerous animals that can directly attack him, bite him, and inflict pain and harm.

Consistent with previous research, Stewart shows an attentional bias related to spiders. Objects like snakes or spiders are especially likely to be associated with such an attentional bias because of their evolutionary relevance (Öhman *et al.*, 2001). The nature and consequences of this attentional bias are not completely understood. Whereas some studies have shown an enhanced attentional bias in individuals with a fear of spiders, others suggest that spider-fearful individuals are more likely to avoid spider-relevant stimuli (for a review, see Mogg and Bradley, 2006). Stewart's attentional bias is expressed by scanning the environment for spiders and by sometimes mistakenly assuming or perceiving the presence of a spider. This then leads to a typical fear reaction, characterized by a racing heart, subjective feeling of fear, and strong desire to leave the situation. In addition to the subjective feeling of fear, Stewart also experiences a feeling of disgust when being confronted with spiders. Refer to Figure 3.1 for an illustration of Stewart's spider problem.

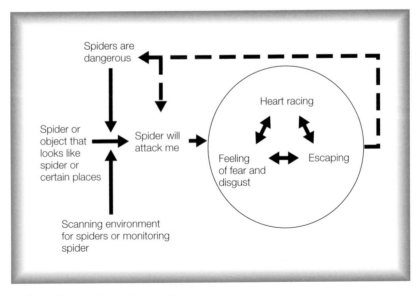

Figure 3.1 Stewart's spider problem.

Treatment Strategies

The primary problem of specific phobia is an excessive and irrational fear of objects or situations. The most effective strategy to target specific phobia is through repeated and prolonged *in vivo* exposure while discouraging the use of any avoidance strategies. Acceptance instructions can further discourage experiential avoidance and encourage the patient to fully experience the emotion.

Another effective strategy is to correct the patient's misinformation about the potential danger of the feared object or situation. This is accomplished through psychoeducation and cognitive restructuring. Attention retraining by encouraging the patient to redirect attention toward nonfearful rather than fearful stimuli can be a useful part of treatment. Finally, breathing retraining exercises can be useful to downregulate the hyperarousal that is often associated with the phobic response, assuming that these breathing exercises are not used as avoidance strategies. Refer to Figure 3.2 for an illustration of how treatment strategies intervene in Stewart's spider problem.

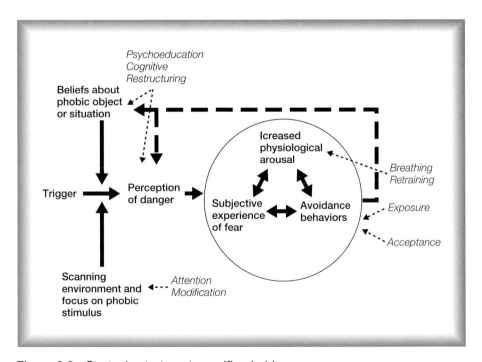

Figure 3.2   Strategies to target specific phobias.

Psychoeducation and cognitive restructuring

People with specific phobias often have irrational beliefs about the phobic object or situation. For example, people with flying phobia often overestimate the probability of getting in a plane crash. When a person with a flying phobia then learns about a recent plane crash, he or she will use this information to support his or her belief that plane crashes are likely events. In fact, they are very unlikely events. One way to get an accurate estimate for the probability of dying in a plane crash is by dividing the number of people who died in a plane crash into the number of total flights all passengers took within a certain time period. Based on this calculation, the annual risk of being killed in a plane crash for the average American is about 1 in 11 million. In contrast, the annual risk of being killed in a motor vehicle crash for the average American is about 1 in 5,000. In other words, it is a lot safer to fly than to drive. A simple discussion of these facts can question some long-held and maladaptive beliefs about the potential danger of a situation or object. The therapist might point the patient to appropriate internet sites to learn about these facts.

Similarly, many people with spider phobias hold incorrect and maladaptive beliefs about the dangers of spiders. Spider bites are very rare. There are about 40,000 species and 109 families of spiders. In the United States, there are many hundreds of species, depending on the states. In Texas, for example, there are about 900 spider species. Only a few are dangerous to humans. Of the spiders that are dangerous to humans, only two species exist in the United States: the black widow and the brown recluse. The bites are painful, but not deadly, unless the victim is allergic to the venom or has a weak immune system. Similar to the chances of dying in a plane crash, it is highly unlikely to get bitten by a dangerous spider, let alone a deadly spider.

Attention and situation modification

Specific phobias are typically associated with a bias in the initial stimulus registration phase of cognitive processing because attention is often rapidly and automatically deployed toward threatening information. Although this shift toward threatening information may be evolutionarily adaptive, it becomes problematic when it leads to hypervigilence (MacLeod et al., 2002; Mogg and Bradley, 1998). Macleod and colleagues (2002) increased anxiety symptoms by manipulating attention in a nonclinical sample by training people to attend to threatening stimuli using a computer task. Subsequent studies showed that encouraging people to attend to nonfearful stimuli can be an effective method to modify the attentional biases and alleviate anxiety symptoms. In Stewart's case, the therapist might ask him to count the number of legs the spider has, describe the color of the spider's hair, examine the movement of his abdomen, or give the spider a name.

Breathing retraining

Exposure to a phobic stimulus can often trigger a panic attack. The phenomenon of panic attacks and their treatment will be discussed in greater detail in Chapter 4. Panic attacks that are triggered by phobic objects or situations are referred to as situational panic attacks. One characteristic feature of panic attacks is hyperventilation, which is associated with the typical panic attack symptoms, such as feelings of lightheadedness, heart racing, and tingling. Breathing retraining can be an effective method to downregulate the physiological hyperarousal associated with the phobic response. A strategy to regulate breathing will be discussed in Chapter 4.

Exposures

Exposure is a highly effective intervention strategy for treating anxiety disorders. Before conducting exposure practices, the therapist has to identify the fear-eliciting cues. In the case of specific phobia, the cues are the situational triggers.

Before conducting exposure practices, the therapist has to have a very good understanding of the patient's fear-provoking and avoided situations. It is often useful to ask patients for ratings to quantify their fear and avoidance (e.g., on a 0–10 point scale).

This information is then used for the exposure practices. It is essential that the patient understands the importance of these practices. The example below provides an example of the basic exposure rationale.

Clinical Example: Consequences of Avoidance and Exposure Rationale

Anxiety and avoidance are obviously very closely connected. Let me explain this by using an example (Figure 3.3). Immediately after you escape (avoid), your anxiety goes down and you feel relief. This is the

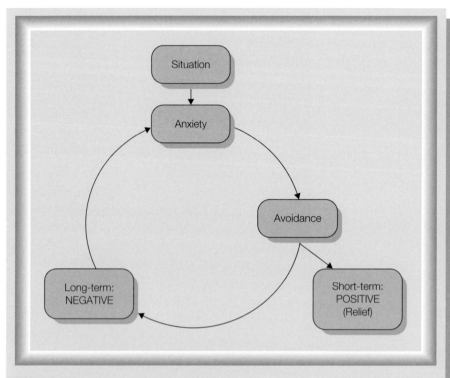

Figure 3.3 Vicious cycle of avoidance.

short-term positive consequence (relief). However, avoidance also has a long-term negative consequence: you will experience anxiety every time you encounter this situation again in the future because you never gave your body the chance to habituate and to learn that the situation or object was not dangerous. Thus, avoidance keeps your anxiety alive, which is the reason why you keep feeling anxious when confronted with a particular situation or object. This is also the reason why anxiety becomes worse after repeated avoidance, and why avoidance tends to spread to other situations and areas of your life (elicit examples).

Let's play a little mind game. Let's think of two scenarios. In the first scenario, you encounter the feared situation or object and you use avoidance strategies. Your anxiety gets greater and greater until avoidance brings it down and you feel relief (Figure 3.4).

However, if you encounter the same situation or object again in the future, nothing changes. You will again feel the same level anxiety when you are confronted with a similar situation or object.

Now let's assume another scenario. Let's assume that you could stay in the anxiety-provoking situation or be exposed to the feared object

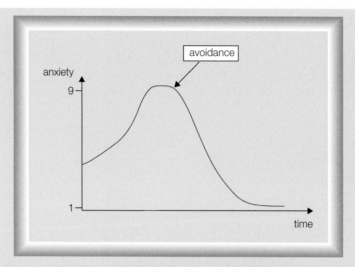

Figure 3.4 Example of an anxiety episode with avoidance.

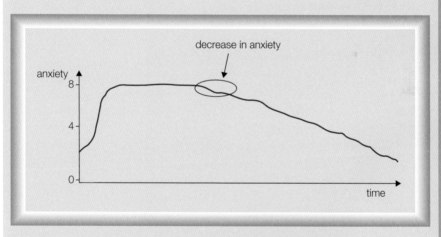

Figure 3.5 Example of an anxiety episode without avoidance.

indefinitely. What do you think would happen to your anxiety if you did not avoid but stayed with your anxiety? (After 1 hour, 8 hours, 20 hours, 1 week, etc.?).

Eventually, your anxiety will decrease. This reduction in your anxiety response happens automatically and naturally (Figure 3.5). Do you know what the underlying biological mechanism is? The reason for this is because your body has regulatory mechanisms that become active after a certain period of time of exposure. Physiologically, your parasympathetic nervous system kicks in and brings your physiological arousal down. In other words, your body eventually adjusts to the anxiety-provoking situation or object. But this process only occurs if you fully experience your anxiety. This means staying in the situation or confronting the object for an extended period of time without using any kind of avoidance strategies.

In addition, this will give you the opportunity to test your beliefs and see if the feared consequence actually occurs. Because you have been avoiding experiencing your anxiety to its fullest extent, you have never given yourself the chance to see what actually happens.

Therefore, exposure works because your body naturally down regulates your anxiety, and because it provides you with an opportunity to test your belief. You can see if the feared outcome is really happening, and, in case it actually does happen, if it is really such as terrible thing.

What do you think will happen the next few times you encounter the same situation or object again after you successfully exposed yourself the first time? You will experience smaller anticipatory anxiety, smaller maximum anxiety, and quicker reduction in anxiety. Your anxiety will not be as bad because you realized that you experienced a reduction in your anxiety. This is a learning process. And, as with any learning process, it will get easier the more often you do it.

Exposure is the only way to eliminate anxiety. If there was an easier and less painful way, we would do it. I know that this all sounds very frightening. But, you really have only two options: You either decide to live with your avoidance, which is likely to become worse and not better, or you take this last and very courageous step by undergoing this effective procedure. However, this treatment can only work if you are willing and committed to do it. Once we start with it, we will have to go through it to the very end.

In preparation for exposure, it is important to develop a hierarchy of situations that the patient typically fears or avoids. Ideally, such a hierarchy should consist of 10 to 15 items, ranging from mildly difficult (e.g., about a 30 on a 0–100 point scale) at the bottom of the hierarchy to very difficult (e.g., 90–100) at the top of the hierarchy. The items on this hierarchy should be specific, concrete, and take into consideration the factors that influence the patient's specific concerns. For example, the task of "looking at a spider" may be broken up into several parts and arranged in order of difficulty based on movement, physical attributes, and physical presence of the spider, in case these are factors that influence the patient's fear. In this case, some items on this hierarchy might include looking at a picture of an animated spider, looking at a photograph of a real spider, watching a video clip of a

Table 3.1   Exposure hierarchy for Stewart's fear of spiders

Item	Description	Fear Rating (0 to 100)
1	Hold a tarantula in the hand.	100
2	Have tarantula crawl over hand.	95
3	Touch tarantula's abdomen with index finger.	90
4	Touch tarantula with a stick.	75
5	Touch window of the terrarium next to the spider.	70
6	Stand directly in front of terrarium with tarantula inside.	65
7	Stand 4 feet away from terrarium with tarantula inside.	50
8	Hold tarantula molt.	50
9	Handle realistically looking rubber spider.	40
10	Watch video clips with close-up of tarantulas.	30

still spider, watching a video clip of a spider moving quickly toward the camera, handling a plastic spider, and looking at a live spider in a terrarium. An example of an exposure hierarchy is provided in Table 3.1.

Stewart was asked to begin the exposure with a task on his hierarchy that is associated with a mild to moderate level of fear. Initially, he watched the documentary *Predator of the Wild,* with close-ups of the tarantula, and then was asked to handle a realistic-looking rubber spider. The initial exposure tasks should range between 40 and 60 on a 0–100 point scale. These initial tasks should be challenging, but the patient should be likely to be able to complete them successfully. Patients can use their fear ratings to gauge their readiness to proceed to the next step. Stewart was asked to stay with a task until his fear decreased to a level at which he was willing to try the next task on the hierarchy. Stewart noticed that the quicker he progressed through his hierarchy steps, the quicker he experienced a reduction in fear. Other patients may prefer to take the exposure steps more gradually and still experience a reduction in fear over time.

It is beneficial to conduct regular checks on the patient's progress by going back to earlier exposure tasks to ensure that the patient can still master the easier steps in the hierarchy. Patients should be encouraged to stay in the situation until their level of discomfort decreases. If they leave the situation, they should be encouraged to return to the situation as soon as possible after leaving. It is desirable, but not necessary, for patients to experience a decrease in discomfort within a single exposure session. In such cases, patients typically still experience a reduction in fear across sessions.

In order to gain a maximum level of benefit from the exposure tasks, the practices should be frequent and planned in advance. Patients should set aside one to two hours for their exposure practices. Longer exposures are often more effective than shorter exposures. It is important that patients do not use any avoidance strategies, such as safety behaviors. Safety behaviors are overt or subtle behaviors that individuals engage in to reduce fear or prevent a feared outcome (e.g., getting hurt) in encounters with their feared object or situation. Over the long term, use of these behaviors may undermine treatment outcome by preventing clients from learning that the feared situation is not, in fact, dangerous.

Empirical Support

In vivo exposure is the most efficacious treatment for specific phobias compared with wait-list and placebo interventions (Choy *et al.*, 2007; Wolitzky-Taylor *et al.*, 2008). The treatment gains are maintained for at least one year, particularly when treatment completers continue exposure practices after treatment has ended (Choy *et al.*, 2007). In the case of blood and needle phobias, the treatment of choice is applied tension. Applied tension involves tensing the muscles of one's body during exposure to feared situations, which triggers a temporary increase in blood pressure and prevents fainting. A study comparing exposure with applied tension to exposure without the tension exercises found that applied tension led to better outcomes for the treatment of blood phobia (Öst *et al.*, 1991).

The most recent innovation for the treatment of specific phobias involves virtual reality. This treatment uses a computer program to generate a three-dimensional, digitized version of the feared object or situation and enables clients to carry out exposure practices in the simulated environment (Rothbaum *et al.*, 2000). This treatment modality can be useful for exposing the patient to objects or situations that are difficult or costly to recreate (e.g., a turbulent flight in the case of flying phobia). It further offers a viable alternative for individuals who refuse *in vivo* exposures.

Conventional psychiatric medication (anxiolytic and antidepressant medication), either in isolation or in combination to CBT, has not been shown to be overly beneficial for treating specific phobias (Choy *et al.,* 2007). However, recent evidence suggests that the use of d-cycloserine (DCS), a partial agonist at the glycine recognition site of the glutamatergic N-methyl-D-aspartate receptor, facilitates exposure therapy of virtual reality-administered flying phobia (Ressler *et al.,* 2004).

Recommended Further Readings

Therapist guide

Craske, M. G., Antony, M. M., and Barlow, D. H. (2006). *Mastering your fears and phobias. Treatments that work,* 2nd edition, therapist guide. New York: Oxford University Press.

Patient guide

Antony, M. M., Craske, M. G., and Barlow, D. H. (2006). *Mastering your fears and phobias. Treatments that work,* 2nd edition, workbook. New York: Oxford University Press.

4 Fighting Panic and Agoraphobia

Sarah's Panic

Sarah is a 45-year-old, white, married woman, and mother of two teenage sons. She works part-time as an accountant. During the last five years, Sarah has been experiencing repeated attacks of extreme fear that are seemingly out of the blue. She remembered her first attack at work, about two months after she began her job. She was asked to hand deliver some paperwork to another office. When she entered a crowded elevator to deliver the package, she had the feeling of suffocating. She remembered that she felt short of breath, her heart was racing, that she was sweating and trembling. People in the elevator noticed her distress and one of the people called an ambulance which brought her to the emergency room. No physical reason for this incident could be identified. Since then, she has had about one to two attacks per month. During these attacks, she typically experiences heart palpitations, feelings of breathlessness, chest pain, feelings of unreality, and sweating. She has undergone many medical tests, but no medical explanation for these attacks has been found. However, she still worries about having more attacks and believes that someday a doctor will be able to identify a medical reason for these attacks. Sarah noticed that these attacks are more likely to happen when she is away from home. She feels somewhat more secure when she knows that there is a hospital close by. She feels especially uncomfortable in crowded places, such as malls and subways. She also avoids traveling by train or plane. She avoids these situations because help is not easily available in case she experiences an attack. She can only travel with her husband and her sister. Sometimes, on a good day, she is able to enter

An Introduction to Modern CBT: Psychological Solutions to Mental Health Problems, First Edition.
S. G. Hofmann. © 2012 S. G. Hofmann. Published 2012 by John Wiley & Sons, Ltd.

malls or take the subway if she carries her cell phone. She thinks that her fear about these attacks is somewhat irrational but wishes she would not have them. Her husband is very supportive and wishes she did not have to suffer from these attacks. She has been seeing a psychiatrist, who has prescribed her various antidepressants and serotonin reuptake inhibitors. These medications have not been effective.

Definition of the Disorder

The DSM-IV defines a panic attack as a discrete episode of intense fear or discomfort. During these attacks, four or more physical symptoms develop suddenly and reach a peak within 10 minutes. Typical symptoms include heart racing or pounding, sweating, trembling or shaking, sensations of shortness of breath or smothering, chest pain or discomfort, nausea or abdominal distress, dizziness, feeling unsteady or lightheaded, feelings of unreality or being detached from oneself, fear of losing control or going crazy, fear of dying, numbing or tingling sensations, and chills or hot flushes.

Panic attacks are intense and sudden fear attacks. These attacks are not unique to panic disorder. That is, a panic attack can occur in a variety of situations, and can be reported by a variety of different patients. For example, a patient who is afraid of social situations may report a panic attack in a social situation, and a patient with a spider phobia may report a panic attack when seeing a spider. There are three types of panic attacks that are differentiated by the presence or absence of situational triggers: unexpected (or uncued) panic attacks, situationally bound (or cued) panic attacks, and situationally predisposed panic attacks. The panic attack of a patient with a spider phobia who sees a spider is an example of a situationally bound panic attack. Situationally predisposed panic attacks are more likely to occur during exposure to a situational trigger, but are not invariably associated with it. For example, a patient with the fear of driving a car may report panic attacks while driving sometimes, but not always. Unexpected panic attacks have no obvious situational trigger and occur out of the blue. These attacks are typically reported by panic disorder patients, whereas patients with a specific phobia typically report situationally bound panic attacks.

Panic attacks in patients with panic disorder are unexpected or situationally bound. In Sarah's case, her first attack happened in an elevator, completely unexpectedly. These attacks were then more likely to occur in crowded places, such as malls and subways, as well as trains or planes. As is typical for patients with panic disorder and agoraphobia, Sarah began avoiding these places and situations because escape might be difficult or embarrassing or because help may not be available in the event of her having a panic attack. Typical agoraphobic situations are air travel, being home alone, driving over a bridge, being in crowded places, driving a car, using public transportation, and riding in an elevator. Often, people with agoraphobia either avoid these situations completely or they experience marked distress or anxiety about having a panic attack when being exposed to these situations. In order to minimize or cope with their distress in such situations, patients with agoraphobia very often carry medication with them, take medication or alcohol prior to entering the situation, or require the presence of a safety person (a spouse or friend) or safety signal (e.g., a "lucky" bracelet or a cell phone). In Sarah's case, her husband serves as an important safety person. Please note that this modern clinical definition of the term "agoraphobia" is quite different from the original Greek translation of the word, which is "fear of open spaces."

Agoraphobia and panic disorder have been linked in the DSM, although there is a current debate whether it might be more meaningful to treat them as completely separate disorders in future revisions of the DSM. The DSM-IV reports that epidemiological studies throughout the world consistently indicate a lifetime prevalence rate of panic disorder with or without agoraphobia between 1.5% and 3.5%. Approximately one-third to one-half of panic disorder patients also have agoraphobia. A much higher rate of agoraphobia is encountered in clinical samples. This discrepancy between clinical and epidemiological prevalence rates might indicate that panic disorder patients with agoraphobia are more likely to seek professional help than panic disorder patients without agoraphobia (Barlow, 2002).

The diagnosis of panic disorder is assigned if the patient reports recurring unexpected panic attacks, and if at least one of the attacks has been followed by a period of at least 1 month of worry about having additional attacks, worry about the implications of the attack or its consequences, or significant changes in behavior related to the attacks. If these panic attacks are not due to a general medical condition or the effects of a substance (e.g., medication, drug, alcohol), it is highly likely that the patient suffers from panic disorder or a related anxiety disorder. If the patient additionally meets the criteria for agoraphobia, the diagnosis of panic disorder with agoraphobia would be assigned. Otherwise, the patient would receive the diagnosis of panic disorder without agoraphobia. In clinical settings, over

95% of patients with agoraphobia have a current or past diagnosis of panic disorder.

Panic disorder with and without agoraphobia must be distinguished from other anxiety disorders that have panic attacks as an associated feature. In particular, the differentiation from specific phobia can be difficult in certain cases. Specific phobic individuals and patients with panic disorder with agoraphobia can fear the same situation for different reasons (e.g., with air travel, people with panic disorder fear having a panic attack, whereas people with a specific phobia fear crashing). However, the fear of panic attacks does not clearly distinguish patients with panic disorder. A study on subjects who are fearful of driving an automobile, for example, showed that 53% reported panic attacks, and 15% reported car accidents, as the primary reason for their phobia, although the majority of driving fearful individuals (69.6%) met criteria for specific phobia (Ehlers *et al.*, 1994). Those patients who reported panic attacks as the primary reason for their phobia were particularly concerned about anxiety symptoms while driving. Similar results were found in a group of individuals with social anxiety disorder and fear of public speaking (Hofmann *et al.*, 1995). The people who attributed their public speaking anxiety to panic attacks were more concerned about their bodily sensations in the public speaking situation than individuals who attributed their fear to other things. It seems that specific phobic individuals and patients with panic disorder are mainly different in the cues that trigger their anxiety. Internally generated cues, such as bodily sensations and cognitive images, seem to be more salient for panic disorder, whereas external, situational cues are more salient for specific phobia (Craske, 1991). In other words, panic disorder patients typically fear their bodily symptoms.

The age of onset for panic disorder and agoraphobia is between late adolescence and mid-30s with considerable variations. On rare occasions, the disorder can begin in childhood, and after the age of 45. In Sarah's case, her first panic attack happened relatively late in life. The course of the disorder varies from individual to individual. Some patients report episodic outbreaks with years of remission in between, whereas others show continuous severe symptomatology. Usually, agoraphobia develops within the first year of the onset of panic disorder, but again, the variation is considerable. In Sarah's case, her agoraphobic avoidance developed soon after the panic attacks started and the course of her illness was continuous and severe.

Panic disorder has been a defining diagnostic category for the DSM. The original conceptualization of the disorder is based on a medical illness model, which assumes the existence of distinct and mutually exclusive syndromes with an inherently organic etiology and specific treatment indications (Klein, 1964; Klein and Klein, 1989). The diagnostic syndrome was identified after Klein observed that some patients with anxiety neurosis responded well to the antidepressant imipramine, whereas others did not. He argued that, similar to an antibiotic which is effective for treating a bacterial infection but which is ineffective for treating a viral infection, the differential response to imipramine identifies two qualitatively different disorders. Clark (1986) later introduced a cognitive model of panic, which assumes that panic attacks result from the catastrophic misinterpretation of certain bodily sensations, such as palpitations, breathlessness, and dizziness. An example of such a catastrophic misinterpretation would be a healthy individual who perceives palpitations as evidence of an impending heart attack. The vicious cycle of the cognitive model suggests that various external (i.e., the feeling of being trapped in a supermarket) or internal stimuli (i.e., body sensations, thought or images) trigger a state of apprehension if these stimuli are perceived as a threat. It is assumed that this state is accompanied by fearful bodily sensations which, if interpreted in a catastrophic fashion, further increase the apprehension and the intensity of bodily sensations. This influential model further assumes that the attacks appear to come from "out of the blue" because patients fail to distinguish between the triggering bodily sensations, the subsequent panic attack, and the thoughts about the meaning of an attack. The model accounts for pharmacological treatment success because any treatment that reduces the frequency of bodily fluctuations also reduces possible panic attack triggers. However, once the medication is withdrawn, the patient is likely to relapse unless the patient's tendency to interpret bodily sensations in a catastrophic fashion has also changed. This model has sparked nothing less than a cognitive revolution within the field of anxiety disorders.

The Treatment Model

The trigger of panic can be a bodily symptom, such as an irregular heart beat, a tingling sensation, or a change in breathing that might lead to feelings of lightheadedness. These symptoms can be easily induced by hyperventilation or even subtle changes in breathing rate and depth. In patients with agoraphobia, a trigger could be a thought of being trapped and unable to reach safety in case a physical or mental catastrophe occurs.

If a person sees him- or herself as being vulnerable and weak, but believes that he or she has to appear strong and resilient, such triggers are more likely to be perceived as threatening and dangerous. For example, typical

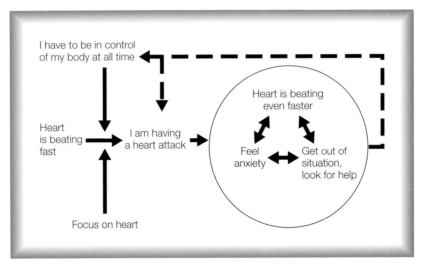

Figure 4.1   Sarah's panic cycle.

maladaptive appraisals of heart palpitations might be "I will have a heart attack" or feelings of dizziness might be "I am going crazy" or "I am going to faint." This then leads to increased physiological symptoms, agitated behaviors, and heightened subjective anxiety. Together, this causes the initial discomfort and anxiety to spiral to a state of panic, which reinforces the person's maladaptive appraisal of a harmless trigger. It also reinforces the schema of the person as being weak and unable to cope with a dangerous world and seemingly uncontrollable bodily sensations. Figure 4.1 shows the cycle of one of Sarah's panic attacks.

An important dispositional variable of panic disorder is anxiety sensitivity. Anxiety sensitivity determines the tendency to respond fearfully to anxiety symptoms. This construct has been developed based on the expectancy model (Reiss, 1991). In contrast to the cognitive model, the expectancy model posits that individuals with high anxiety sensitivity believe that high arousal itself can lead to harmful consequences, without necessarily misinterpreting any physical sensations (McNally, 1994). Although the expectancy model and the cognitive model show important theoretical differences, the model-specific treatment strategies are relatively similar. The biggest difference is that the cognitive model places relatively more emphasis on the misinterpretation of bodily symptoms, whereas the expectancy model places a relatively greater emphasis on exposure techniques, maladaptive beliefs, and expectancies concerning the anxiety symptoms.

Treatment Strategies

The vicious panic cycle depicted in Figure 4.1 can be interrupted at various points. If the person does not interpret a harmless trigger as a threat, the cycle will not initiate in the first place. For this reason, psychoeducation about the nature of panic attacks, bodily symptoms, and the influence of breathing on physiology are important common elements of panic disorder treatment protocols. Cognitive restructuring is another important component. Cognitive restructuring explores and challenges maladaptive schemas (e.g., "I always have to appear strong" or "I have to be in control over my body at all times"), as well as maladaptive, catastrophic cognitive appraisals of harmless bodily symptoms (e.g., "my pounding heart beat is a sign of an impending heart attack" or "my dizziness is a sign that I will go crazy"). Breathing exercises can be very useful to slow down the physiological aspects of panic attacks, thus stopping the vicious cycle from building up. Moreover, changing breathing in general can reduce the likelihood that changes in breathing rate or depth can lead to physiological symptoms that trigger panic. Finally, exposing patients to panic-related and fear-provoking sensations or situations while encouraging them to accept these experiences without using avoidance strategies are highly effective methods to treat panic. The types and number of exposure practices depend greatly on the level of agoraphobic avoidance. If patients report a high level of agoraphobic avoidance, situational exposures are the most beneficial components of treatment. If the level of agoraphobic avoidance is low, exposure exercises typically focus on activities and situations that provoke fearful bodily symptoms. Newer protocols also include acceptance-based strategies. These strategies are summarized in Figure 4.2 and will be described in more detail below.

Psychoeducation

Panic attacks are extremely frightening experiences. Naturally, patients try to explain these unexplained phenomena. Even after repeated negative medical tests, patients often assume that these attacks are a signal or symptom of a serious medical health problem. A very effective initial therapeutic step is to educate patients about the nature of panic attacks. Patients are often surprised to learn that a significant number of other people suffer from the same problem, that panic attacks are not qualitatively different from extreme fear when confronted with real danger, and that these attacks are actually

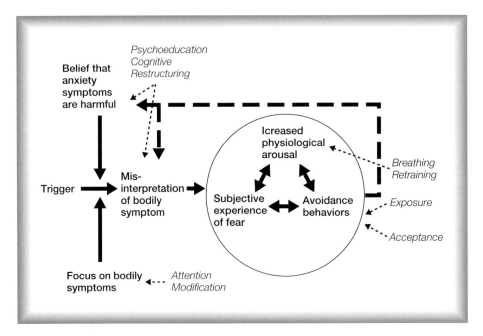

Figure 4.2 Strategies to target panic.

part of an evolutionary adaptive fight-flight response system, which functions to protect the person. The difference from normal and adaptive fear episodes that we experience when confronted with dangerous situations, such as a near car accident, is that panic attacks happen for no apparent reason. Therefore, panic attacks can be viewed as false alarms of our biological fight-flight response system. As is the case for other fear episodes, the symptoms that are experienced during a panic attack are neither dangerous nor harmful. Rather, they are adaptive and protective because they serve to mobilize and energize the organism. Such a discussion about the nature of panic attacks normalizes and demystifies the experience, and provides groundwork to explore alternative viewpoints. In order to demystify the panic experience, the following information about the nature of panic and panic disorder may be provided:

Clinical Example: Psychoeducation about Panic

Panic disorder is a condition in which people experience intense fear or discomfort for no apparent reason. When people avoid situations or activities because of these attacks, the diagnosis of panic disorder with agoraphobia is given. Panic disorder and agoraphobia are common problems. Although these panic attacks are extremely frightening, they are not actually dangerous to your physical health. This does not imply that the panic attacks you are experiencing are not real. They are absolutely real and you are suffering from a real problem. However, the good news is that these attacks will not cause you any physical harm and they can be treated very effectively with a specific psychological intervention, called cognitive behavioral therapy.

Before we discuss the specific treatment techniques, you should know something about these attacks. First of all, panic attacks are not at all uncommon. In fact, everybody knows what these attacks feel like because everybody has occasionally experienced episodes of extreme fear. Usually, these anxiety attacks happen when we perceive danger. For example, imagine you are driving your car on a highway in the left lane. Suddenly, the car in front of you slams on the breaks. You see the break lights, slam on your breaks and almost crash into it. The car behind you does the same. You and the other two cars almost got into a very bad accident. You will likely experience intense anxiety. Your breath might become faster and heavier, you might feel hot flushes, your heart might pound fast, and you might have sweaty hands. These are symptoms of extreme fear and you experience these symptoms because you almost crashed into the person in front of you. These feelings are normal and adaptive and are designed by Mother Nature to prepare our bodies for action in order to avoid danger. These feelings had important survival function for our ancestors who needed to flee or fight potential predators or enemies. In the case of panic disorder, these symptoms happen for no apparent reason. This does not make them less real. However, it is important to realize that these anxiety attacks are not qualitatively different from the fear attacks in response to obvious threat. In the case of panic attacks, the cues that trigger the fear attacks are more subtle and less obvious. But they are not qualitatively different from other episodes of intense fear. One important goal of treatment is to find out why these attacks keep recurring.

Attention and situation modification

Panic attacks are typically perceived as coming from out of the blue and occurring for no apparent reason. However, when patients are asked to closely monitor the time, situations, and circumstances of these attacks, patterns often become apparent. For example, Sarah noticed that her attacks more often occurred when she was emotionally labile. In fact, some of her worst attacks happened within hours after arguments with her husband. Knowing this demystified the nature of the attacks and gave Sarah some control over them.

She also reported that she felt very uncomfortable during a yoga class because she does not like focusing in her body. She found that focusing closely on her heart beat and breathing can easily trigger a panic attack. Again, knowing that panic attacks can be triggered by focusing her attention on specific symptoms gave Sarah a sense of control, made the attacks more predictable, and reduced her anxiety about them. In addition, raising curiosity about an experience can help reduce the fear of it.

Breathing retraining

Many panic patients overbreathe (hyperventilate). Therefore, some theories assume that abnormalities in breathing and hyperventilation or hypocapnia (lower than normal levels of PCO_2) cause panic symptoms (Klein, 1993; Ley, 1985). For example, Ley (1985) proposed that chronic hyperventilation leads to a lowered threshold for panic, and Klein (1993) assumed that panic is a result of an overly sensitive suffocation alarm response system. Therefore, breathing exercises are a usual component of psychological interventions. More recent studies support the unique contribution of breathing retraining for treating panic disorder (Meuret *et al.,* 2010).

Breathing results in an exchange of oxygen and carbon dioxide. The body is particularly sensitive to changing levels of carbon dioxide. As a result of hyperventilating, the blood becomes more alkaline (less acidic), blood vessels in the body constrict, and less oxygen is carried through the blood to the tissues, including the brain, which leads to the typical hyperventilation symptoms such as dizziness, lightheadedness, breathlessness, and feelings of unreality.

Breathing retraining exercises teach patients a breathing technique designed to slow their respiration rate and promote diaphragmatic breathing. This approach aims to reduce the frequency of panic attacks by helping patients attribute their symptoms to overbreathing and by teaching patients to correct breathing habits that attenuate the intensity of such symptoms. The following breathing retraining instructions might discourage patients from hyperventilating:

Clinical Example: Breathing Instructions

The way you breathe has a direct effect on your body. Specifically, hyperventilating can trigger or worsen panic attacks. You hyperventilate if you breathe in and out too deeply and too quickly. Breathing brings oxygen into your body and carbon dioxide out of your body. When you hyperventilate, you breathe in more oxygen than your body really needs. Paradoxically, your body compensates for this change by transporting less oxygen to the various parts of your body, including some areas of your brain. This then triggers a number of automatic biological mechanisms that leads to the typical sensations of hyperventilation, such as tingling, hot flushes, sweatiness, dizziness, and feelings of derealization (the sensation that you are in a dream-like state and that this is not really happening). When you stop hyperventilating, these symptoms quickly diminish and your body returns to normal. Some people have an unhealthy way of breathing. They breathe too hard, too deeply, too often, or irregularly. This can trigger or worsen a panic attack in a given situation. Some people also habitually breathe in such an unhealthy way. This can make it more likely that little changes in your bodily can trigger panic attacks.

In order to retrain yourself to breath in a more healthy way, set aside at least 10 minutes every day. Sit comfortably in a chair, place your right hand on your chest and the left hand on your belly. Notice how your hands are moving. A healthy way of breathing causes your left hand on your belly to slowly move up and down, while your right hand on your chest stays still. Breathe slowly, gently, and avoid deep breaths. Pause for about one second right before you breathe in. If this exercise is too boring, listen to some relaxing music while you do it.

Cognitive restructuring

Many maladaptive cognitions of patients with panic disorder are misconceptions due to the cognitive error of probability overestimation (overestimating an unlikely and undesirable event) and catastrophic thinking (blowing things out of proportion). We will discuss catastrophic thinking in Chapter 5. Here, we will discuss probability overestimation in more detail.

During cognitive restructuring, the patient's maladaptive thoughts are treated as hypotheses. Patients are encouraged to become objective observers and, similar to scientists, explore the nature of their anxiety with the goal of finding effective strategies to deal with it. In order to identify and challenge maladaptive thoughts, the therapist and patient critically discuss the evidence for and against a particular assumption through a debate (or Socratic dialogue). This is done by using information from the patient's past experiences (e.g., what is the probability based on your past experience?) and by delivering more adequate information (e.g., what are the high risk factors of cardiovascular diseases?). The purpose of this discussion is to correct maladaptive cognitions. Whenever possible, the therapist should also explore ways to test the validity of these thoughts by, for example, encouraging patients to expose themselves to the feared and/or avoided activities or situations. The following dialogue between Sarah and the therapist illustrates the Socratic questioning method to explore probability overestimation.

Clinical Example: Probability Overestimation

Therapist: What happens when you feel these symptoms?
Sarah: I get very afraid.
Therapist: Why exactly are you afraid?
Sarah: I think that something is wrong with me, that I may have a heart attack.
Therapist: Why do you think that these symptoms are caused by a heart attack?
Sarah: Well, because these are typical symptoms of a heart attack.
Therapist: Have you ever had a heart attack?
Sarah: No, my doctor says that everything is O.K.
Therapist: So how do you know that those are typical symptoms of a heart attack?
Sarah: (Laughs) Well, I guess I don't. But I am afraid that they might be.
Therapist: So you *think* that these symptoms are related to a medical condition. How high would you rate the probability that these symptoms are related to a heart problem using a 0 to 100 scale?
Sarah: Well, I know that my doctor did not find anything. I would therefore only give it a probability rating of 40%.
Therapist: So you are saying that you believe that there is a 40% chance that you are having a heart attack when you experience the symptoms of palpitations, chest pain, and breathlessness.
Sarah: I guess that sounds about right.
Therapist: Just to review, a probability of 40% means that you are saying that 4 out of 10 times that you experience these symptoms it is because you are having a heart attack. Let's find some evidence for

this assumption based on your past experience. What do you think is the total number of panic attacks that you have had in your life?

Sarah: Oh, my gosh. Maybe 50 or 60?

Therapist: Okay. So according to your estimation, you should have had at least 20 heart attacks by now, because 40% of 50 is 20. But how many heart attacks did you actually have?

Sarah: (Smiles) None.

Therapist: Right. So how accurate do you think your probability estimation is that these symptoms are indeed related to a heart attack based on your past experience?

Sarah: I guess it must be much lower than 40%.

Therapist: I agree. If we use past experience, it would be 0 divided by 50, which is 0%. Right?

Sarah: Right.

Therapist: So why don't we keep track of this from now on. I would like you to estimate the likelihood that you will die of a heart attack at the beginning of each week and after you had an attack, I want you to write down how likely you thought that it would end up in a heart attack using a scale from 0 (not likely at all) to 100 (very likely). So that we can experiment more with these attacks, I suggest that you go into situations that make it more likely that these attacks are going to happen. What do you think?

Exposure

Exposure is a highly effective intervention strategy for treating anxiety disorders (see Chapter 3 for general exposure instructions). Before conducting exposure practices, the therapist has to identify the fear-eliciting cues. In the case of panic disorder, the cues are often the physiological symptoms, and in the case of agoraphobia, the cues are often the situational triggers.

Before conducting exposure practices, the therapist has to have a good understanding of the patient's fear-provoking and avoided situations. It is often useful to ask patients for ratings to quantify their fear and avoidance (e.g., on a 0–10 point scale). For example, consistent with the model depicted in Figure 4.1, Sarah misinterprets her accelerated heart rate as an impending heart attack, leading to a panic attack, which results in avoidance behaviors.

Exposure to physical sensations. Sarah experiences discomfort when she feels that her heart is beating fast. As a result, she avoids physical exercise. Upon further exploration, Sarah reported that she also avoids other situations that induce strong physiological symptoms, including going to a sauna (because of feelings of suffocating) and drinking strong coffee (because of caffeine-induced arousal). In Sarah's case, some of the feared sensations could be induced in the therapist office. Some of the examples include holding one's breath (to induce feelings of breathlessness and suffocation), breathing through a thin cocktail straw (to induce feelings of suffocation), spinning (to induce dizziness), staring at a bright light and then trying to read (feelings of unreality), and, of course, hyperventilation. Repeated exposure to those practices (e.g., hyperventilating for one minute three times in a row every day) can lead to a significant reduction in the patient's fear of certain sensations. Other exercises might include watching scary movies and going on roller coaster rides.

Exposure to agoraphobic situations. Exposure is the single most effective strategy to target agoraphobic avoidance. One of the most challenging aspects of this treatment is to motivate patients to engage in feared activities without using any avoidance strategies. For this reason, it is critically important that the patient understands the reason for confronting some of his or her worst fears. The following is an example of how a skilled therapist might be able to motivate the patient to engage in these unpleasant practices. It also clarifies what is meant by the term "avoidance."

Clinical Example: Defining Avoidance

You experience anxiety in a variety of situations that are not anxiety-provoking for other people. Because certain situations make you feel so uncomfortable and anxious, you either escape from those situations as quickly as possible, or you avoid entering those situations so that you do not have to experience your anxiety.

Today, I would like to discuss the negative and positive aspects of avoidance. The term "avoidance" usually means "not doing something." However, we will use the term "avoidance" more generally. For now, let's just define "avoidance" as any type of behavior that keeps you from facing your fear. This includes: getting out of a situation, not getting into a situation, taking pills, drinking alcohol, distracting yourself, or having a close friend or your spouse next to you. Therefore, avoidance behaviors can be active (getting out of a situation) or passive (not entering a situation).

Avoidance has two consequences, one short-term positive and one long-term negative consequence. Let me give you an example to illustrate the short-term positive consequences of avoidance. The *x*-axis indicates the time (events), and the *y*-axis your level of anxiety (0–10). Please plot your anxiety to indicate how anxious you felt at certain points in time (e.g., during the first, worst, and most recent episode) and write down anything that you have done or that happened, which caused your anxiety to decrease (e.g., taking medications, safety behaviors and signals, distraction) or increase (e.g., the situation changed, physical sensations become more intense). Figure 4.3 shows examples of avoidance behaviors.

Avoidance strategies don't always eliminate your anxiety. Instead, avoidance strategies simply bring your anxiety down to a more tolerable level. You might also have noticed that at some point your anxiety increased even before you got into the fearful situation. This initial increase in your anxiety is called "anticipatory anxiety," which is another consequence of avoidance behavior. The more you avoid, the greater your anticipatory anxiety will be in the future.

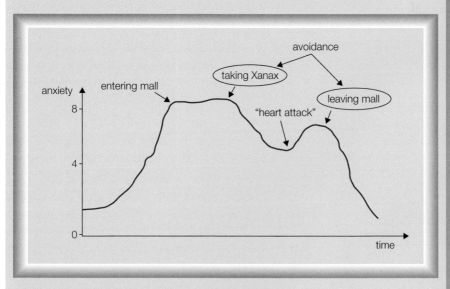

Figure 4.3   Example of avoidance behaviors.

Once avoidance is clearly defined, the therapist should introduce the idea that avoidance is associated with positive short-term but negative long-term consequences. It is important not to simply dismiss the patient's attempts to use avoidance strategies and to assume the patient is well aware of the negative consequences of these maladaptive coping strategies. As was discussed in Chapter 2, people do not necessarily change or eliminate problem behaviors even if they are aware of the maladaptive nature of them. Patients proceed through stages of change. Simply being aware of behavioral consequences is a necessary but not a sufficient condition to promote long-lasting behavioral change. For behavioral change to happen, the patient needs to be fully aware of the long-term consequences of the maladaptive behaviors, and the patient needs to realize that these maladaptive consequences are significantly more problematic than the short-term negative consequences of the exposure practices.

Exposure therapy is painful to patients. Gradual exposures (i.e., slowly moving up an exposure hierarchy) can increase the likelihood for dropouts because every successful experience is colored by the dread of having to confront an even more frightening situation. Therefore, some therapists, including myself, prefer very brief nongradual massed exposures. As part of the massed exposures, patients engage every day for four to six hours for a period of three to five days of therapist-guided exposure practices. Contrary to gradual exposure, nongradual and massed exposure practices do not begin with easier (i.e., less fear-provoking) situations first. Instead, the initial exposures are the ones that induce a great degree of fear. It is advisable to choose those practices as initial exposures that provide little room for avoidance. For example, elevator, train, or plane rides are more suitable than driving a car or standing in line, because the cues that induce anxiety are more under the control of the therapist and less vulnerable to manipulation by the patient. If the therapist decides to conduct nongradual massed exposure, it is advisable not to discuss specific situations until shortly before the patient enters these situations under the guidance of the therapist. The patient is then simply told that he or she will be informed shortly before the exposure session in order to reduce anticipatory anxiety.

Because this requires a big commitment and a "leap or faith" on the part of the patient, it is important that the patient is making an informed decision that leads to a firm commitment to undergo treatment. I usually give patients at least three days to think about it, and we usually arrange for a call after the three days to decide whether or not they will undergo these exposures. This strategy results in a very low refusal rate (see Chapter 2 for motivational strategies).

Empirical Support

Clark's 1986 article was a brief theoretical paper that became the second most frequently cited article in the entire field of psychology, among more than 50,000 articles published between 1986 and 1990 (Garfield, 1992). Other prominent proponents of the model include Beck and Emery (1985), Barlow (1988), and Margraf *et al.* (1993). A number of studies have shown the efficacy of CBT protocols in randomized controlled trials (e.g., Hofmann and Smits, 2008). The largest treatment trial compared CBT to imipramine, a pill placebo, and combinations of CBT with imipramine or a pill placebo (Barlow *et al.*, 2000).

A total of 312 panic disorder patients with mild or moderate agoraphobia were randomly assigned to imipramine, CBT, CBT plus imipramine, CBT plus placebo, or placebo only. Participants were treated weekly for three months. In addition, responders were seen monthly for six months and then followed up for an additional six months after treatment discontinuation. The results of this study showed that combining imipramine and CBT had limited advantage acutely, but more substantial advantage in the longer term: Both imipramine and CBT were superior to placebo on some measures for the acute treatment phase and were even more pronounced after the six monthly maintenance sessions. Six months after treatment discontinuation, however, people were more likely to maintain their treatment gains if they received CBT, either alone or in combination with a pill placebo. Individuals who received imipramine were more likely to relapse than those who did not receive the antidepressant. Interestingly, more than a third of all eligible patients refused participation in the study because they were unwilling to take imipramine. In contrast, only one out of more than 300 potential participants refused the study because of the possibility of receiving psychotherapy (Hofmann *et al.*, 1998).

Similar results were also reported with a CBT protocol that focuses more on cognitive restructuring. For example, a study by David M. Clark and his colleagues compared CBT, applied relaxation, imipramine, and a wait-list control group. At posttreatment, 75% of the CBT patients were panic-free, compared with 70% in the imipramine condition, 40% in the applied relaxation condition, and 7% in the wait list control condition. CBT was superior to the wait-list control group on all panic and anxiety measures, while imipramine and applied relaxation were better than the wait-list control group on approximately half of the measures. At nine-month follow-up, after imipramine had been discontinued, the panic-free rates were 85% for CBT, 60%

for imipramine, and 47% for applied relaxation. These results are consistent with reviews and meta-analyses of treatment outcome studies utilizing *in vivo* situational exposure, suggesting that 60–75% of treatment completers experience clinical improvement with fairly stable treatment gains at treatment follow-ups. More recently, we examined the use of d-cycloserine as an augmentation strategy to CBT and found that this agent can significantly enhance the efficacy of CBT for panic disorder when administered acutely before the exposure practices (Otto *et al.,* 2010).

The delivery of CBT for panic disorder differs slightly, depending on the specific clinical trial. Although all treatment protocols are based on the same basic treatment rationale, they vary in the number of treatment sessions, length of treatment, and emphasis on the particular treatment components (such as the number and type of exposures).

Recommended Further Readings

Therapist guide

Craske, M. G., and Barlow, D. H. (2006). *Mastery of your anxiety and panic: Therapist guide.* New York: Oxford University Press.

Patient guide

Barlow, D. H., and Craske, M. G. (2006). *Mastery of your anxiety and panic,* 3rd edition, workbook. New York: Oxford University Press.

5   Conquering Social Anxiety Disorder

Seymour's Shyness

Seymour is a 50-year-old single postal worker. He recently decided to see a psychiatrist because of his excessive shyness and depression. During the diagnostic interview, Seymour told the psychiatrist that he has always been very shy. He also reported that he feels inadequate and depressed. Seymour told the therapist that he cannot remember ever feeling comfortable in social situations. Even in grade school, his mind would go blank when somebody asked him to speak in front of a group of his parents' friends. He avoided going to birthday parties and other social gatherings when he could, or he would just sit there quietly if he had to go. He used to be a very quiet kid in school and would only answer questions in class when he wrote down the answers in advance. But even then, he would frequently mumble or not be able to get the answer out clearly. He usually met new children with his eyes lowered, fearing that they would make fun of him.

  As he grew older, Seymour had a few playmates in his neighborhood, but he never really had a "best" friend. His school grades were fairly good, except for those in subjects that required classroom participation. As a teenager, he was especially anxious in interactions with members of the opposite sex. Although he would like to have a relationship with a woman, he has never gone on a date or asked a woman out because of a fear of rejection. Seymour attended college and did well for a while. But when he was expected to give oral presentations in his classes, he stopped attending class and eventually dropped out. For a few years after that, he had trouble finding a job because he didn't think that he was capable of going on job interviews. Eventually, he found some jobs for which only a written

An Introduction to Modern CBT: Psychological Solutions to Mental Health Problems, First Edition.
S. G. Hofmann. © 2012 S. G. Hofmann. Published 2012 by John Wiley & Sons, Ltd.

test was required. A number of years ago, he was offered a job in the post office to work the evening shift. He was offered several promotions, but refused them because he feared the social pressures. Seymour told the therapist that he has a number of acquaintances at work, but no friends, and avoids all invitations to socialize with coworkers after his shifts.

Seymour is terrified of most social situations. He avoids them as much as possible. If he can't avoid them, he overprepares and often develops scripts prior to entering social situations so he knows what to say. But despite this, he feels extreme fear when confronted with social situations. He often monitors and observes himself in social situations and is often disgusted by his own incompetence. He simply does not think he has what it takes to handle social situations. He often feels that his anxiety is out of control. He then feels strong physiological sensations, such as a racing heart, sweaty palms, and trembling. He has been trying to control his anxiety in social situations with propranolol, a beta-blocker. Recently, his doctor advised him to try paroxetine. However, he does not like the idea of taking medication.

Definition of the Disorder

Social anxiety disorder (SAD; also known as social phobia) is a frequently diagnosed psychiatric condition. Epidemiological studies report lifetime prevalence rates between 7% and 12% in Western countries. The disorder affects females and males fairly equally. SAD often begins in the mid-teens, but can also occur in early childhood. During childhood, SAD is often associated with overanxious disorder, school refusal, mutism, separation anxiety, and, unsurprisingly, extreme shyness. If untreated, the disorder typically follows a chronic, unremitting course and leads to substantial impairments in vocational and social functioning (for a recent review, see Hofmann and DiBartolo, 2010).

Many different social situations can cue social anxiety, including performance situations such as speaking, eating, or writing in public, initiating or maintaining conversations, going to parties, dating, meeting strangers, or interacting with authority figures. When the person's fears are related to most or all social situations, a generalized subtype is assigned. In addition, people can receive an additional Axis II diagnosis of avoidant personality disorder. As a result, the diagnostic category of SAD shows a great degree of heterogeneity. However, it remains uncertain whether the diagnostic subgroups are different in kind or whether they are only different in the severity of their social anxiety (for a review, see Hofmann et al., 2004). Seymour met the diagnostic criteria for both the generalized subtype of SAD and avoidant personality disorder.

The Treatment Model

People with SAD typically believe that the social world is a dangerous place. They assume that they are expected to meet a particular social standard by behaving in a particular way, that this social standard is high, and that they lack the competence to meet this standard. When entering social situations, people with SAD tend to focus their attention to these alleged deficiencies, thus directing attention to negative aspects of themselves. As a result, they fear negative evaluation by others and believe that this would result in negative, long-lasting, and irreversible consequences.

Consistent with other individuals with SAD, Seymour believes that the social standards are unattainable and that he does not possess the competency to cope with this threat adequately. The allocation of attention resources to negative aspects of himself, away from task-relevant aspects, further strengthens his fear of negative evaluation. He fears that negative evaluation would result in negative and long lasting social consequences.

As a result of these maladaptive cognitions and cognitive processes, Seymour experiences a fear response that can be described as panic attacks in some cases and extreme withdrawal in others. More typical, however, are the panic-like symptoms which include increased heart rate, sweating, trembling, and intense feelings of fear and anxiety. To cope with this anxiety response, Seymour engages in subtle avoidance strategies. For example, he overprepares and develops scripts for anticipated social situations and takes beta-blockers to calm himself down. Although these avoidance strategies lead to relief from his anxiety in the short term, they lead to negative consequences in the long term. The primary negative consequence is the reinforcing effect on the maintenance of his social anxiety. Because of these avoidance strategies, Seymour never has a chance to test whether the worst case scenario is, in fact going to happen, and, if it happens, what the actual consequences would be.

Seymour, like other people with SAD, believes that social mishaps would have irreversible or long lasting disastrous consequences. However, the truth is that social situations are generally harmless events. Negative evaluation by others rarely, if ever, leads to any actual negative consequences and, even if they do, the effects are short-lived. Rare exceptions are major social blunders that result in a divorce, or the loss of a job or friends. However, it is difficult

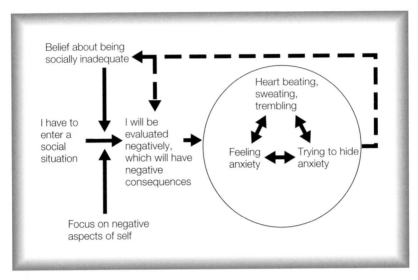

Figure 5.1   Seymour's social anxiety.

to imagine any mishaps that necessarily and reliably lead to such consequences. Clearly, the feared stimulus is imaginary and fictitious, rather than
real. The social world is created by people, and the rules of this world show
a remarkable degree of tolerance and flexibility. Seymour, however, does not
see the rules of the social world as flexible and tolerable. He perceives these
rules as rigid and difficult to adhere to. One of these rules is not to show
anxiety in social situations. This, paradoxically, induces a great degree of
anxiety. Because he experiences strong subjective and physiological anxiety,
the situation appears to be threatening as a result of emotional reasoning
and self-perception. Moreover, people with a high degree of social anxiety
often ruminate about past social situations. This process, which is also
referred to as postevent processing, often focuses on negative aspects, turning
ambiguous, or even initially pleasant experiences, into unpleasant and negative events. This reinforces the negative self-perception and anxiety-inducing
self-statements, leading to a positive feedback cycle and a self-maintaining
system. Seymour's social anxiety is illustrated in Figure 5.1.

Treatment Strategies

Effective psychotherapy provides patients with a range of learning experiences that modify the patient's anxiogenic beliefs and expectations, while

making other interpretations and beliefs available. I have recently formulated a comprehensive psychological treatment model of SAD (Hofmann, 2007a) that has been translated into specific treatment strategies (Hofmann and Otto, 2008). Earlier models have been developed by Clark and Wells (1995) and Rapee and Heimberg (1997).

Our model (Hofmann, 2007a; Hofmann and Otto, 2008) assumes that individuals with SAD are apprehensive in social situations in part because they perceive the social standard (expectations and social goals) as being high. They desire to make a particular impression on others but doubt that they will be able to do so, partly because they are unable to define specific and attainable goals and select specific, achievable behavioral strategies to reach these goals. This leads to a further increase in social apprehension and increased self-focused attention, which triggers a number of additional cognitive processes. It is predicted that, once a situation is perceived as holding the potential for social evaluation, individuals with SAD become preoccupied with negative thoughts about themselves and the way other people perceive them. The negative impression is assumed to often occur in the form of an image from an "observer" perspective in which people with SAD see themselves as if from another person's vantage point. Therefore, it can be assumed that the treatment is most effective if it targets dysfunctional cognitions directly and systematically via CBT.

Consistent with this notion are results from studies showing that socially anxious individuals believe that negative social events are more likely to occur than positive social events. Additionally, they assume that most people are inherently critical of others and are likely to evaluate them negatively. The belief system of individuals with SAD appears to magnify the competitive aspects of interpersonal relationships but minimizes the cooperative, supportive aspects. My model has been derived based on a large and consistent literature (see Hofmann and Otto, 2008). The primary intervention strategies, psychoeducation, attention modification, cognitive restructuring, and exposure procedures, have been well-validated. Moreover, acceptance-based strategies have recently been investigated and show promising results (Darymple and Herbert, 2007).

Psychoeducation

As noted earlier, social anxiety disorder is a heterogeneous disorder in terms of types and number of feared situations and other problems that may be associated with social anxiety, such as self-perception and social skills. Nevertheless, the model described in Figure 5.2 can be applied to most, if

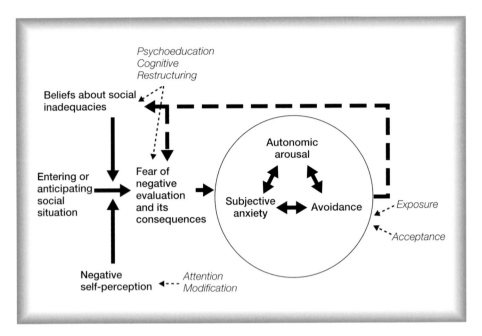

Figure 5.2   Strategies to target social anxiety.

not all, individuals presenting with these problems. It is important that patients understand and accept the explanation for their social anxiety. Patients who are initially resistant to the idea of being able to overcome social anxiety using these strategies often argue that shyness is a personality trait and social anxiety is simply part of their personality. This may certainly be correct, but this does not mean that social anxiety has to cause distress and interfere with their lives. Furthermore, as will any form of anxiety, social anxiety will decrease after being exposed repeatedly to the feared situation without using any avoidance strategies. The exposure rationale is an important part of the intervention that will be discussed in more detail below. In addition to exposure practices, a number of other strategies will provide the patient with opportunities to correct misperceptions and misattributions that maintain the problem. Thus, the treatment is not intended to change the personality of the individual, but to give the patient concrete techniques to handle social situations more effectively and to eventually overcome his/her anxiety in social situations. It can be very helpful to spell out the concrete goals and expectations of treatment in the form of learning objectives.

Learning Objectives

Here is what you will learn:

- You will realize that social anxiety is a vicious cycle and that you can stop this cycle.
- You will learn that you are more critical toward yourself than other people are toward you. Therefore, it is important that you become comfortable with the way you are (including your imperfections in social performance situations).
- You will learn how you perform in social situations when you do not use anxiety as a barometer of your social performance.
- You will learn that your feeling of anxiety in social situations is a very private experience. Other people cannot see your racing heart, your sweaty palms, or your shaky knees.
- You will realize that you overestimate how much other people can see what's going on in your body.
- You will realize that even if a social encounter objectively did not go well, it is simply not a big deal. Social mishaps are very normal; they happen all the time. But what makes people different is the degree to which these mishaps (or, better, the possibility of mishaps) affect a person's life.
- You will also realize that your actual social performance is not nearly as bad as you think it is. If fact, there are plenty of people in this world whose social skills are much poorer that yours, but who are not socially anxious.
- You will have a chance to be in social situations long enough to allow your anxiety to dissipate naturally.
- You will have a chance to learn how to coach yourself more accurately before, during, and after social performance.
- You will learn that using avoidance strategies (either overt or subtle) is part of the reason why social anxiety is so persistent and tends to generalize.

Attention and situation modification

When people with SAD anticipate social threat or have to enter a social situation, they typically shift their attention to detailed monitoring and observations of themselves, especially to personal weaknesses and perceived incompetence. This attentional shift produces an enhanced awareness of feared anxiety responses which then interferes with processing the situation and other people's behavior. For example, when Seymour had to give a speech last week, he focused on negative aspects of himself. This led to greater anxiety and the attention that he could have used for a successful social performance was spent on monitoring his own anxiety. This established a vicious cycle that made him feel out of control. As a result, he used behavioral and pharmacological strategies to bring his anxiety down. These avoidance strategies gave him short-term relief, but they are ineffective and detrimental in the long term.

An effective strategy to stop this vicious cycle from forming in the first place is to encourage Seymour to focus his attention on task-relevant things (e.g., thinking of questions to ask during a conversation or thinking of the delivery and content of a speech) rather than fear-relevant things (e.g., heart racing, negative self-focused thoughts). This can be done by instructing Seymour to voluntarily focus his attention on different stimuli when being in an anxious state. For example, before giving a speech or engaging in an interaction, Seymour might be instructed to focus his attention on (1) himself and his anxiety, (2) aspects of the environment that causes him anxiety (e.g., audience members, a podium), (3) aspects of the environment that do not cause him anxiety (e.g., pictures on the wall), and (4) the content and delivery of the speech he is about to give. It is important that Seymour not use any strategies to suppress his anxiety (i.e., avoidance strategies). Instead, he is instructed to stay in the present moment and nonjudgmentally observe how changes in his focus of attention lead to changes in his anxiety without trying to suppress it.

Cognitive restructuring

People with SAD typically overestimate how negatively they are evaluated by other people. Furthermore, prior to and after a social event, individuals with SAD often think about the situation in detail, focusing primarily on past failures, negative images of themselves in the situation, and other predictions of poor performance and rejection. People with SAD further see themselves as being confined in a social world that consists of rigid and unclear rules. They are constantly concerned about violating social norms and believe that others expect them to meet social standards that are difficult for them to reach because they feel deficient in the necessary social skills or are unclear about the precise definition of these standards.

Cognitive restructuring is effective in uncovering, challenging, and correcting maladaptive beliefs about the probability of a negative outcome of a social situation and, even more importantly, about the consequences of this outcome. For example, Seymour fears that he will be evaluated negatively in social situations. His overarching belief is that social situations are dangerous and he is incompetent in handling them. He further focuses on negative aspects of himself. The following is an example of a therapist-patient dialogue that illustrates the process of challenging Seymour's overestimatation of the occurrence of negative outcomes:

Seymour: When I have to talk to somebody new, I won't be able to think of anything to say.

Therapist: What do you mean when you say "I won't be able to think of anything to say?"

Seymour: It means that I have nothing to say. My mind simply goes blank.

Therapist: So let's be more specific. Let's say you are invited by one of your co-workers to a party. You decided to go, and you just stand there, unable to have a conversation with anybody.

Seymour: This would be awful.

Therapist: A real catastrophe?

Seymour: Yes.

Therapist: But what exactly would be so terrible about it?

Seymour: It would be embarrassing!

Therapist: Why would it be embarrassing?

Seymour: Because I will make a fool of myself and people will think that I am weird.

Therapist: What would happen if people think that you are weird.

Seymour: They would laugh about me and think that I am a total loser?

Therapist: How do you know what other people think of you?

Seymour: What do you mean?

Therapist: You are making a number of assumptions here that may or may not be correct. Interestingly, you choose out of many possible alternatives the ones that are most threatening and unpleasant. Specifically, you are assuming that if you don't have anything to say, everybody will laugh at you, and think that you are weird. Now first of all, you don't know that everybody will think that you are weird. In fact, the likelihood that everybody thinks that you are weird because you are not talking is extremely low. Why am I saying this?

Seymour: Maybe because there are other reasons why people are quiet?

Therapist: Absolutely, what are some possible reasons?

Seymour: Maybe people are quiet because they are tired or uninterested.

Therapist: Right, very good. In fact, chances are very high that most people don't even notice you because they are busy with themselves and their own conversations or worries. But let's assume that there are one or two or even more people who notice that you're not talking and think that you are weird. How bad would that be?

Seymour: Bad!

Therapist: Sure, but how bad? What would that mean to you, your life, your future, and so forth.

Seymour: I don't know.

Therapist: Well, would this be a life-changing event? Would this have long-lasting, irreversible, catastrophic consequences because a handful of people think you are weird?

Seymour: (Laughs)

Therapist: Well, would it?

Seymour: No. Many people think I am weird.

Therapist: And I am sure many people think that I am weird as well. So what? The goal in life is not to please everybody and it is unreasonable to assume that everybody you meet in life will like you. Many people will not like you and some will think that you are very weird. But this is not the goal in life. Is it?

Seymour: No. I guess not. You can't please everybody.

Therapist: You are absolutely correct! So what we have to do is to make you familiar with the experience of people showing you their disapproval or rejection. In other words, we want to put you in situations that make it very, very likely that your worst-case scenario comes true so that you can experience that there is absolutely nothing dangerous about social situations. Social mishaps and embarrassing situations are completely normal and they happen to everybody. What distinguishes people from one another is not so much the mishaps per se, but the way those mishaps can bother people. It simply is not a big deal if they happen. Life goes on. The consequences are short-lasting and minor. Once you realize this, you will be able to break out of your self-imposed social prison. Are you ready to step outside of your self-imposed social prison and experience the freedom?

Exposures

Exposure to feared social situations is one of the most important, and quite possibly the single most important, component of treatment (see Chapter 3 for a general description of the exposure rationale). There are many reasons why exposure practices are so central. First, without the use of any avoidance strategies, exposures create a high level of emotional arousal, which provide the patient with the opportunity to use acceptance strategies to cope with anxiety.

Second, exposures provide an opportunity to demonstrate the effects of attentional focus on subjective anxiety. Before every exposure situation, the therapist asks the patient to focus his or her attention toward the self and the anxiety symptoms and to give an anxiety rating (0–10). The therapist should then ask the patient to direct his or her attention to his/her physical sensations, to describe the feelings, and to rate his or her anxiety.

Third, exposures provide an opportunity for the patient to re-evaluate his or her social self-presentation. For this purpose, video feedback can be used to re-examine the patient's prediction of his or her performance. Specifically, this technique includes a cognitive preparation prior to viewing the video during which patients are asked to predict in detail what they would see in the video. They will then be instructed to form an image of themselves giving the speech. In order to compare the imagined/perceived self-presentation with the actual self-presentation, individuals will then be asked to watch the video from an observer's point of view (i.e., as if they were watching a stranger). Additional strategies to target self-perception include mirror exposure exercises and listening to their own audiotaped speech. During mirror exposures, patients are asked to objectively describe the appearance of their mirror image and to audiotape this description. The reason for these exercises is to correct the person's distorted self-perceptions, and to become used to one's own appearance.

Forth, exposures provide an opportunity to practice goal settings and to re-evaluate social standards. For this purpose, the therapist should discuss with the patient what the social expectations (standards) of a given situation might be, and should help the patient to state at least one clear (behavioral, quantifiable) goal (e.g., asking a particular question). It is important to provide very clear instructions as to what the exposure task should look like. Thus, the therapist's role during these early exposures is similar to that of a movie director who provides the patient with a clear script of his or her expected behavior. If the situation requires a complex social interaction (e.g., returning an item to the same sales person from whom it was purchased minutes before) the therapist should clearly specify when a particular action should be shown. For example, rather than simply instructing the patients to "Return a book minutes after you bought it," the therapist should instruct the client to "Purchase the newest Harry Potter book, walk with it toward the exit door, and when reaching the exit doors, turn around, find the same sales person again, and ask for a refund of this book by saying: 'I want to exchange this book that I just bought because I changed my mind.'" The goal of this task may be *to say this particular sentence.*

Finally, and perhaps most importantly, *in vivo* exposure situations that model social mishaps (e.g., dropping a pastry on the floor) provide an ideal opportunity to test distorted assumptions about the social cost of situations and other assumptions. The use of safety behaviors makes maladaptive cognitions immune to empirical tests because they prevent people from critically evaluating their feared outcomes (e.g., "I will shake uncontrollably") and catastrophic beliefs (e.g., "I will be humiliated and will never be able to show my face there again.").

Examples of Exposure Tasks

- Go to a crowded restaurant and ask women sitting at tables: *Excuse me, but is your name Catherine?* (Goal: Ask five women.)
- Go into a restaurant, get seated. When the waiter comes, say: *May I please have a glass of tap water?* When the waiter brings the water, drink a sip, get up, and leave. (Goal: Drink water without ordering anything else.)
- Order a slice of pizza, "accidentally" drop it on the floor and say: *I just dropped my pizza. May I please have a new slice?* (Goal: Get another slice without paying.)
- Go to a restaurant and sit at the bar. Ask a fellow patron whether he has seen the movie *The Hangover*. In case he/she has not seen it, tell him/her the story plot. In case he/she has seen it, ask him if he/she liked it and what his/her favorite scene was. (Goal: Discuss the funny parts of the movie.)
- Stand on a street corner and loudly sing "Old MacDonald Had a Farm" for 10 minutes.
- Ask a bookstore clerk for *The Joy of Sex*. When he or she locates it, ask: "Can you recommend a more modern version?"

Effective exposure situations for individuals with SAD differ from exposure situations to treat other phobic disorders. The main differences are as follows: (1) social exposures often require performance of complicated chains of interpersonal behavior; (2) the social phobic patient's specific anxiety-eliciting situations are not always easy to create. For example, an agoraphobic individual may go for a walk away from home at almost any time, but the social phobic may confront that feared staff meeting only once per week. Other situations may occur more rarely. Therefore, the therapist might have to create opportunities for exposure situations. Public speaking situations are especially useful for this. These situations give the therapist a great degree of control over the situation (e.g., by choosing different speech topics or modifying the situation by bringing in additional audience members or instructing the audience to behave in certain ways) and are realistic (rather than role play) situations.

Exposure practices should not be restricted to the therapy session, but should be assigned systematically as homework practices between sessions. When reviewing homework practices, the therapist should be careful not to spend too much time with the review of the practices. In fact, too much review might serve the function of postevent rumination. Therefore, patients should be discouraged from giving long and elaborate descriptions of the situation. Instead, the situation should be summarized succinctly and followed by specific and guided questions with the following purpose:

1. What were the anxiety-provoking aspects of situation? Summarize what exactly made the situation so anxiety provoking.
2. What was the main goal the patient wanted to achieve and what did the patient think other people's expectations were?
3. What kind of social mishap was the patient afraid of, and what would have been the social consequences?
4. Did the patient focus on self and anxiety? What impact did the situation have on his or her self-perception?
5. What were the safety behaviors and avoidance strategies the patient used?
6. How long did the situation and its feared consequences linger on? Did the situation irreversibly change the patient's future life?

Empirical Support

The efficacy of earlier formulations of CBT for SAD has been demonstrated in a number of well-designed studies. Treatment drop-outs are generally low and not systematically associated with any patient variables. Traditional group CBT is administered by two therapists in 12 weekly 2.5-hour sessions to groups consisting of four to six participants. A comparison between fluoxetine (a popular SSRI), CBT, placebo, CBT combined with fluoxetine, or CBT combined with placebo showed that all active treatments were superior to placebo. Interestingly, the combined treatment was not superior to the other treatments. The response rates in the intention-to-treat sample were 50.9% (fluoxetine), 51.7% (CBT), 54.2% (CBT plus fluoxetine), 50.8% (traditional CBT plus placebo), and 31.7% (placebo only). Although these results emphasize the efficacy of CBT, either alone or in combination with pharmacotherapy, the data also show that many participants remain symptomatic (Davidson *et al.*, 2004). More recent trials suggest that d-cycloserine can significantly enhance the efficacy of CBT for SAD when administered acutely prior to exposure practices (Hofmann *et al.*, 2006; Guastella *et al.*, 2008).

More recent formulations of CBT for SAD specifically target some of the core maintenance factors, safety behaviors, self-focused attention, and perceived social cost. The efficacy of these targeted CBT protocols has considerably improved that of over earlier, more traditional CBT protocols. The treatment efforts of targeted CBT are directed toward the systematic teaching of an alternative cognitive framework for understanding social situations, social performance, and social risk. Interventions are richly cognitive in nature, as they ask patients to examine their expectations about social situations and the social costs of imperfect social performances. Patients then specifically examine the veracity of these expectations as evaluated by logical evaluation, and particularly by specific "behavioral experiments" that are designed to test anxiogenic expectations. An effect size analysis of such a targeted CBT approach showed that the uncontrolled effect size of the severity rating based on the clinical interview was 1.41 (pretest to post-test) and 1.43 (pretest to 12-month follow-up) in the targeted CBT group. The composite score was associated with an uncontrolled pre-post effect size of 2.14 (Clark *et al.*, 2003). These are exceptionally strong effects, suggesting that CBT for SAD can be significantly improved by targeting specific maintenance factors.

Recommended Further Readings

Therapist guide

Hofmann, S. G., and Otto, M. W. (2008). *Cognitive-behavior therapy of social anxiety disorder: Evidence-based and disorder specific treatment techniques*. New York: Routledge.

Patient guide

Hope, D. A., Heimberg, R. G., and Turk, C. L. (2010). *Managing social anxiety: A cognitive-behavioral therapy approach*, 2nd edition, workbook. New York: Oxford University Press.

6 Treating Obsessive-Compulsive Disorder

Olivia's Obsessions

Olivia is a 42-year-old married woman with three children. Since her husband, who is 25 years her senior, retired as a dentist, she has started a lucrative business as an antique furniture seller. Olivia has been struggling with obsessive-compulsive disorder (OCD) for as long as she can remember. She is unable to drive by herself because she is afraid of hitting people. In the past, when she had to drive her children to school, she often checked the route she had driven to make sure she had not hit anyone. She often thought that she may have heard a scream, seen a shadow out of the corner of her eyes, or felt an unusual bump. She also frequently checked the local news for hit and run accidents. She even repeatedly called the local police to check on reported hit and runs and became known by the police department. In addition to her "hit and run" OCD, Olivia is concerned that her actions may cause harm and death to others. When discussing medical conditions, she is concerned that she will misrepresent information and that people will die as a result of her providing misinformation. This is particularly the case regarding dental issues because she feels people would assume that she is knowledgeable because her husband was a dentist. This has led to strained relationships with friends and family members because she feels an irresistible urge to contact them after discussing medical issues to make sure that they did not misunderstand the information she gave them. In addition to her problems with OCD, she has also been struggling with depression. She has had occasional hypomanic episodes in the past, but most of the time, her depressive episodes are unipolar, lasting for many weeks at a time. During these episodes, she experiences feelings of worthlessness, self-blame, lack of energy, and a strong urge to stay in bed, often until early afternoon. Her husband has been supportive. Olivia has tried many anti-anxiety and antidepressant medications with variable success.

An Introduction to Modern CBT: Psychological Solutions to Mental Health Problems, First Edition.
S. G. Hofmann. © 2012 S. G. Hofmann. Published 2012 by John Wiley & Sons, Ltd.

Definition of the Disorder

Obsessions are persistent, unwanted, and involuntary thoughts, images, or impulses that intrude into the mind unbidden and cause marked distress. In contrast, compulsions are deliberate and repetitive behaviors or mental acts that are intended to reduce feelings of distress or are completed to prevent a feared event from occurring. Epidemiological studies suggest that the lifetime prevalence of OCD ranges between 1.6% and 2.5% (e.g., Kessler *et al.*, 2005). The gender distribution for OCD is roughly equal, with women showing a slightly higher prevalence than men. The disorder typically develops at 13–15 years for males and 20–24 years for females.

OCD is a rather heterogeneous disorder. For example, obsessions can involve unwanted aggressive thoughts, images, or impulses to harm oneself or others (e.g., pushing a random person over a bridge), sexual and religious/blasphemous intrusions (e.g., thoughts about Jesus Christ's genitals), persistent thoughts of doubt (e.g., "Did I turn off the gas stove?"), or fears of being harmed or contaminated by germs or dirt (e.g., "What if I get germs from touching a contaminated doorknob?"). In turn, compulsions range from excessive hand washing, cleaning, checking (e.g., stove, lights), counting, ordering and arranging, hoarding, tapping, touching, and mental rituals (e.g., repeating prayers, words, or songs). Such behaviors are expressed in a ritualistic form, such as the repetition of a prayer for a specified number of counts, or washing one's hands in a specific order (e.g., washing the left hand before the right and starting with specific fingers) out of a fear that unless the ritual is performed, a catastrophic consequence will occur (e.g., "If I don't align my shoes correctly, my father will die").

A common characteristic associated with OCD is a difficulty for patients to separate cognitions from behaviors. In other words, thinking a "bad" thought is just as horrible and distressing as performing the "bad" behavior. This phenomenon has become known as thought-action fusion (TAF). It has been proposed that TAF is comprised of two discrete components (Shafran *et al.*, 1996). The first component refers to the belief that experiencing a particular thought increases the chances that the event will actually occur (likelihood), whereas the second component refers to the belief that thinking about an action is synonymous to actually performing the action (morality). For example, the thought of killing another person may be considered morally equivalent to performing the act. This moral component is assumed to be the result of the erroneous conclusion that experiencing "bad" thoughts is indicative of one's true nature and intentions.

Important factors that are related to TAF include an inflated sense of responsibility, religiosity, or superstitious and magical thinking (Rachman, 1993; Rassin and Koster, 2003). Olivia's case is a good example of such an inflated sense of responsibility. She believes that giving people inaccurate information will result in harm and death which is ultimately her responsibility. Olivia also shows strong magical and superstitious thinking. This refers to the belief that thinking of the possibility of an event somehow increases the likelihood that the event is going to happen. As a result, the person attempts to suppress the thought, which in turn increases the likelihood of experiencing the thought (see Chapter 1; Wegner, 1994). Mindfulness and meditation practices that promote decentering (i.e., taking a present-focused, nonjudgmental stance in regard to thoughts and feelings; see Chapter 7) can be effective at targeting these maladaptive beliefs.

The Treatment Model

Unwanted thoughts, images, and impulses are very common. Over 90% of people in community and analogue samples report the presence of those intrusions, including urges to harm or attack someone and thoughts of sexually inappropriate acts (Salkovskis and Harrison, 1984). The CBT model of OCD emphasizes the appraisal of unwanted thoughts (Rachman, 1998; Salkovskis, 1985). Patients with OCD believe that these intrusions are meaningful. As is typical for patients with OCD, Olivia holds an exaggerated sense of responsibility. She also believes that failing to prevent harm (i.e., "sin of omission") is as bad as deliberately causing harm ("sin of commission"). This exaggerated sense of responsibility negatively interacts with intrusive thoughts. For example, Olivia's thought "Did I hit somebody?" leads to feelings of distress, an urge to check the route, and an urge to call the police to make sure she has not hit and killed people with her car. Therefore, in Olivia's mind, the death of other people is only preventable by checking, and not checking suggests that she wants to harm others.

Another characteristic feature of OCD is the overimportance placed on thoughts, suggesting that the mere presence of a thought provides evidence of its importance (i.e., "It must be important because I think about it, and I think about it because it is important"). In addition, people with

OCD overestimate the likelihood and severity of harm and view situations as dangerous unless proven safe despite the fact that most people assume the opposite (Foa and Kozak, 1986). These different faulty beliefs are not mutually exclusive, but often present in combinations according to the particular intrusion and resultant appraisal (Freeston *et al.*, 1996). For example, Olivia's thoughts about harming someone by giving the wrong medical information involve overestimations of danger, TAF, and exaggerated responsibility.

Given the importance patients with OCD place on obsessional thoughts, they have a strong desire to suppress these distressing thoughts and neutralize them with compulsions. However, attempts to suppress these thoughts make them even more intrusive. Similarly, attempts to neutralize them with compulsions in order to reduce the distress and subvert any feared catastrophic consequences are ineffective long-term strategies. Because compulsions lead to a temporary reduction in feelings of distress, they can quickly become a coping mechanism, and thereby increase the probability of subsequent neutralizing. In addition, given the nonoccurrence of feared consequences following neutralization, the absence of negative outcomes becomes reinforcing and can be construed as evidence for the validity of obsessional beliefs. Thus, faulty appraisals are maintained by a failure to adequately evaluate alternatives (Salkovskis, 1985). Figure 6.1 depicts the cycle of Olivia's hit-and-run obsession.

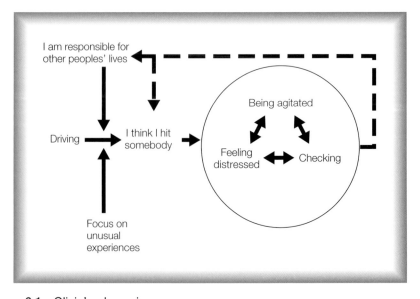

Figure 6.1   Olivia's obsessions.

Treatment Strategies

People with OCD typically have an inflated sense of personal responsibility for others and similar maladaptive beliefs. In addition, they try extremely hard to act in accordance with these beliefs in order to avoid harm. Psychoeducation and cognitive restructuring are central to effectively target a sense of inflated responsibility, superstitious beliefs, and overestimations of catastrophic events.

Obsessions about concrete situations arise when triggers are present and the person starts focusing on stimuli that provide support for the obsessive thoughts. This process can be averted at an early stage by focusing on stimuli that are inconsistent with the beliefs or by modifying the situational triggers directly. However, there is an unlimited number of potential triggers that can be interpreted as being consistent with the maladaptive beliefs. Therefore, the maladaptive beliefs should be the primary target of treatment. Cognitive restructuring techniques can effectively challenge and modify these maladaptive beliefs and obsessional thoughts. Furthermore, mindfulness meditation can be potentially useful to target the rumination process of obsessions by encouraging the person to focus on the present rather than the future (the catastrophic outcome) or the past (the action that might cause the harm). Relaxation strategies can also be beneficial for targeting autonomic arousal. Finally, exposure and acceptance strategies can interrupt the vicious and self-reinforcing cycle between distress, arousal, and compulsions. These strategies are summarized in Figure 6.2., and some of these strategies will be highlighted in more detail below.

Attention and situation modification

Olivia frequently watches the news to find out whether there were any reports of hit and run accidents or unexplained deaths. Focusing her attention on information in her environment consistent with her obsession further intensifies the problem. Obviously, it is under Olivia's voluntary control to decide whether or not she scans the environment for evidence supporting her obsessive beliefs, despite her urge to do it. Therefore, a therapeutically beneficial strategy is to resist her urge to scan her environment for information that provides confirming evidence for her obsessional beliefs and to learn how to tolerate and resist a strong urge. In this context, mindfulness meditation can be very useful (see also Chapter 7). Rather than responding to an urge to check by watching the news, Olivia might use the

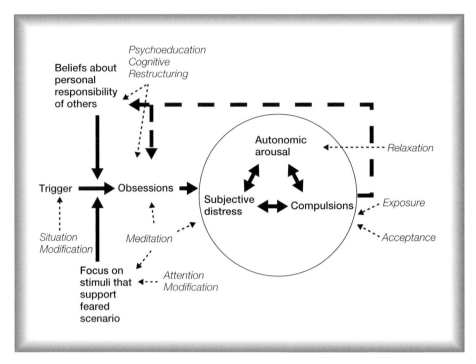

Figure 6.2   Strategies to target Olivia's obsessions and compulsions.

urge as a trigger to practice mindfulness meditation in order to learn how to gradually prolong the time between the initial impulse to check and the checking behavior.

Psychoeducation

The two most important messages that need to be conveyed in treatment during the psychoeduction phase are: (1) Unusual and strange thoughts, images, and impulses are normal; having these experiences is not indicative of one's personality or future action; (2) attempts to suppress these thoughts, images, and impulses paradoxically increase the likelihood of their occurrence. As described in Chapter 1, the paradoxical effect of thought suppression can be illustrated using the White Bear experiment (Wegner, 1994).

White Bear Experiment

Close your eyes. Picture a fluffy, white bear. Picture his fluffy fur, his nose, his ears, and his paws. Picture is as clearly as you can. Hold this image. Next, please think about anything you like, *except* this white bear. Every time the bear pops into your mind, please say "white bear." I will keep track of time and will also count for you how many times you say white bear within the next one-minute period. So again, please think of anything but the white bear. When it pops into your mind say "white bear." Please start now.

This experiment is used to demonstrate that attempts to suppress a random thought increase the likelihood of having the thought. The minute, or even hours and days, before the suppression instruction was given, the patient probably did not think about a white bear even once, because there was simply no reason to do so. The only reason why the bear became an intrusive image is because the patient was actively trying not to have the image.

There are many images, thoughts, and impulses that are odd. Everybody has them. The thought about pushing an elderly woman in front of traffic is certainly an odd thought. It becomes an obsessive thought if we believe that it carries special meaning. For example, having certain thoughts might be seen as a reflection of one's personality or character. A devout Catholic, for example, might believe that having certain thoughts is a sin because thinking is almost as bad as doing—the essence of thought-action fusion. As a result, the person with OCD attempts to suppress the thought, causing the thought to occur more frequently, making the thought even more significant.

Cognitive restructuring

As is the case for other anxiety disorders, people with OCD overestimate the likelihood of a negative outcome (i.e., assume that a negative outcome is likely going to happen) and exaggerate the degree of the negative outcome (i.e., assume that a negative outcome would likely be a catastrophic event). The former cognitive error is often referred to as probability overestimation and the latter error is known as catastrophic thinking. Olivia believes that giving medical advice would cause death, an example of probability overestimation. The example below illustrates how probability overestimation can be targeted by encouraging Olivia to critically examine the logic of her thinking. In this example, the therapist explores the worst-case scenario by identifying a sequence of events that would need to happen for the worst-case scenario to come true. Each of these events is then assigned a probability.

Although Olivia still overestimates some of these single events, it becomes clear that the catastrophic outcome (i.e., death of a person) at the end of this sequence is extremely unlikely, given that all of the events need to converge.

Clinical Example: Targeting Probability Overestimation

Scenario: Olivia told Sarah's husband that aspirin is used to treat inflammation. She is concerned that he will take too much aspirin, which will irritate his stomach and cause him to bleed to death internally.

Subjective probability that Sarah's husband misinterpreted this, leading to death: 75%

Realistic probability:

1. He will take too much aspirin: 1/5
2. His stomach will get irritated as a result of the aspirin: 1/5
3. His stomach will bleed as a result of the irritation: 1/100
4. He will continue taking aspirin despite experiencing stomach problems: 1/20
5. He will not consult anyone about his stomach irritation: 1/1000
6. The bleeding stomach will result in death: 1/2

Logical probability:

$$\frac{1 \times 1 \times 1 \times 1 \times 1 \times 1}{5 \times 5 \times 100 \times 20 \times 1000 \times 2} = \frac{1}{100,000,000} = 0.000001\%$$

The purpose of this exercise is to identify the specific negative assumptions that are related to the obsession. This can be facilitated by asking specific questions, such as "What did you expect might happen?" and "What will happen next?" The primary message of this exercise is to illustrate that real catastrophes are unlikely to happen. Even if the single events that might lead to the catastrophic outcome are overestimated and relatively high (e.g., a 50% chance that stomach bleeding would result in death), the chance that these different individual steps will align to finally lead to the catastrophic event (the person dies because Olivia advised him about taking aspirin) is highly unlikely (0.000001%). This probability is then compared to the subjective probability identified by the patient (75%).

Meditation and relaxation

The basic premise underlying mindfulness practices is that experiencing the present moment nonjudgmentally and openly can effectively counter the effects of stressors, because excessive orientation toward the past or future when dealing with stressors can lead to psychological distress. A particularly important component of mindfulness practices is the slow and deep breathing exercises that alleviate bodily symptoms of distress by balancing sympathetic and parasympathetic responses (Kabat-Zinn, 2003).

During mindfulness meditation, people are encouraged to pay attention to what is happening inside and around them in the very moment, acknowledging thoughts and feelings just as they are, and letting go of the need to critically judge, change, or avoid their inner experiences. Patients should identify one particular cue they can use in their daily life to help them stay focused in the present moment. This cue is typically their own breathing, but it can also be the ticking of a clock, the sound of waves, or any other rhythmic, recurring sound. This cue is intended not to distract patients, but to help them focus and anchor themselves in the present. Patients come to associate this cue with the emotional experience of nonjudgmental present-focused awareness. The following mindfulness exercise is an example of how the therapist may introduce mindfulness practice.

Mindfulness Practice

Please make yourself comfortable, close your eyes, and follow my voice. Please focus your attention on the present moment. Notice how it feels to be sitting in the chair. Notice how your body feels and any sensations you experience. Notice your body resting on the chair; notice your feet touching the ground. Notice your breathing. Notice your chest moving as you breathe in and out. Notice the cold air flowing in as you breathe in and the warm air as you breathe out. Please simply notice it; don't try to change anything (pause). Focus on your breathing as it is happening right now, at the present moment. Use your breath to help anchor yourself to the here and now (pause). Let your thoughts come and go. Simply notice what you're thinking, but don't try to keep the thoughts or push them away. Just let them come and go (pause). Allow yourself to watch your thoughts for a few moments—and as you do, notice how they come and go (allow a brief period of silence). As you take note of these thoughts, start to shift and explore how you're feeling. Emotions, just like thoughts, are constantly changing. Sometimes emotions come in waves, sometimes

> they linger; sometimes they are brought on by certain thoughts, other times they seem to come out of nowhere. Simply acknowledge how you're feeling in this very moment (pause). Allow yourself to observe your emotions, without judgment. Notice how they go up and how they come down (allow a brief period of silence). Continuing to use your breath to anchor you, begin to take note of your entire experience—how your body feels, what you are thinking, what emotions you are experiencing. Notice whatever you're experiencing in this very moment (pause). Notice your breathing to anchor yourself in the present moment. Allow your awareness to shift and flow to your sensations so you can take in what's going on around you. Notice the temperature (pause). Notice the sounds in the environment (pause). When you are ready, bring yourself back. Picture yourself and open your eyes.

Exposure and acceptance

Targeted behavioral experiments can be very helpful in realistically assessing the potential danger of the feared activity. Prior to engaging in a behavioral exercise, a hypothesis regarding outcome is formulated. For example, Olivia predicted that driving alone in the parking lot of a supermarket would almost certainly result in her accidentally hitting and killing a person with her car. The patient and therapist may estimate how many people will be killed if Olivia drives around a particular section of the parking lot. In order to discourage the patient from checking (i.e., as a form of response prevention), the patient may be allowed to drive a section only once. It is advisable to construct the exercise in such a way as to maximize the likelihood of experiencing the worst outcome.

An important aspect of this exercise is to transfer the responsibility of the worst outcome to the therapist. In other words, in case Olivia kills somebody, the therapist takes full responsibility for this action. It is very useful to make this arrangement explicit in a written contract (e.g., "If a hit and run accident occurs, it will be the responsibility of the therapist"). Such a contract should be carefully designed in collaboration with the patient and repeatedly referred to when the patient assigns an unreasonable degree of responsibility to him- or herself for events over which the patient has little control.

An essential initial step for constructing the exposure exercises is to construct a fear hierarchy, which lists a range of situations the patient fears. The situations from the hierarchy are then used to construct the actual exposure practices. Developing such a list is very useful for identifying the relevant dimensions of the patient's fear. For example, in Olivia's case, the more people and less structured the traffic situation is, the more discomfort she

Table 6.1   Clinical example: Olivia's fear hierarchy for driving

Items	SUDS
1. Driving in a supermarket parking lot alone with people walking around.	100
2. Driving in a supermarket parking lot with my husband in car.	95
3. Driving around a residential area alone	90
4. Driving around a residential area with my husband in car	85
5. Driving on a busy highway with my husband as a passenger	80
6. Driving on empty highway while my husband talks on the phone.	70
7. Driving on an empty highway while my husband sits attentively next to me.	60
8. Being a passenger in the car with an inexperienced driver who is driving on an empty highway	50
9. Being a passenger in the car with an experienced driver who is driving on a busy highway	40
10. Being a passenger in the car with an experienced driver who is driving on an empty highway	30

experiences (i.e., driving in supermarket parking lots is more challenging than driving on highways). Furthermore, it is apparent that when her husband is present she experiences less fear than when she has to drive alone. Therefore, her husband serves as a safety signal, and this needs to be explicitly addressed in treatment (i.e., the exposure should be conducted without her husband).

In generating a hierarchy, as in Table 6.1, it is advisable to begin with situations that produce relatively little anxiety and that the patient is confident of successfully completing the exposure. Subsequent steps are gradual and progressively challenging. Therapist modeling and full response prevention can also be very useful.

Other exposure exercises may be designed to encourage reality testing. Specifically, hitting another person with the car is typically an unmistakable event that results in a crash. People without OCD typically do not confuse little bumps on the road with hitting a person or object. Therefore, it can be useful for the patient to sit in the driver's seat with the engine running, put the car in the park position, and place their foot on the accelerator while the therapist loudly bangs his hands against the hood of the car screaming loudly. This exercise can approximate the experience of hitting a person while driving and can be used to contrast the patient's experience of hitting bumps on the road.

Such an exercise is further useful to encourage the patient to fully experience and accept the discomfort of experiencing the noises, bangs, and screams of a person in front of the car. Encouraging the patient to adopt a mindful, accepting stance toward these distressing stimuli can effectively counter automatic avoidance strategies (including emotional avoidance strategies). Thus, the patient should be instructed to experience their discomfort to its fullest, while the therapist approximates the worst-case scenario. When Olivia experienced intrusive images and a strong urge to put the car in the drive position and to run over the therapist, it was used as an opportunity to target TAF by illustrating the difference between action and thoughts.

Empirical Support

CBT has been shown to be effective for treating OCD (van Oppen and Arntz, 1994; Whittal *et al.*, 2005). A meta-analytic review of randomized controlled studies (Hofmann and Smits, 2008) showed that CBT for OCD was associated with a large effect size as compared to a placebo condition (Hedges' $g = 1.37$).

The effects of CBT for OCD may be enhanced to some degree by traditional anxiolytic medications (e.g., Hofmann *et al.*, 2009), and augmentation medications such as d-cycloserine (Kushner *et al.*, 2007; Wilhelm *et al.*, 2008).

Recommended Further Readings

Therapist guide

Foa, E. B., and Kozak, M. J. (2004). *Mastery of obsessive-compulsive disorder: A cognitive-behavioral therapist guide. Treatments that work.* New York: Oxford University Press.

Patient guide

Abramowitz, J. S. (2009). *Getting over OCD: A 10-step workbook for taking back your life.* New York: NYL Guilford Press.

7 Beating Generalized Anxiety Disorder and Worry

Walter's Worries

Walter is a 42-year-old, white, married man and father of two girls, aged 8 and 5. He works as a financial advisor at a large financial service company where he meets with individual clients, primarily handling their retirement accounts. He has been married to his wife June, a 34-year-old librarian, for almost 7 years. Their two children are adopted. Walter describes himself as a worrywart. He worries excessively about the family's finances, their health, his children's college funds, politics, and the environment, as well as minor matters such as car repairs and shopping for clothes. As a result of these worries, Walter likes to plan for the future. For example, he already has a well-developed plan for his children's college education. In the past, his worries about car repairs resulted in regular visits to a car shop in addition to the usual checkup times in order to get his car inspected even before anything turned out to be wrong. On various occasions, the car shop did find potential problems. Other worries, such as his concerns about world politics and the environment, cannot be solved with future planning, which he finds frustrating. Walter often has trouble sleeping and feels tense and stressed out. June recognizes these worries as being excessive and often teases him about it. However, she also appreciates his devotion to the family and she feels that Walter is taking very good care of her and the children. At the same time, she wishes that Walter would be less stressed over minor matters and could relax more and enjoy life. Walter has tried numerous anti-anxiety medications prescribed by a psychiatrist. While these medications helped him to some extent, he did not like the side effects and stopped taking them.

An Introduction to Modern CBT: Psychological Solutions to Mental Health Problems, First Edition.
S. G. Hofmann. © 2012 S. G. Hofmann. Published 2012 by John Wiley & Sons, Ltd.

Definition of the Disorder

The defining feature of generalized anxiety disorder (GAD) is excessive anxiety and worry amount a number of things, such as work, family, finances, health, community, world affairs, and minor matters (such as car repairs and clothes shopping).

In order to meet the DSM-IV criteria, worrying has to present more days than not for a period of at least 6 months and is typically associated with restlessness, feeling keyed up or on edge, being easily fatigued, having difficulty concentrating, being irritable, having muscle tension, and having sleep problems. The worries also need to cause clinically significant distress and interference with social, occupational, and other important areas of functioning. The disorder is relatively low in the DSM hierarchy, because GAD cannot be assigned if the worries are related to other mental disorders. Epidemiological studies have found that the average age of onset for GAD is 31, with 50% of patients reporting that the disorder began between the ages of 20 and 47 (Kessler *et al.,* 2005). Further, these studies typically report that the prevalence of GAD is higher in women, white people, and those with low income.

Walter's worries are clearly excessive. Although he has a stable and well-paying job, his family is healthy, and he lives in a safe country, he worries excessively about his family's finances and health, politics, and minor matters, such his car. He finds these worries uncontrollable and interfering with his life. Walter has a general tendency to worry a lot and worrying is perceived as part of his personality. At the same time, these worries are distressing and interfering. In most cases, he feels that he can't control them. In other cases, the worries seem to be adaptive, because they seem to protect him from undesirable situations in the future. For example, Walter's worries about his car cause him to have his car checked out by a mechanic before anything is even wrong and, in some cases, the mechanic was able to fix a minor problem that might have caused a much bigger and more expensive problem.

Worrying is an interesting phenomenon. Worrying about a future event is not the same as simply anticipating an event (Hofmann *et al.,* 2005). Worrying is a cognitive process that involves primarily verbal activity and, to a lesser extent, imagery. Imagery and verbal processes are two cognitive processes that have different effects on the psychophysiological response to emotional material. For example, verbalizing a fearful situation typically induces less cardiovascular response than visually imagining the same situation, possibly because verbalizations are used as a strategy for abstraction and disengagement. This suggests that the verbal activity during worrying is less closely connected to the affective, physiological, and behavioral systems than images are, and might therefore be a poor vehicle for processing emotional information (Borkovec *et al.*, 1998). For example, in one classic study by Borkovec and Hu (1990), a group of speech-anxious students were asked to visualize a fearful public speech as subjective anxiety and heart rate response were recorded. Before the visualization, one group engaged in relaxed thinking, another group engaged in worried thinking, and a third in neutral thinking. Those in the worry group reported the greatest subjective anxiety but had lower physiological reactivity than those in the neutral condition, who had lower reactivity than those in the relaxed condition. These results seem to suggest that worrying inhibits the emotional processing of distressing material and thus preserves cognitive-affective fear structures. Therefore, worrying can be conceptualized as a cognitive avoidance strategy. For example, Walter's worries about losing his job may be a strategy to avoid thinking about a much more catastrophic event. For example, he might be concerned that if he loses his job, he would stay unemployed, his wife and kids would leave him, and he would be abandoned and die as beggar under a bridge. Thus, worrying about finances, jobs, and health is a way to avoid the worst case scenario. Often, such a worst case can be best described as an image and a moment in time (such as dying lonely and abandoned as a beggar under a bridge).

Some researchers believe that an aspect of worrying, and possibly a cognitive vulnerability factor and dispositional variable, is intolerance of uncertainty. Intolerance of uncertainty is defined as a set of beliefs about the uncertainty of the world. Individuals with a high level of intolerance of uncertainty are assumed to perceive many sources of danger in their daily lives when confronted with uncertain and/or ambiguous situations. For example, somebody who is concerned that an unforeseen event could spoil one's career or personal life might feel anxious and engage in excessive worrying about these issues as a way to respond to such uncertainties (Ladouceur *et al.*, 2000). This construct is fully compatible with the cognitive model.

The Treatment Model

A number of different things can trigger worries—events in the workplace, world affairs, politics, news about the economy, or reports of illnesses, to name only a few. In Walter's case, the economic downturn triggered his worries about losing his job. As is the case for many patients who worry excessively, Walter holds the implicit belief that worrying can prevent the worst case scenario from happening (i.e., "worrying about my job will help me keep it"). Such overarching beliefs about the function of worrying are called metacognitions. Metacognitions are cognitions that control, monitor, and appraise thinking (Wells, 2009). These meta-cognitions can be classified into positive metacognitive beliefs (e.g., "worrying about the future means I can avoid bad things from happening") and negative metacognitive beliefs (e.g., "Worrying can damage my brain" or "I am unable to control my worries").

Excessive worrying typically leads to feelings of anxiety, muscle tension, and safety behaviors such as reassurance seeking. These subjective, behavioral, and physiological aspects of the emotional reactions to worrying reinforce each other and also reinforce the meta-cognitive beliefs about worrying and worrying itself. As a result of emotional reasoning, the negative thinking patterns become reinforced in part because they produce negative emotions. For example, if thinking about a future event causes distress (muscle tension, anxiety, seeking reassurance, etc.), then the vulnerable person is more likely to interpret this as a reason to worry about this event. This in effect closes the positive feedback loop, leading to the maintenance of worrying. Figure 7.1 depicts the cycle of one of Walter's main worries, his worry about losing his job.

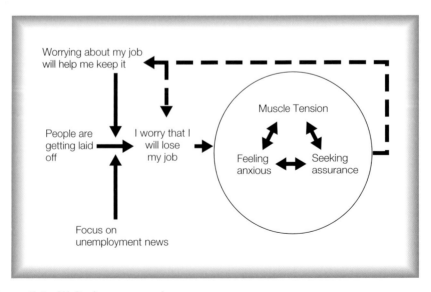

Figure 7.1   Walter's worry cycle.

Treatment Strategies

At the heart of this model are the processes of worrying, the beliefs about worrying, and the consequences of worrying, including the psychophysi-ological consequences, the feeling of anxiety, and the reassurance-seeking behaviors. Different strategies can effectively target these various compo-nents of the worry cycle. First, raising awareness of the function of worrying and then discussing the maladaptive beliefs about worrying can stop the cycle at its initial state. For example, Walter's worries appear to be part of his personality. He is a worrywart, a loving husband and father who is concerned about the well-being of his family. He believes that he is loved and appreciated partly because of this personality trait. Walter has also experienced proof that his worrying can prevent bad things from happen-ing in the future. For example, he can avoid costly car repairs and inconvenience by bringing his car in regularly for a checkup even outside the usual checkup times. Because of this, worrying appears to have positive consequences in addition to the negative effects. The most negative effect is that worrying about losing his job increases his anxiety and results in reassurance seeking behaviors. For example, Walter would follow very closely the news about the economic situation and discuss it with colleagues at work. This further increased his worries about his job and further rein-forced the belief that worrying about his job was one reason why he was still employed.

This vicious cycle between worrying, beliefs about worrying, and the psychophysiological, subjective, and behavioral consequences of worrying can be targeted with a number of different strategies. These strategies include psychoeducation and cognitive restructuring to target worrying and metacognitions about worrying, meditation to target worrying and the associated consequences, and relaxation strategies to target the auto-nomic inflexibility often associated with worrying. These components can further be modified during worry exposure and by use of acceptance strate-gies. These strategies are summarized in Figure 7.2 and will be described in more detail below.

Attention and situation modification

Worrying is a response to external triggers that are perceived as potentially threatening. Therefore, if the triggers change, the worrying response will naturally be affected as well. In Walter's case, the news about the economic

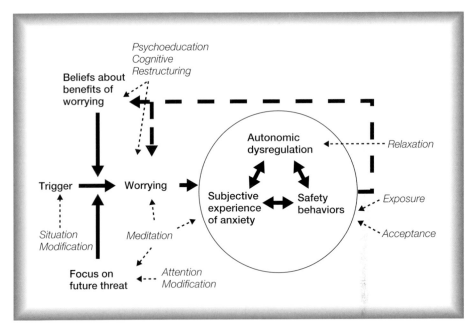

Figure 7.2   Strategies to target worrying.

situation triggered his worrying. Attempts to suppress focusing on the triggers are a reliably ineffective strategy to control them. Similar to thought suppression, the conscious attempt not to focus on something paradoxically increases the likelihood that we do focus on whatever we are trying not to focus on. Therefore, it would be counterproductive to ask Walter not to focus on the news about the economic situation. However, it would be reasonable to instruct him to focus on other, more pleasant things. Instead of watching shows on television about politics and the economic situation, he might be instructed to watch other shows, perhaps sitcoms or movies or (even better) spend more time outdoors doing light physical exercise, such as hiking, playing golf, or gardening. Without specifically instructing Walter to suppress any thoughts, urges, or impulses, the therapist was able to get Walter concentrate on more pleasant tasks that are unrelated to his worries. He took a beginner class in golf and greatly enjoyed this new sport. This also encouraged mild outdoor physical exercise, which has a general benefit for overall well-being. This also gave Walter the experience that life is much more than an accumulation of worries and worry behaviors and that there are many pleasant activities that are worth exploring.

Psychoeducation

At the beginning of treatment, Walter thought that there are many more pros than cons to worrying and that worrying is, generally speaking, an adaptive strategy to prevent the worst thing from happening. After all, worrying prepares us for the future and protects us from having to deal with undesirable events or situations in the future. Walter sees the unpleasant consequences of worrying as being a necessary evil of a generally very adaptive response. When the therapist introduced the idea to Walter that worrying might be the primary problem, he responded with skepticism and surprise, as shown below. The following dialogue between Walter and the therapist illustrates the technique used to compare the advantages and disadvantages of worrying.

Clinical Example: The Pros and Cons of Worrying

Therapist: Tell me a bit more about your worries about your job. I understand that your job is pretty secure. Why do you worry about it?

Walter: I think it is just in my nature. I am just a worrywart.

Therapist: You mean you worry a lot about a number of things?

Walter: Yes, it's in my nature.

Therapist: Do you like to worry?

Walter: I don't think there is anybody in the world who likes to worry. No, I don't like to worry. But I do.

Therapist: Would you like to worry less?

Walter: Sure, I would. In the perfect word, I would not worry at all.

Therapist: But we don't live in a perfect world. Things can go wrong, right?

Walter: Absolutely.

Therapist: And some things can go seriously wrong, right?

Walter: Yes.

Therapist: Can you tell me some of the things that could go seriously wrong in your life?

Walter: Oh, lots of things.

Therapist: Like what?

Walter: I could become sick or lose my job and not be able to support a family.

Therapist: You mean you could become unemployed and not find another job again.

Walter: Yes.

Therapist: How likely is that?

Walter: Well, that's hard to say. The economic news is quite troubling. So far, I have been able to keep my job. But the unemployment rate in the US is still close to 10% and all the economic indicators show that we are still in a recession.

Therapist: So far you are still employed in the middle of a recession.

Walter: That's right, I am still very lucky.

Therapist: Is it just luck?

Walter: Well, probably not. I think I am more aware of the situation than most of my colleagues and friends.

Therapist: You are more prepared?

Walter: Yes, I think I am. I follow the news very closely and I have been avoiding a bad situation.

Therapist: How do you avoid a bad situation from happening, such as getting laid off?

Walter: I do anything in my power to avoid it. I read the paper, regularly watch MSNBC, get news from the internet, and discuss things with co-workers and even my boss.

Therapist: So worrying about getting laid off prepares you well so that you can avoid it. You have been worrying about it a lot and it seems to work because you have not getting laid off. Obviously, we don't know whether or not you would have lost your job if you had not worried and prepared yourself so much. We would only know this for sure if we lived in a parallel universe. In fact, the only way of knowing whether your worrying in fact helps you keep your job is by doing what?

Walter: I don't know. Maybe by stop worrying?

Therapist: That's right! The only way to know for sure whether worrying helps you keep your job is my stop worrying. If you stop worrying and lose your job, there is a good chance that worrying before helped you to keep it. Obviously, this is a scary experiment, because losing your job is something we both want to avoid. But let's assume for a moment that, all things being equal, worrying is, in fact, completely unrelated to your employment situation. If that was the case, which situation would you prefer – being worried or not being worried?

Walter: Well, if I could be sure that I keep my job, I rather not worry about it.

Therapist: Why?

Walter: Because it doesn't feel good to worry. I get very anxious and tense and have problems sleeping when I worry.

Therapist: Okay. So worrying has some possible positive but clearly also some negative consequences. Worrying might help you avoid the worst case scenario, such as getting fired. On the other hand, it also has a number of negative consequences. You are often tense, feel anxious, and seek reassurance from your coworkers and your boss. In the best case scenario, worrying is a necessary evil, and in the worst case scenario it makes you feel miserable for no good reason and perhaps even makes it more likely that the worst case scenario is going to happen. This is known as a self-fulfilling prophecy—trying too hard to avoid the worst case scenario could actually make the worst case scenario more likely to happen. What do you think?

Cognitive restructuring

In order to identify and modify maladaptive cognitions, the patient may be asked to engage in active worrying (Borkovec and Sharpless, 2004).

Clinical Example: Worrying Practice

1. The therapist and patient identify one issue the patient frequently worries about.
2. The patient is asked to close his/her eyes and worry about this topic in his/her usual fashion for 1 minute.
3. The therapist asks the patient to describe in detail the specific thoughts, images, and flow of associations that happened during the worrying period.
4. Repeat the 1 minute of worrying and ask patient to verbalize the cognitive activities.
5. Ask the patient to pay attention to the specific contents each time he/she starts worrying, and encourage patient to identify the worry triggers.

The goal of this exercise is to identify the specific negative cognitions that accompany the worries. This can be done with questions, such as "What did you expect was going to happen?" and "What did you tell yourself?" In the final step, the maladaptive thoughts are corrected and replaced using the methods that have already been discussed in previous chapters.

Meditation and relaxation

Meditation practices are potentially useful in a variety of disorders, especially if the problem is related to ruminative thinking (thinking about past events), such as in SAD and depression, or worrisome thinking (thinking about future events), such as in GAD and OCD. Mindfulness practices help the individual to focus on the present moment and to encourage nonjudgmental awareness to directly counter the preoccupation with past or future events.

Imagery-focused meditation strategies can further be beneficial to gain distance to undesirable thoughts, images, or impulses (see Chapter 6). As discussed in Chapter 1, thought-action fusion is a result of an inability to gain distance (i.e., become decentered) from these internal experiences. Imagery-focused medication strategies might instruct the patient to detach him- or herself from these experiences. For example, a patient may be asked to turn a particular worrisome thought into a leaf that is floating on the surface of a creek and then to watch the leaf float away, or to turn the worrisome thought into a cloud in the sky and to watch the wind carry the cloud way. This strategy can facilitate the distancing/decentering experience and patients learn that "I am not my thoughts," "A thought and worry is a product of my mind and not reality," and "I can simply let go of my worries and it will be okay."

Many meditation practices and mindfulness exercises are potentially useful, and there is no single practice generally superior to any others, but, rather, it depends on the specific person and problem. Further, it is much more a matter of preference because some practices are more sensory focused, others are more breathing focused, and others are more imagery focused. Traditional Zen or yoga practices can be very helpful to get one acquainted with the meditation practices. Certain yoga practices that are focused on breathing can be helpful to reduce the autonomic hyperarousal in some GAD patients. An example of such a practice is given below.

Clinical Example: Yoga breathing practice (Pranayama)

Sit on the floor on a blanket or yoga mat in a yoga posture (legs crossed and pulled toward you, back straight, with arms resting on your thighs). Then do the following:

1. As you inhale, focus on the path your breath is taking going through your body. Breathe naturally, neither trying to slow nor to speed it up.
2. Clear your mind of unwanted images and thoughts. Let these thoughts come and go. Gently refocus on your breath.
3. Begin to inhale deeply through your nose.

4. Practice abdominal breathing by keeping your chest area still and by only expanding and contracting the abdominal area. Expand and contract your belly like a balloon as you breathe in and out. Pay close attention to how your abdominal area expands and contracts. Continue with deep breaths while keeping your chest area still. Do this for about five breaths.

5. Next, practice your chest breathing by keeping your abdomen still and by only expanding and contracting your chest area. Notice how your chest moves up and down. Continue with deep breaths while keeping your abdominal area still. Do this for about five breaths.

6. When you exhale, let the breath go out first from the upper chest, then from the rib cage, letting the ribs slide closer together. Finally, let the air go out from your abdomen.

7. Practice this three-part breathing exercise for about 10 breaths.

Exposure and acceptance

Worrying is an inherently superstitious behavior. It is an attempt to control the uncontrollable (i.e., the future). It is impossible to prevent adverse events from happening. Everybody will sooner or later have to deal with tragedies, deaths in a family, sicknesses, failures, and disappointments. It is simply a matter of time until we are personally confronted with such events. Some people experience more of those stressors, adverse events, and tragedies than others. To some extent these events can be avoided by anticipation and by proactive engagement in behaviors that decrease the likelihood of occurrence. Many other events, however, cannot be easily anticipated or they happen despite taking precautionary measures. The human desire to be in control of one's own destiny and to prevent catastrophic events, such as death, disabilities, and natural and man-made disasters are the reasons why the insurance business is such a lucrative industry.

Worrying, as was discussed earlier, is an abnormal expression of this natural and evolutionary adaptive desire to prepare ourselves for the future and to avoid negative events from happening to us or our kin. Excessive worrying, however, is maladaptive. Although worrying itself is an unpleasant activity, it is maintained because the distress associated with worrying validates worrying itself through emotional reasoning. In addition, safety behaviors are avoidance strategies that immunize worrying from falsification and that thereby preserve worrying because the patient is unable to examine whether the worried outcome will, in fact, happen or not.

Worry exposure and acceptance strategies target the processes that preserve worrying. Worry exposure encourages the patient to imagine the worst case scenario that is being avoided by worrying. In other words, worrying is conceived as a verbally mediated cognitive avoidance strategy of worst case scenarios. These scenarios can be effectively explored using imagery scripts. The following is an example of the worry exposure technique.

Clinical Example: Worry Exposure

Therapist: Let's explore a bit your worry about being unemployed. What exactly are you worried about?

Walter: I am worried that I would not be able to find another job.

Therapist: And then what?

Walter: This would be very horrible. I have a family to support, pay my mortgage, pay off our credit card debts, our car loan, my kids' school.

Therapist: You are carrying a lot of responsibility. What would happen if you did not have any money to pay for all these things?

Walter: I don't know. We would probably have to use up our savings.

Therapist: And what would happen if you used up all of you savings and still could not find another job?

Walter: Wow, I don't know. I would probably have to refinance our house and take out cash.

Therapist: What if all the money is gone. You have nothing left in your savings and nobody is willing to give you any money. What would happen?

Walter: I don't know. My wife would probably leave me, taking the kids so somebody else can support them, and I would have to live on the street.

Therapist: Yes, this would be a bad situation. What do you think the likelihood is that you end up on the street alone and abandoned if you lose your job?

Walter: I don't know; probably not very likely.

Therapist: Why don't you give me a number on a scale from 0% (not likely at all) to 100% (very likely).

Walter: Maybe 30?

After discussing the concept of probability overestimation (see Chapter 4), Walter acknowledges that the probability of living on the street must be much smaller. After some discussions, he estimated it to be approximately 1%.

Therapist: Now let's consider for a moment this worst case scenario. Please imagine for a moment that your worst fears have come true:

you lost your job, were unable to find a new job, used up all of your savings. Your wife and kids left you and you live on the street. Can you think of a particular image that represents all of this?

Walter: Sure. I am sitting underneath the BU bridge, covered with one of those grey blankets.

Therapist: Great. What season is it?

Walter: It's cold. Maybe late fall. I am shivering. It is cold and I am drained from the rain.

Therapist: You are doing great! So you are cold, wet, covered in a grey blanket, sitting under a bridge, poor and lonely. Please close your eyes now and imagine this scene. Try to put yourself in the situation and experience it to its fullest. Simply accept it as is. If you have distracting thoughts or a desire to push this image way, simply acknowledge it and gently refocus on the image again. Experience the feelings that the image produces without judging it and without trying to make it better. Handle it just the way you did when you did the mindfulness exercise we did earlier. But this time, put yourself in the situation when you are sitting under the bridge, wet, cold, and alone. Should we try it?

This exercise is likely to induce negative feelings. The natural tendency is to suppress the negative emotion or to use other strategies to lessen the negative experience. In conjunction with this exercise, it can be very helpful to introduce acceptance as a different approach to dealing with those negative emotions. An example for introducing acceptance is given below (from Campbell-Sills *et al.*, 2006).

Clinical Example: Acceptance Strategy

People often think that negative emotions must be controlled or stopped. They may learn from an early age that they can and should control negative thoughts and feelings. People are told things like "just stop worrying" or "put it behind you." Moreover, you see people controlling their feelings on many occasions, such as at funerals or in crisis situations, and you may come to believe that people should always try to control their emotions.

Given that you have most likely experienced some difficulty with emotions like anxiety or sadness in your life, efforts to block these feelings are quite understandable. However, although self-control may work in many areas of your life, there are situations involving emotions where it might be difficult or even impossible. Struggling against relatively natural emotions can actually intensify and prolong your distress, rather than make the situation better.

So, am I suggesting that you just give up on changing your emotional experiences? No, what I'm suggesting is that there is an alternative to struggling or battling with your emotions and it is called acceptance. Accepting your emotions means that you are willing to experience them fully and that you don't try to control or change your emotions in any way.

Am I proposing that you should just put up with discomfort and distress? No, what I'm suggesting is that one way to think about your emotions is not as something that always needs to be contained or controlled in order for you to be okay, but as natural reactions that occur, peak, and fade without leading to any awful consequences and without you having to struggle or fight with your feelings at all.

Accepting emotions like anxiety and sadness may be difficult, especially when common sense tells you that these emotions are bad. There are times in life, however, when our common-sense reactions get us into trouble. Have you ever driven your car on a sheet of ice and lost control? Usually, the mistake people make is that they try to correct the situation by turning in the opposite direction from which they are skidding. This seems to make sense, but the more effective approach is to do the opposite—to turn the wheel in the direction of the skid.

What I am suggesting is that dealing effectively with your emotions may be very similar. It is against your natural reaction to allow yourself to feel negative feelings. However, just like turning into the direction of the skidding is a better way of dealing with icy road conditions, leaning into your emotions and fully experiencing them may be a better way of dealing with emotional situations.

So, if emotions occur during your viewing of the following series of pictures, allow yourself to accept and stay with your emotions without trying to get rid of them. Refrain from attempts to distract yourself or otherwise lessen your feelings, and instead allow yourself to feel your emotions as fully as possible. Just let your emotions run their natural course and see how that goes.

Empirical Support

A number of meta-analyses have been conducted to examine the efficacy of CBT for GAD (e.g., Borkovec and Ruscio, 2001; Hofmann and Smits, 2008).

These studies showed that CBT is effective at reducing symptoms of GAD in both the short and long term. For example, the Borkovec and Ruscio study reviewed 13 outcome studies involving CBT for GAD. CBT was found to produce decreases in anxiety at post-treatment that were on average more than one standard deviation (1.09) greater than waiting-list control groups. A comparison between CBT and a credible placebo treatment showed a moderate effect size (Hedges' $g = 0.51$) at post-treatment (Hofmann and Smits, 2008). However, it should be noted that these CBT protocols did not include many of the more novel intervention strategies, such as mindfulness training and metacognitive strategies that target the beliefs about the potential benefits of worrying.

Recommended Further Readings

Therapist guide

Craske, M. G., and Barlow, D. D. (2006). *Mastery of your anxiety and worry: Workbook.* New York: Oxford University Press.

Patient guide

Leahy, R. L. (2005). *The worry cure: Seven steps to stop worry from stopping you.* New York: Harmony Books.

8   Dealing with Depression

Martha's Mood

Martha is a 39-year-old white married woman and mother of a son, aged 14. She has a college degree in English literature and has been a stay-at-home mom since her son Frederick was born. In her spare time, she writes poetry and theatrical plays. Her husband (Frederick Sr.) works as an architect. The relationship with her husband is at times "rocky." Her husband agrees that they have marital conflicts at times, but does not think that they indicate any serious marital problems. They both agree that her depression often negatively affects her relationship with her husband. Similarly, disagreements with her husband often trigger a depressive episode. In fact, even minor arguments can set off a depressive episode. These arguments reinforce her feeling of being worthless and unlovable, and at times she is convinced that her husband is going to leave her. However, her husband has never threatened that he would. When she feels depressed, she typically withdraws from the relationship with her husband and her family and experiences a strong feeling of emptiness and hopelessness. She typically perceives herself as being worthless and unlovable. She usually blames herself for arguments with her husband, attributing her disagreements to her inadequacy as a woman and wife. During the depressive episodes, she typically loses interest in her hobbies (writing, reading, and going to theatrical plays with her husband) and loses her appetite. All she wants to do is to disappear. She finds comfort by staying in bed and sleeping a lot. During these depressive episodes, which can last 6 months or a year at a time, she feels unable to take care of the basic tasks around the house. At times, she contemplates suicide, but never had a plan and denies being at risk of committing suicide. She would not do this because of her family, but sometimes fantasizes about suicide

An Introduction to Modern CBT: Psychological Solutions to Mental Health Problems, First Edition.
S. G. Hofmann. © 2012 S. G. Hofmann. Published 2012 by John Wiley & Sons, Ltd.

as a way to escape the feeling of emptiness. Martha reports experiencing her first depressive episode at the age of 25, shortly after she gave birth to her son. Since that time, her depression has reoccurred at least once each year. The times are unpredictable, although they happen to be more likely after major changes in her life, such as after moving her home.

Definition of the Disorder

Depression is one of the most common psychiatric problems. The 12-month prevalence rate of unipolar depression is 6.6%, and the lifetime prevalence rate is 16.2% (Kessler *et al.*, 2003). Martha's case of depression is not atypical. Females are consistently twice as likely than males to experience depression. The disorder most often begins in mid-to-late adolescence and early adulthood. About 25% of adults with depression report an onset before their young adulthood, and 50% report an onset by age 30 (Kessler *et al.*, 2005). Consistent with these statistics, Martha's depression began at age 25, and developed into a chronic condition. Whereas the majority (approximately 70%) of individuals recover within a year, many experience significant problems even 5 years after the initial onset (for a review, see Gotlib and Hammen, 2009). Unless depression is adequately treated, it usually lasts between 4 months and a year. Relapse and recurrence of depression is common; the majority (between 50% and 85%) of depressed patients experience multiple episodes (Coyne *et al.*, 1999; Solomon *et al.*, 2000). As in Martha's case, these episodes can be associated with stressors, but this is not necessarily the case. Sadly, only a minority (21.7%) of patients receive adequate treatment within a 12-month period.

Martha's depression appears to be linked to interpersonal problems. It is not unusual that depression is linked to social and interpersonal problems or changes, such as marriage, divorce, or marital conflict, loss of a significant other, loss of a job, a move to a new neighborhood, or the birth of a child. Therefore, understanding the social and interpersonal context of depression can lead to new ways to deal with current depression and future episodes. The therapeutic techniques to explore and alter interpersonal and social factors that might contribute to depression are the basis for interpersonal therapy (IPT; Weissman *et al.*, 2007). Although IPT is not incompatible with traditional cognitive-behavioral treatment of depression, there are a number of notable differences. Most importantly, IPT does not assume that maladaptive cognitions are associated with depression. Instead, depression is conceived of as a medical illness, and interpersonal problems can contribute to the symptoms of this illness. Therefore, interpersonal therapy focuses much less on cognitions and addresses grief, interpersonal role disputes, interpersonal deficits, and role transitions.

The Treatment Model

There are many reasons for becoming depressed, but only a minority of people experience a full-blown (major) depressive episode. Unexpected things happen often, and some of these things are highly undesirable and even traumatic. We might lose a job, a relationship might end, or a child might suffer from a serious illness. None of these serious tragedies is likely to happen at any given moment, but it is very likely that people experience some tragedies at some point in the future. This is simply because the world is to a great degree unpredictable and we have limited control over our future. To make things worse, even if things are going well at any point in our lives, everything is eventually going to end because we will die sooner or later and all good things will come to an end. Clearly, there are many reasons to become depressed. The question which then arises is, "Why don't more people develop depression?"

The reason why healthy people are protected from getting depressed is a positive bias. Healthy people are likely to attribute positive events to themselves and attribute negative events to other causes (Menzulis *et al.*, 2004). This *self-serving attributional bias* seems to be missing or deficient in people with depression, who tend to attribute negative events to internal (something about the self), stable (enduring), and global (general) causes (e.g., lack of ability, personality flaws). Such an attributional style implies that negative events are likely to recur in the future across a wide variety of domains, leading to widespread hopelessness (Abramson and Seligman, 1978). In addition to the self-serving attributional bias, healthy people show an illusion of control over stressors (Alloy and Clements, 1992). Depression is characterized by a breakdown or absence of these positive cognitive biases, resulting in a more realistic assessment of the uncontrollable and unpredictable nature of stressors. This has been referred to as *depressive realism* (Alloy and Clements, 1992; Mischel, 1979). This is consistent with the notion that, in contrast to people with depression, healthy people show a remarkable degree of resiliency when confronted with tragic events. When asked to anticipate how one will feel in the future, people are typically unable to ignore the current state and will base this future prediction partly on the current moment (Gilbert, 2006). As a result of this affective forecasting, people with depression cannot imagine liking future events very much when they think about them (MacLeod and Cropley, 1996).

Stress is a common trigger for depression. In Martha's case, prolonged stress (e.g., the move to a new house or a new job) and acute stressors (e.g., arguments with her husband) can easily trigger a depressive episode. Interpersonal stressors are especially powerful triggers. As is typical for people with depression, Martha has strong negative beliefs (schemas) about herself (e.g., "I am worthless and unlovable"), which are expressed as a negative prediction about her relationship (e.g., "my husband will want to leave me"). It is not clear whether the relationship problems are the primary cause for the Martha's depression. Her husband acknowledges relationship problems, but does not believe that these problems are out of the ordinary. He further believes that the depression is as much a consequence as it is a cause for the arguments and thinks that their relationship would be much improved if her depression was under control. However, the critical point is that Martha appears to be dissatisfied. Epidemiological data suggest that dissatisfied spouses are almost three times more likely than satisfied spouses to develop a major depressive episode over the course of a year, and almost 30% of new occurrences of depression are associated with marital dissatisfaction (Whisman and Bruce, 1999). Therefore, it can be highly beneficial to include the significant other in the treatment (O'Leary and Beach, 1999), and to consider interpersonal therapy, especially as maintenance treatment of depression in elderly people (Reynolds et al., 2006). In Martha's case, the therapist considered interpersonal therapy, couples therapy, or individual CBT. A careful analysis of Martha's depression suggested that CBT in combination with strategies borrowed from interpersonal therapy would be the best treatment option.

When the therapist and Martha explored the contributing factors of some of her depressive episodes, it became clear that social factors were often at the forefront. For example, her decision to become a stay-at-home mom brought a number of challenges. Although she loves her family and would do anything for her son, she felt that she had to give up a lot of her dreams for the family. During treatment, at times she expressed resentment, which was associated with feelings of guilt about feeling resentful and "selfish." Some of the worst episodes of depression occurred after arguments with her husband. When exploring the reason for her response, it became clear that fears of abandonment contributed to some of her depressed feelings. Martha remembered that her relationship with her father was very conflictual, and she often felt misunderstood and unloved by him. Although she does not think that her husband would ever leave her, she is worried that he will find another woman and abandon her. Martha realized that her fears of abandon-ment and her worries about not being loved by her father may be related to her fears and worries about the relationship with her husband. Although the fights with her husband do not seem to be overly intense, she tends to rumi-nate about them excessively, even weeks after they have passed. Martha reported that at times her husband could not even remember the fights that Martha had ruminated over for weeks.

Martha also showed a number of maladaptive beliefs and thoughts related to these interpersonal problems. Specifically, she quickly jumps to cata-strophic beliefs (e.g. "my husband wants to leave me") after these fights. This leads to low energy, depressed mood, and social isolation. She withdraws from social relationships and her marriage is negatively affected by her depression. It also appears that that the marital conflicts trigger, and even cause, her depression. A close examination of a depressive episode revealed a close association between Martha's relationship stressor, her maladaptive beliefs ("I am worthless and unlovable"), her automatic thoughts ("my husband wants to leave me"), and her depressed mood, low energy, and social isolation. These depressive syndromes reinforce her maladaptive beliefs and automatic thoughts. This is in part due to emotional reasoning to rationalize her depression and in part because her depression creates conflicts with her husband, which seems to validate her concerns about the relationship. Figure 8.1 illustrates Martha's depression.

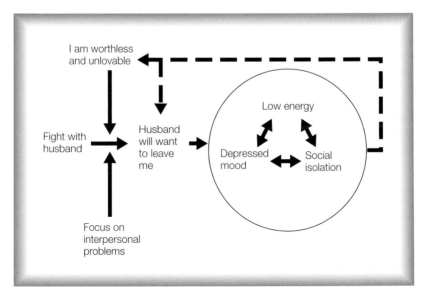

Figure 8.1   Martha's depression.

Treatment Strategies

Negative events, tragedies, and personal losses are virtually unavoidable in a person's lifetime. It is normal to experience episodes of low mood or temporary feelings of depression when those events happen. However, few people develop a mental illness and major depression as a result of it. What distinguishes people with depression from those who are not depressed is not so much their experience of stressors *per se* but their response to them. Therefore, depression is, generally speaking, a result of maladaptive coping strategies to stressors, combined with a negative view of oneself, the world, and the future, and heightened attentional focus on the negative aspects of the trigger. Coping strategies can be broadly classified into problem-focused strategies and emotion-focused strategies (e.g., Carver *et al.*, 1989; Lazarus, 1993). Examples of problem-focused coping strategies are attempts to modify the situation and triggers; other possible strategies are emotion-focused interventions. These strategies are summarized in Figure 8.2 and will be described in more detail below.

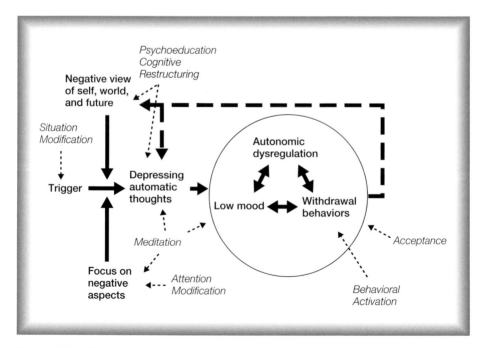

Figure 8.2   Strategies to target depression.

Situation modification

Martha's depression is closely tied to relationship problems with her husband. These marital conflicts frequently trigger depression and can be accentuated by depression, forming a vicious cycle. Working with her husband Frederick to identify and resolve some of the martial problems can effectively modify some of the triggers of Martha's depression.

Attention modification

Encouraging Martha to focus her attention on positive aspects of her life she is taking for granted can be an effective strategy. These aspects might include positive parts of her relationship, her family, and her life in general. Focusing on those positive aspects as alternatives to her triggers of depression can intervene at an early stage of the process. In order to encourage Martha to focus on these aspects, she might be asked to keep a diary of events, people, and things she feels positive about and is thankful for.

Psychoeducation and cognitive restructuring

The original formulation of the CBT model of depression posits that people with depression hold a negative view of themselves, the future and/or the world. These schemas give rise to specific maladaptive automatic cognitions in specific situations. CBT proceeds by identifying and challenging the maladaptive cognitions and then by eventually exploring and correcting the maladaptive beliefs and schemas. It is assumed, and it has been shown, that correcting maladaptive automatic cognitions and beliefs also changes the associated emotional response (Beck *et al.*, 1979).

Clinical Example: Exploring and challenging maladaptive depressive beliefs

Therapist: Tell me a little about the fight you had last week.

Martha: Fred announced on Friday evening that he would have to go to the office on the weekend. This ruined our entire weekend's plans. I am still very upset.

Therapist: How long did he go into the office?

Martha: Maybe 3 hours on Saturday. He would have stayed a lot longer if I hadn't brought it up.

Therapist: So you were upset with him that he went to the office on Saturday and you had other plans.

Martha: Yes, I wanted to do something outdoors with our son. I am still upset that he puts the family second place.

Therapist: You are upset because he does not prioritize spending time with you?

Martha: Yes; with me and our son.

Therapist: What does it mean that he does not spend enough time with you?

Martha: I don't know. What do you mean?

Therapist: I am trying to understand where the feeling of being upset is coming from. I understand if you were feeling disappointed because you were looking forward to spending some time with your husband and the family. But my sense is that you are not only feeling disappointment but you are also upset and perhaps even angry. Where do you think the feeling of being upset and angry is coming from?

Martha: I don't know. I guess I don't feel like he is treating me with respect and values me.

Therapist: I see. Great work identifying and describing your emotions. So you are feeling upset and angry because he is not valuing you. Let's explore this feeling even a bit further. Please imagine that your husband was sitting next to you. Please say what you are feeling inside and why, using I-statements.

Martha: I am hurt and upset because you treat me like dirt. I don't want to play second fiddle. I have the right to be treated with respect.

Therapist: Great work! It sounds to me that you feel worthless when he shows this behavior.

Martha: Yes, very.

Therapist: What else?

Martha: He doesn't really care for me.

Therapist: That he doesn't love you?

Martha: Yes.

Therapist: And if there is anybody who loves you, it should be your husband, right?

Martha: Yes, but I don't think anybody loves me. I can't even love myself.

Therapist: So you feel like nobody loves you and that you are not worthy of other people's love. This feeling of worthlessness and not being loved is a very important piece of your depression. The way you interpret things around you greatly depends on the beliefs you have. So if you believe that you are worthless and unlovable, then you are more likely to interpret a neutral, or even positive behavior of your husband toward you more negatively and perhaps even as a sign that he does not love you even though that would not be the case. I wonder if we can clarify the specific uncaring behaviors your husband would show and then set up experiments to see if we are correct with our assumption that he does not care for you. What are some of the specific behaviors that would tell you that he does not care for you?

Meditation

Depression is an unpleasant state. The natural response to it is to suppress this feeling and to ruminate about past events that might have led to this state. As a result, the person becomes preoccupied with depression, focuses on him/herself, and loses touch with the outside, and, in particular, the social world. This leads to social isolation and exacerbation of the depressive cycle of social and interpersonal isolation and rumination. Mindfulness practices encourage the person to focus on the present moment nonjudgmentally and openly. Thus, depression leads to isolation, rigidity, and distancing, whereas mindfulness practices encourage openness, flexibility, and curiosity.

This can end the depression cycle. Instead of ruminating about past failures, lost opportunities, and the future, mindfulness encourages the person to let go of these negative thinking patterns and feelings. It increases cognitive and affective flexibility by allowing the patient to experience, rather than suppress, negative feelings, by exploring other future options, and by then moving forward without obsessing over past mistakes.

It has been shown that patients with depression treated to remission with either antidepressant medication or CBT showed different patterns of cognitive reactivity following a negative mood induction, and that this cognitive reactivity predicted depression relapse (Segal et al., 2006). Specifically, medication responders showed more cognitive reactivity as compared with CBT responders. Further, treatment responders, irrespective of the treatment they received, also showed cognitive reactivity and had an increased risk for relapse in the subsequent 18 months as compared with participants with minimal or no cognitive reactivity. These findings suggest that cognitive reactivity following an emotionally challenging task may confer vulnerability for depression relapse or recurrence and that CBT may target this vulnerability more effectively than pharmacotherapy.

In addition to cognitive restructuring, it has been suggested that cognitive reactivity can be effectively targeted by meditation strategies that promote decentering. Decentering refers to the capacity to take a present-focused, nonjudgmental stance in regard to thoughts and feelings and the ability to accept them (see also Segal *et al.*, 2002). An example of such a present-moment/breathing-focused mindfulness practice has been discussed in the previous chapter that discussed worrying, a cognitive process that is closely related to rumination.

In addition to the maladaptive ruminative processes, depression and problems that are closely linked to it, such as suicide (Joiner *et al.*, 2009), are also associated with interpersonal and social difficulties. One particularly promising meditation strategy to target interpersonal problems is loving kindness meditation (LKM), a particular meditation technique from the Buddhist tradition. It should be noted, however, that LKM has not be applied—at least to my knowledge—to the treatment of depression in any clinical trials. Nevertheless, due to its potentially very useful application, it will be described here in some detail.

Whereas contemporary mindfulness meditation encourages nonjudgmental awareness of experiences in the present moment by focusing on breathing and other sensations, LKM focuses on the happiness of others. More specifically, it involves a range of thoughts and visualizations with the goal of evoking specific emotions (i.e., love, contentment, and compassion). One important goal of LKM is to gain happiness by cultivating positive feelings toward other people. This, in turn, can dispel false assumptions about the sources of one's happiness and shift a person's basic view of the self in relation to others, increasing general empathy (Dalai Lama & Cutler, 1998).

Loving Kindness Meditation (LKM)

LKM proceeds through a number of stages that differ depending on the focus of the exercise. These steps typically include:

(1) Focus on self
(2) Focus on a good friend (i.e., a person who is still alive and who does not invoke sexual desires)
(3) Focus on a neutral person (i.e., a person who typically does not elicit either particularly positive or negative feelings but who is commonly encountered during a normal day)
(4) Focus on a "difficult" person (i.e., a person who is typically associated with negative feelings)

(5) Focus on the self, good friend, neutral person, and difficult person (with attention being equally divided between them); and eventually
(6) Focus on the entire universe.

At each stage, the meditation exercise consists of thinking about specific wishes (aspirations), including the following:

(1) May the person be free from enmity
(2) May the person be free from mental suffering
(3) May the person be free from physical suffering; and
(4) May the person take care of him/herself happily (see Chalmers, 2007).

The typical period of the practice is 1 hour and the preferred position is the full lotus posture (i.e., with both legs crossed, bottom of the feet facing upward, the back being straight, and the hands on the lap with the palms on top of each other, facing upwards).

Behavioral activation

Depression is often associated with withdrawal behaviors and inactivation. As a result, the lives of people with depression become devoid of reinforcements, gratification, and pleasure. Due to low energy, depressed people may not have enough energy to examine beliefs, automatic thoughts, and other aspects that might maintain the depression. Therefore, behavioral activation is highly recommended, especially at the beginning of treatment in order to lift the patient's energy level.

As the first step, patients are asked to monitor their activities during the week. In its simplest form, the activity log includes the time and date, location, a brief description of the activity, and a rating how pleasant the activity was on a scale from 0 (not pleasant at all) to 100 (very pleasant). In the next step, the therapist and patient explore the reasons why some activities are pleasant and why others were rated as unpleasant. The goal is to build and increase the number of pleasant activities and to decrease the unpleasant activities and periods of inactivity during a normal week. In addition, it is desirable to establish routines in the patient's daily life and to implement regular eating and sleeping patterns.

Clinical Example: Behavioral Activation

Below is a portion of Martha's activity diary on one day.

Martha's diary for December 12, 2010

Time	Activity	Mood Rating 0 (low) 100 (high)
6:00-7:00	Woke up, got ready	10
7:00-7:30	Woke up Fred Junior, prepared breakfast and luncheons	10
7:30-8:00	Had breakfast	40
8:00-9:00	Went back to bed	50
9:00-11:00	Watched TV	20
11:00-12:00	Cleaned up	10
12:00-1:00	Read paper	20
1:00-2:00	Talked to Paula	60
2:00-3:00	Went over bank statements	40
3:00-5:00	Went to store to buy groceries and run errands	20
5:00-6:00	Cooked dinner	30
6:00-7:30	Had dinner with Fred and Junior	40
7:30-9:00	TV	50
9:00-10:00	Argued about money	0
10:00-11:00	Got ready for bed	20

A review of Martha's diary illustrates a number of issues: (1) her mood ratings were overall low and her highest mood rating was when watching TV; (2) her repertoire of enjoyable activities was very small and ranged primarily around chores, food, and watching TV; (3) her routine was inconsistent because she went back to bed after she got out of bed earlier in the morning; (4) fights with her husband resulted in a drop in her mood; and (5) further explorations revealed that her lowest mood ratings in general were during unstructured times and on weekends when she ruminated about her life, her relationship, and her future. Finally, it was evident that Martha did not do any physical exercise, an important detail that can lead to dramatic changes in mood.

Some important questions that activity logs might answer include: How withdrawn and isolated is the patient from normal daily activities? Are there enough opportunities to experience pleasant situations? How disrupted is the patient's daily routine because of the depression? And finally, does the patient have the necessary motivation and resources to implement the behavioral strategies? The last point is of particular importance because the primary symptom of depression is often a lack of motivation and anhedonia. However, pleasant activities can be self-reinforcing. This vicious cycle between inactivity, social isolation, and depression can be effectively disrupted by slowly and persistently introducing patients in creative ways to a range of pleasant activities.

As her homework assignment, the therapist asked Martha to come up with a list of pleasant tasks. This list included reading English literature, reading and watching modern theater plays, writing novels and poetry, going for walks, playing cards with her friends, and watching newly released movies. These activities were gradually built into her homework exercises. Martha was also instructed to begin and maintain a regular eating and sleeping routine, to join a gym to do cardiovascular exercise twice a week, and to go for a walk on the days when she does not go to the gym. Because her gym was closed on the weekend, the therapist and Martha agreed that it be best to go for long walks (at least 40 minutes) on Saturdays and Sundays and to go to the gym on Tuesdays, Wednesdays, and Thursdays. These walks later became important social events when she started asking one or two friends to join her.

Empirical Support

A large number of clinical trials have supported the efficacy of CBT for major depressive disorder (Butler *et al.*, 2006). A particular benefit of CBT relative to antidepressant medication is that fewer patients (i.e., approximately half) relapse (Glogcuen *et al.*, 1998). In their meta-analysis of the efficacy of CBT for depression, Glogcuen and coworkers reported that the average risk of relapse (based on follow-up periods of 1 to 2 years) was 25% after CBT, compared to 60% following antidepressant medication. Some research data also suggest that patients who receive CBT alone are no more likely to relapse after treatment than are those individuals who continue to receive medication (Dobson *et al.,* 2008; Hollon *et al.,* 2005). CBT has also been compared to antidepressant treatment (SSRIs) for severe depression (DeRubeis *et al.,* 2005; Hollon *et al.,* 2005). Both interventions resulted in equal outcomes of remission in the acute phase of treatment, but the risk of relapse at 1-year follow-up was favorable for individuals treated with CBT even compared to those who continued to receive medication (Hollon *et al.,* 2005).

Recommended Further Readings

Therapist guide

Beck, A. T., and Alford, B. A. (2009). *Depression: Causes and treatment,* 2nd edition. Philadelphia: University of Pennsylvania Press.

Patient guide

Leahy, R. L. (2010). *Beat the blues before they beat you: How to overcome depression.* Carlsbad, CA: Hay House.

9 Overcoming Alcohol Problems

Chuck's Alcohol Problems

Charles (Chuck) is a 35-year-old white male. He works as a construction worker and is married without children. His wife, Rose, works as a part-time secretary. Chuck is slightly overweight, has high blood pressure, mild cirrhosis (fatty liver), and chronic back pain. The back pain appears to be caused by years of hard physical labor. Chuck and Rose have been married for 10 years and both describe their relationship as "rocky." The biggest point of contention for Rose is Chuck's friends. He regularly gets together with them to have drinks at local bars. Chuck's best friend is Joe, an old high-school buddy. He is also close friends with two of his coworkers, Dave and Tom. He regularly meets them right after work to have a few drinks. He also frequently sees Joe at his favorite bar one or two times a week and often on weekends. Chuck and Joe often consume a large amount of alcohol, primarily beer, and tend to drink the most on weekends. Chuck reports that he has always had a very high tolerance for alcohol, especially beer. On a normal week, Chuck estimates that he might drink about 30 bottles of beer (39 standard drinks) per week (one bottle of beer equals 1.3 standard drinks) and does not think that this is a problem. Moreover, he usually takes his car to and from the pub. He thinks that he is a very safe driver, even after he has had "a few beers too many." Rose does not like Chuck's drinking or his drinking buddies. They often get into arguments over it, which increase on weekends when Chuck is recovering from his hangover on Sunday. In addition to the relationship problems, the drinking has caused him to miss some work. Not only has his boss urged him to look for help to reduce his drinking, but his doctor has also strongly urged him to stop drinking.

An Introduction to Modern CBT: Psychological Solutions to Mental Health Problems, First Edition.
S. G. Hofmann. © 2012 S. G. Hofmann. Published 2012 by John Wiley & Sons, Ltd.

Definition of the Disorder

Substance use disorders are among the most common psychiatric disorders and constitute a major public health problem. Epidemiological surveys in the United States have reported lifetime prevalence rate of DSM-IV substance use disorder of 14.6% in the general population (Kessler *et al.*, 2005). Alcohol is the most common and hazardous substance, inflicting a significant risk to the person's health, as well as an economic burden to society.

Chuck's behaviors meet the diagnostic criteria for alcohol abuse. Alcohol abuse is diagnosed based on problems in at least one of four areas, including failure to fulfill major social role obligations at work, home, or school (Chuck is often late at work); drinking repeatedly in a manner that creates potentially dangerous situations (he often drives his car while under the influence of alcohol); continuing to drink despite known social or interpersonal problems that result from drinking (his drinking causes marital conflicts), and incurring repeated alcohol-related legal consequences. Although Chuck meets some of the criteria for alcohol dependence (three of seven criteria), he does not meet the minimum number required for alcohol dependence. The criteria for alcohol dependence includes impaired control, physical tolerance, physical withdrawal, neglect of other activities, increased time spent using alcohol, and continued use despite knowledge of recurrent physical and psychological problems related to use. Although he shows impaired control of his drinking, the time he spent drinking has remained constant and is limited to the meetings with his friends. Although he consumes a large number of drinks, he has not yet developed physical tolerance and does not show physical withdrawal symptoms, aside from his hangovers on Sunday.

It is important to note that drinking alcohol and using substances are behaviors. Abuse is a maladaptive behavior because it has negative consequences on the person's social life, career, and self-perception. In order to change maladaptive behaviors, the person needs to recognize that the behavior is a problem, must be motivated to change it, and has what it takes to implement specific strategies to change it.

The Treatment Model

Drinking has an important role in Chuck's life and it defines the friendship with his best friend Joe and his coworkers Tom and Dave. However, it has also caused him problems with his wife, Rose, and his employer. He spends a lot of time with his friends drinking, which takes away time spent with his wife Rose and intensifies the conflict between them. Moreover, his drinking is particularly excessive during the weekends. As a result, he spends a lot of time in bed on Sundays recovering from his handover. Additionally, this behavior has gotten him into trouble with his employer in the past.

Chuck does not fully appreciate the difficulties drinking has caused him or the problems he might face in the future from drinking to this extent. He is currently at risk of getting divorced from his wife and of losing his job and may be at risk for health problems in the future (e.g., liver problems). Yet Chuck does not believe that he has a drinking problem. For him, there is nothing wrong with having a few drinks with friends; it is a way to enjoy the time with his friends and to "blow off some steam." He works hard and feels that he has the right to some enjoyable moments in his life. Drinking relaxes him and it makes him feel good, which further maintains his drinking behavior. However, he does admit that he has a hard time stopping once he starts drinking, especially when he is hanging out with Joe at his favorite bar. Just thinking about it during the day can result in a large urge to drink, which leads him to call Joe to arrange another get-together. Figure 9.1 illustrates some of the important factors that maintain Chuck's drinking problem.

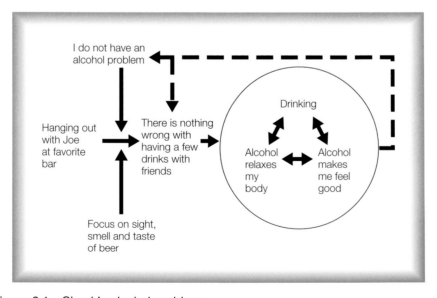

Figure 9.1   Chuck's alcohol problem.

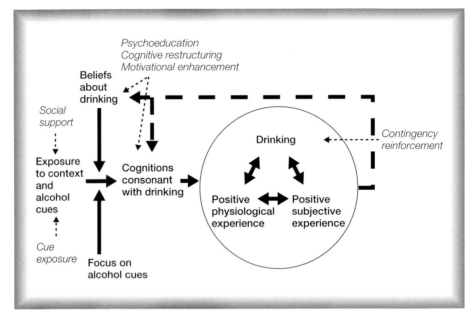

Figure 9.2 Strategies to target Chuck's alcohol problem.

Treatment Strategies

Chuck's alcohol problem can be most effectively targeted through three main areas: (1) psychoeducation, cognitive intervention, and motivational interviewing to raise awareness of the negative consequences of his behavior and to create adaptive cognitive dissonance, (2) cue exposure to lower his urge to drink, and (3) reinforcing his nondrinking behaviors using contingency reinforcement. Figure 9.2 illustrates treatment strategies.

Psychoeducation

Alcohol is a social drug and its cues constantly confront people due to their high prevalence in everyday life, though some of these cues are more subtle than others. Virtually every social gathering includes alcoholic beverages and people are constantly bombarded with beer and liquor commercials. In essence, alcohol is part of "normal" social life. As a result, people who are abusing alcohol are often unable to separate normal from abnormal or out-of-control behaviors. Therefore, it is important to provide the patient with simple, factually correct information about average consumption and diagnostic definitions of alcohol problems. The therapist should be aware that the patient might be defensive and deny having any problems. These obstacles can be effectively targeted using motivational interviewing techniques, as will be further discussed below. The psychoeducation portion of the therapy should be provided in a neutral, matter of fact, nonjudgmental, and nonargumentative fashion. Below is an example how this information can be presented.

Clinical Example: Psychoeduction

Therapist: I am glad you came to see me, Chuck. I understand that your wife urged you to come see me, but that you don't share her concerns. Is that right?

Chuck: Yes, she thinks that I'm an alcoholic, but I'm not.

Therapist: Your diagnostic evaluation showed that you do not meet criteria for alcohol dependence. However, you drink a large amount of alcohol every day during the week. During a normal week, you drink as much as 30 bottles of beer. Is this correct?

Chuck: Yes.

Therapist: Do you know what is considered normal drinking?

Chuck: I don't know. I guess quite a bit less.

Therapist: Yes. For men, it is two drinks a day or 14 drinks a week; for women it is one drink a day or seven drinks a week maximum. So you drink about three times as much as most people who drink alcohol would drink. Obviously, there are a lot of people who don't drink any alcohol. Thirty bottles of beer per week puts you above the 92nd percentile. This means that out of 100 people, 92 of them drink less than you do.

Chuck: But this does not make me an alcoholic.

Therapist: No, it does not. However, it can in the future. Alcohol is a highly addictive drug. People can develop a tolerance and dependence for it. Tolerance means that people need to drink more and more to achieve the desired effect. Dependence means that people will require alcohol in order to avoid unpleasant feelings. Some people with alcohol dependence, but not all, need to drink in the morning in order to be able to function normally. Hangovers are obvious negative effects of alcohol. Other negative effects are withdrawal symptoms that can happen when people with alcohol dependence have to stop drinking. Dependence happens both on a psychological and physiological level. The reason why I am telling you this is not to suggest that you suffer from alcohol

> dependence. Rather, I am telling you this to make sure that we are using the same words when we talk about dependency, abuse, withdrawal, and the like. Do you have any questions for me so far?
> *Chuck:* No, I don't think so.
> *Therapist:* Great. Now, if I understand you correctly, you don't think that you are alcohol dependent. However, you are consuming more alcohol on a regular basis than most people do. Would you agree with this?
> *Chuck:* Perhaps. Yes, I guess that's correct.

In order to determine the percentile of standard drinks the patient is consuming per week, Table 9.1 can be used as a guide. One standard drink is a 12 oz can, one 5 oz glass of wine or one mixed drink containing one shot of liquor. One of Chuck's 16 oz beer bottles equals 1.3 standard drink units (see National Institute on Alcohol Abuse and Alcoholism, 2011).

Cognitive restructuring

We usually behave in ways that are consistent with our beliefs. If beliefs and behaviors are inconsistent, we experience an uncomfortable psychological

Table 9.1   Some percentiles for alcohol use in men and women (modified from Epstein and McCrady, 2009)

Standard Drinks per Week	Men	Women
1	46	68
2	54	77
7	70	89
9	73	90
15	80	94
28	90	98
41–46	95	99
49–62	97	99

tension. This tension can be resolved by changing either our beliefs or our behaviors. Based on the influential cognitive dissonance theory (e.g., Festinger 1957; Festinger and Carlsmith, 1959), behavior change is determined by the relationship between beliefs that are consistent with one's behaviors (consonant cognitions) and beliefs that are dissonant with one's behaviors (dissonant cognitions). If the frequency and importance of dissonant cognitions outweigh the frequency and importance of consonant cognitions, the behavior is likely going to change. However, if people have been tricked into doing something that is not consistent with their own beliefs and there are no alternative ways to justify their behaviors, they are likely to change their beliefs to make them consistent with their behaviors.

The cognitive dissonance theory can predict whether people will change their behaviors, depending on the frequency and importance of consonant and dissonant cognitions (the cognitive dissonance ratio). For example, it is well known that smoking is bad for one's health. At the same time, people want to live a long and healthy life. Thus, the wish to live a long and healthy life is dissonant with the smoking behavior. This dissonance can be resolved or reduced by changing the behavior (i.e., quitting or reducing smoking) or by changing one's beliefs about smoking. In order to change one's belief about smoking in order to continue smoking, one could search for reports questioning the connection between poor health and smoking (i.e., reducing the frequency of dissonant cognitions), argue that smoking reduces psychological tension and is, therefore, good for one's health (i.e., adding consonant cognitions), argue that the health risks of smoking are negligible compared to the risks of dying in a car crash, etc (i.e., reducing the importance of dissonant cognitions), and argue that smoking is simply an important part of one's life (i.e., increasing the importance of consonant cognitions).

Chuck is not convinced that he has a problem with alcohol (i.e., he devalues dissonant cognitions). Perhaps even more important is the value he places on drinking in his life. For Chuck, drinking serves an important role in his friendships with Joe and also with his coworkers Dave and Tom. This is a powerful consonant cognition ("I have a better time with my friends when we drink together"), which maintains his drinking behavior. Cognitions that are dissonant with his drinking behaviors are related to his wife ("I don't want to get divorced"), his employer ("I want to keep my job"), and his health ("I don't want to die soon"). Chuck is likely going to initiate a change in his behavior if the frequency and importance of dissonant cognitions outweigh the frequency and importance of consonant cognitions.

As already mentioned in Chapter 2, Prochaska and coworkers (1992) have developed a model to describe how people change such problem behaviors. People who are not considering change are considered to be in the *precontemplation* stage. For those patients, it is most helpful to begin to raise the level of awareness of the risks and problems associated with their current behaviors. Once people have become aware of the negative consequences of their behaviors, they enter the *contemplation* stage. This is the stage in which they consider whether or not they should change their behavior. Here, people compare the pros and cons of changing versus not changing their problem behavior. Typically, patients are ambivalent at this stage because they are conflicted between the reasons for change versus continuing to drink. Once the internal conflict decreases, ambivalence also declines. Patients then make comments such as, "I've got to do something about this, but I don't know what!" This stage is referred to as the *preparation* stage and it is considered the "window of opportunity." Once patients are ready to change their behavior, they enter the *action* stage of change to pursue their goals. At the next stage, the *maintenance* stage, patients develop new habits and are in the process of maintaining them. Finally, the termination phase is reached when the person has no temptation and is very confident that he or she will not fall back to the old and maladaptive behavioral or cognitive patterns. The model assumes that many people relapse into old patterns of behavior several times before the change is permanent.

Motivational interviewing

Motivational interviewing (or motivational enhancement therapy) is particularly helpful to raise awareness of the negative consequences of maladaptive behaviors (in Chuck's case, drinking) and to further increase the dissonance between Chuck's personal goals, values, and beliefs on the one hand (enjoying life, being a loving husband, good employee, and so on) and his maladaptive and dissonant behaviors (drinking, which could lead to divorce, unemployment, and poverty).

Motivational interviewing or motivational enhancement therapy (MET) is a brief intervention that is directly derived from Prochaska and colleagues' stages of change model (Prochaska *et al.*, 1992). MET directly targets the cycle of change and assists patients in moving toward change. It is specifically designed to address ambivalence in the early stages of change by moving patients from contemplation to action. It is based on the inherent assumptions that the patient brings a basic capacity for the actualization of a positive self and is responsible for changing to the therapy session. The therapist's role is to create the conditions which enhance the likelihood that a patient will engage in behavior change efforts. The elements underlying motivational interviewing involve four basic principles: (1) express empathy, (2) develop discrepancy, (3) roll with resistance, and (4) support self-efficacy (Miller and Rollnick, 1991). The six common elements to enhance motivation to change can be summarized in the acronym FRAMES. This stands for: (1) personalized feedback (F) to the patient about his/her status, (2) emphasis on personal responsibility (R) of the patient's change, (3) provision of clear advice (A) about the need for change, given in a supportive manner, (4) providing the patient with a menu (M) of options for how to implement the change, (5) providing treatment in an empathic (E), warm, and supportive environment, and (6) enhancing the patient's perceived self-efficacy (S) for change.

Clinical Example: Motivational Interviewing Techniques

Therapist: Please help me understand some of the good things about drinking.

Chuck: I don't know. It makes me feel good. It's really more like a habit. After work, I get together with Dave and Tom and we drink, because that's what we do together.

Therapist: So you drink after work because it is how you spend your time with your coworkers after work.

Chuck: Yes.

Therapist: What would happen if you didn't drink when you get together with Dave and Tom?

Chuck: I don't know. I have never tried it. It would probably be not as much fun and my buddies would go, "Hey, what is wrong with you, man?"

Therapist: So it's hard to imagine not drinking when you are with your friends and it might even be boring without alcohol.

Chuck: Yes.

Therapist: What would be the alternative? What would you do if you did not go out drinking with Dave and Tom?

Chuck: I don't know. Stay home? But that would not be much fun.

Therapist: Staying home is not a solution for you because you would be bored?

Chuck: Yes. Not just bored. It would be depressing.

Therapist: It would be depressing because you can't be alone?

Chuck: I guess.

Therapist: Maybe drinking helps you deal with depression?

Chuck: Sure.

Therapist: But drinking also has some negative consequences, right?

> *Chuck:* Yes, it can get me into trouble.
> *Therapist:* It can cause problems with your wife and your boss, right?
> *Chuck:* Yes.
> *Therapist:* What kind of problems?
> *Chuck:* Well, my wife tells me that she will leave me if I don't stop. And my boss will fire me.
> *Therapist:* So you might lose your job and wife because of your drinking. How does this make you feel?
> *Chuck:* Angry and depressed.
> *Therapist:* It looks like drinking helps you deal with your depression and loneliness in the short term, but leads to possible negative long-term consequences. In the short term, drinking helps when you hang out with your friends, but in the long term it might cause a number of very negative personal, social, and professional consequences. Do I understand this correctly?

It can be very helpful to directly compare the pros and cons of drinking and not drinking. Table 9.2 presents an example of some of the positive and negative aspects of drinking. Listing the pros and cons of drinking and not drinking clarifies the factors that reinforce the drinking behaviors. It also provides an opportunity for the therapist to explore the short-term and long-term consequences of drinking. Of particular importance here are, obviously, the long-term negative consequences of drinking. The problems with his wife and his employer can easily lead to significant and undesirable consequences, such as, but not limited to, divorce, unemployment, poverty, and homelessness. Once Chuck realizes the negative consequences of his

Table 9.2   The pros and cons of drinking

	Pros	Cons
Drinking	Makes me feel good. Important for friendship.	Gets me into trouble with Rose and boss. Hangover feels bad.
Not drinking	Relationship to Rose and boss improves. Feel better about myself.	Difficult to blow off some steam without beer. Less fun when hanging out with buddies.

behavior he will be ready to entertain the possibility of changing his behavior.

Cue exposure

Raising awareness and motivation to change is an important aspect of treatment. Other important factors that contribute to the initiation and maintenance of behavior change are provided by the situational context. In Chuck's case, sitting with Joe, Dave, and Tom provides strong situational cues to drink alcohol. The urge is particularly strong when a glass of Chuck's favorite beer is placed in front of him while he is in this setting. Repeated exposure to this specific cue (his favorite drink), while resisting the urge to drink, can effectively target Chuck's drinking behavior. During such cue exposure practices, Chuck might be asked to repeatedly (e.g., every 3 minutes for a period of 20 minutes) lift the class of beer and smell it while resisting drinking it.

Other cues are considerably more complex and might require changes or eliminating the context altogether. This might require changing the places he spends his time in, the people he spends time with, and the routines (i.e., he might have to decide not to meet Dave and Tom after work). In order to alter the maintenance factors related to his friends, Chuck might require assertiveness training in order to say "no" to his friends when it comes to drinking.

Social support

Chuck's drinking is closely tied to his social group, and in particular to Joe, Dave, and Tom. As a result, it might be necessary to offer an alternative social context in case his friends do not accept Chuck's new approach toward drinking. One particularly promising intervention for gaining social support is through Alcoholics Anonymous (AA) and the intervention approach based on it, which is the Twelve Step Facilitation Therapy (TSF) for alcohol problems (Nowinski and Baker, 1998). The TSF is a brief, 12- to 15-session treatment to facilitating early recovery from alcohol abuse, alcoholism, and other substance abuse problems. It is closely based on the behavioral, spiritual, and cognitive principles of Twelve-Step fellowships of AA. These principles emphasize willpower-sustained sobriety and spirituality within a supportive group environment. Each new participant is assigned to a sponsor, a person further along in recovery, to provide the new participant with guidance through the process. The Twelve Steps of AA, which form the basis of the TSF process, are the following.

Twelve Steps of AA and TSF

1. The person admits that he/she is powerless over alcohol and that his/her life has become unmanageable.
2. The person comes to believe that a power greater than him/herself could restore him/her to sanity.
3. The person makes a decision to turn his/her will and life over to the care of God as the person understands Him.
4. The person makes a searching and fearless moral inventory of him/herself.
5. The person admits to God, to him/herself, and to another human being the exact nature of his/her wrongs.
6. The person is entirely ready to have God remove all these defects of character.
7. The person humbly asks God to remove his/her shortcomings.
8. The person makes a list of all persons he/she has harmed, and becomes willing to make amends to them all.
9. The person makes direct amends to such people wherever possible, except when to do so would injure him/herself or others.
10. The person continues to take personal inventory and, when wrong, promptly admits it.
11. The person seeks through prayer and meditation to improve his/her conscious contact with God *as we understand Him*, praying only for knowledge of His will for us and the power to carry that out.
12. Having had a spiritual awakening as the result of these steps, the person tries to carry this message to other alcoholics, and to practice these principles in all our affairs.

Adapted from: Twelve Steps and Twelve Traditions of Alcoholics Anonymous World Series, Inc., www.aa.org.

Note: These Twelve-Step guiding principles have been altered to emphasize principles important to particular fellowships and to remove gender-biased or specific religious language.

Contingency reinforcement

The use of alcohol can be viewed, in part, as a learned behavior that is maintained through the reinforcing effects of the pharmacological actions of alcohol in combination with social and other reinforcement derived from the alcohol-abusing lifestyle. Learned behaviors can be modified by changing their consequences (i.e., contingencies). The contingency reinforcement approach targets drinking by modifying these contingencies and by improving the individual's skills and social context that play a role in maintaining problematic drinking behaviors. This approach has been well developed for illicit drug use, such as cocaine dependence (Higgins and Silverman, 1999), but also applies to alcohol problems. The overarching goal of this treatment is to systematically weaken the influence of reinforcement derived from alcohol use and the alcohol abusing lifestyle, and to increase the frequency of reinforcement derived from healthier alternative activities, especially those that are incompatible with continued substance use and abuse.

As part of the contingency reinforcement approach, the patients are encouraged to functionally analyze their alcohol use by recognizing anteced-ents and consequences of their alcohol use. Drinking is conceptualized as a behavior that is more likely to occur under certain circumstances than others. By learning to identify the circumstances that make drinking more likely, it will be possible to reduce the likelihood of future alcohol use.

Patients are encouraged to restructure their daily activities in order to minimize contact with known antecedents of drinking (going to the familiar bar with drinking buddies), to find alternatives to the positive consequences of drinking, and to make explicit the negative consequences of drinking. In this context, it is important to teach alcohol-refusal skills, as patients are likely to be offered opportunities to use alcohol at some point in the future. Patients are taught to handle this type of situation with assertiveness. Therapists should explain the rationale for alcohol-refusal skills training, engage the patient in a detailed discussion of the key elements of effective refusal, assist the patient in formulating his/her own refusal style (incorpo-rating the key elements), and role play potential scenarios wherein the patient may be offered alcohol.

Moreover, helping patients to develop new social networks that support a healthier lifestyle is important. Having them get involved with recreational activities that are enjoyable and do not involve alcohol or other drug use is a key component to changing behaviors and should be addressed. It can be helpful to explore with patients other activities that they might want to explore, as these changes play a key role in helping them reduce or eliminate alcohol consumption.

As with Chuck, drinking is often not the only problem that requires inter-vention, but is part of a larger, more complex system of interrelated problems. In Chuck's case, drinking has multiple functions, one of which is a means of coping with his depression. Therefore, in order to effectively target Chuck's drinking problem, it might be necessary to also target his depression, his marriage problems, and his dissatisfaction with his career.

Empirical Support

The Project MATCH compared the efficacy of traditional CBT, MET, and TSF (Allen *et al.*, 1997, 1998). To assess the benefits of matching alcohol dependent patients to traditional CBT, MET, or TSF with reference to a variety of patient attributes, two parallel but independent randomized clinical trials were conducted, one with alcohol-dependent clients receiving outpatient therapy ($N = 952$; 72% male) and one with patients receiving aftercare therapy following inpatient or day hospital treatment ($N = 774$; 80% male). Patients were randomly assigned to one of the three treatments that were conducted over 12 weeks. Patients were then monitored over a 1-year post-treatment period. The results showed significant and sustained improvements in drinking outcomes from baseline to 1-year post-treatment by the patients assigned to each of these treatments. There was little difference in outcomes by type of treatment. Only one attribute, psychiatric severity, demonstrated a significant attribute by treatment interaction in that outpatient patients who were low in psychiatric severity had more abstinent days after TSF than after traditional CBT. However, neither treatment was clearly superior for patients with higher levels of psychiatric severity. Two other patient attributes showed time-dependent matching effects: motivation among outpatients and meaning-seeking among aftercare clients. Patient attributes of motivational readiness, network support for drinking, alcohol involvement, gender, psychiatric severity, and sociopathy were prognostic of drinking outcomes over time. In general, all three treatments were beneficial at the 1-year follow-up (Allen *et al.*, 1997).

The study further examined the prognostic effects of the patient matching attributes and the overall outcomes at 3-year follow-up (Allen *et al.*, 1998). Patient anger demonstrated the most consistent interaction in the trial, with significant matching effects evident at both the 1-year and 3-year follow-ups. Patients high in anger did better in MET than in the other two MATCH treatments (traditional CBT and TSF). Conversely, patients low in anger performed better after treatment in traditional CBT and TSF than in MET. Significant matching effects for the support for drinking variable emerged in the 3-year outcome analysis, such that patients whose social networks were more supportive of drinking derived greater benefit from TSF treatment than from MET. A significant matching effect for psychiatric severity that appeared in the first year post-treatment was not observed after 3 years. Readiness to change and self-efficacy emerged as the strongest predictors of long-term drinking outcome. With regard to the overall outcomes, the reductions in drinking that were observed in the first year after treatment were sustained over the 3-year follow-up period: almost 30% of the subjects were totally abstinent at the 3-year follow-up. Those who did report drinking remained abstinent an average of two-thirds of the time. As in the 1-year follow-up, there were few differences among the three treatments, although TSF continued to show a slight advantage.

Recommended Further Readings

Therapist guide

Daley, D. C., and Marlatt, G. A. (2006). *Overcoming your alcohol and drug problem: Effective recovery strategies. Therapist guide*, 2nd edition. New York: Oxford University Press.

Patient guide

Epstein, E. E., and McCrady, B. S. (2009). *Overcoming alcohol use problems: A cognitive-behavioral treatment program workbook*. New York: Oxford University Press.

10 Resolving Sexual Problems

David's Erection Problem

David is a 56-year-old African-American public high school teacher and vice-principal of his school. He is married to his wife Karen and has four children, aged 13, 15, 35, and 38. David is physically very healthy and he does not take any medications on a regular basis. David and Karen have been having sexual problems for about 10 years, around the time when he took on the job as a vice-principal of his school. This was also the time when he began to have problems with erectile dysfunction. Specifically, he has problems getting fully aroused and he often loses his erection during intercourse. David expressed a great degree of distress about it. He feels ashamed and embarrassed about this problem because he always thought of himself of being a great lover. On average, David and Karen used to have sex two times a week. Before his sexual dysfunction began, he described his sex life as very satisfying for most of his marriage. However, the frequency of intercourse with his wife has decreased to once weekly and, at times, once every month, in part because he feels so nervous about trying it. He initially attributed his problems to the stress at work caused by the increased responsibilities with the initial start of his job. A separate interview with his wife showed that she had been supportive and accepting of David and did not demand sex from him. However, she has been missing the physical closeness and intimacy with him. David and Karen have been fighting more about children, finances, and family issues, and attribute this partially to their lack of intimacy. However, both acknowledged that their two teenage daughters might also contribute to the relationship stress. David has tried Viagra, but disliked the side effects. He also did not feel that it worked very well. Seeing a psychologist for this problem was a big step for him.

An Introduction to Modern CBT: Psychological Solutions to Mental Health Problems, First Edition.
S. G. Hofmann. © 2012 S. G. Hofmann. Published 2012 by John Wiley & Sons, Ltd.

Definition of the Disorder

Sexual dysfunctions are characterized by problems in sexual desire and in the psychophysiological changes associated with the sexual response cycle in men and women. The disorders are categorized based on the triphasic model of the sexual response cycle (desire, excitement, and orgasm) as proposed by Kaplan (1979). Accordingly, sexual dysfunctions are divided into sexual desire disorder (including hypoactive sexual desire and sexual aversion disorder), sexual arousal disorder (including female sexual arousal disorder and erectile disorder), orgasmic disorders (including female and male orgasmic disorder and premature ejaculation), and sexual pain disorders (including dysparaneunia and vaginismus).

Sexual disorders are classified into several subtypes, including the generalized or situational, lifelong (primary) or acquired (secondary), and psychological or medical factors. For example, primary psychogenic erectile dysfunction refers to the lifelong inability to achieve successful sexual performance, whereas secondary psychogenic erectile dysfunction occurs after a period of satisfactory sexual performance. Examples of secondary psychogenic sexual dysfunctions are erectile problems that are associated with substance abuse or a major psychiatric disorder (e.g., depression, generalized anxiety disorder). In David's case, the erectile dysfunction started about 10 years ago, after a period of normal sexual activity. His sexual problems started at around the time when he took on a more stressful position at work. Medical tests did not show any physical problems, and he does not take any medication that could interfere or be associated with his sexual problems. Therefore, he is likely to have a secondary psychogenic erective dysfunction.

David's problem involves both getting and maintaining an erection. Erectile dysfunction is defined as a consistent or recurrent inability to obtain and/or maintain penile erection sufficient for satisfying sexual activity. However, David is not alone in having these problems. Erectile dysfunction is a commonly occurring male sexual arousal disorder, especially among older men. In general, sexual dysfunctions are very common in both sexes. In fact, large epidemiological studies (Laumann et al., 1999) report prevalence rates of sexual dysfunction at 43% in women and 31% in men.

Erectile dysfunction is the most prevalent sexual disorder in men seeking treatment services in sex therapy clinics (Rosen and Leiblum, 1995). Community studies show that the prevalence rate of erectile dysfunction is 5% and, therefore, the second most common male sexual dysfunction, followed by premature ejaculation (21%), which is defined as the inability to delay ejaculation on vaginal penetrations (Laumann *et al.*, 1999). The ejaculation often occurs before or shortly after vaginal penetration and is associated with distress and frustration. Popular medications, such as sildenafil (Viagra), can produce erections by relaxing the corporal smooth muscle tissue. However, these drugs can be associated with a host of unpleasant and potentially dangerous side effects. In women, the most common problems are low sexual desire (22%), sexual arousal problems (14%), and dyspareunia (pain during sexual activity; 7%).

Sexual dysfunctions are associated with various demographic characteristics. For women, the prevalence of sexual problems tends to decrease with increasing age except for those who report trouble lubricating. In contrast, erection problems and low sexual desire for sex increases as men grow older. For example, men aged 50–59 years of age are more than 3 times more likely to experience erection problems and low sexual desire problems than men aged 18 to 29 years (Laumann *et al.*, 1999).

Overall, women and men with lower educational attainment report less pleasurable sexual experience and raised levels of sexual anxiety. The rates are similar across different races and ethnicities, with blacks having slightly more and Hispanics slightly fewer sexual problems, as compared to whites. Interestingly, marriage appears to be a protective factor: married people are at much lower risk for having sexual problems than nonmarried people. Other factors that contribute to sexual problems include general health (especially cardiovascular problems and diabetes); psychiatric problems, especially sexual trauma; smoking and other substance use problems; education level; and sociodemographic variables. Not surprisingly, the least sexual problems are reported by healthy and educated people without a trauma history who attained a high sociodemographic status and who do not smoke or abuse other dugs (Laumann *et al.*, 1999).

Because of the very wide range of sexual dysfunctions, a number of unique treatment strategies have been developed to target these problems. It would be impossible to cover these techniques in a single chapter. An excellent, yet older, review of these procedures is provided by Kaplan (1987).

The Treatment Model

David shows a strong fear of failure. He views himself as a "real" man, but feels his symptoms interfere in his ability to live up to this label. He has always been very comfortable in the role of a calm, self-assured, strong, and

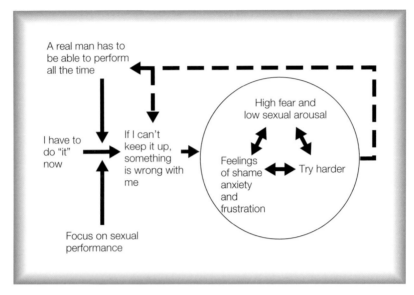

Figure 10.1   David's sex problem.

tough man who supports and protects his family. One important aspect of this male role is to be able to satisfy his wife and to be able to perform intercourse whenever he wants. In order to have sex, he depends on his penis to become and remain erect. Not being able to perform suggests to him that something is wrong with him and, more specifically, his penis. The idea of this causes him great distress, as he feels ashamed for not meeting the fundamental demands of a functional man. Additionally, he feels anxiety about performing and is frustrated with himself and angry at his penis. When he feels that his erection is not happening or when he starts losing his erection, he becomes fearful and sometimes even panicky. This fear results in intense physical symptoms including sweating, heart palpitations, and increased breathing. In order to avoid losing his erection, he tries harder by stimulating himself vigorously or by thrusting during intercourse. The psychological factors that contribute to David's sex problems are summarized in Figure 10.1.

Treatment Strategies

Effective strategies to interrupt this vicious cycle are through attention and situation modification, correcting maladaptive beliefs and the concrete worries about his sexual performance, meditation, relaxation, adequate

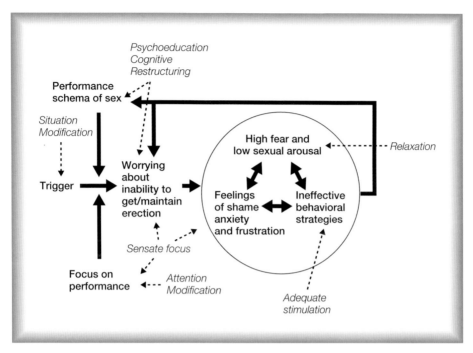

Figure 10.2   Strategies to target David's sex problems.

stimulation, and sensate focus techniques. A summary of these strategies are depicted in Figure 10.2 and discussed in more detail below.

Attention and situation modification

Sexual activity is an evolutionarily primitive process in which little or no prior training is necessary. Moreover, the response is controlled by specific and known external (sexual) stimuli. Despite of the clear stimulus-response pattern, it is important that this process can be stopped at any moment in case any situational demands require the individual to shift his or her attention to other sources. For example, animals quickly stop their sexual activities if a predator is approaching them. Their ability to stop sexual activities by refocusing attention to nonsexual stimuli is evolutionary highly adaptive. If this refocusing of attention had not occurred, it would have been unlikely that the species could have survived. In other words: sexual activities can be easily initiated and carried out by the members of a species, unless there are factors that inhibit the activity or draw attention away from the sexual stimuli. Therefore, paying attention to nonsexual stimuli (i.e., cognitive distraction) can easily disrupt sexual arousal (e.g., Barlow, 1986). In the case of erectile dysfunction, the man with performance anxiety critically examines his own behaviors as a spectator and thereby redirects attention from the erotic stimuli to anxiety-related cues (Masters and Johnson, 1970). Men tend to be more susceptible to the distracting effects of anxiety and sexual performance demands than women (Rosen and Leiblum, 1995). The situational context also plays a critical role because it provides the range of sexual stimuli that one's attention can be focused on. Therefore, a "romantic" set-up (e.g., candlelight and soft music) and stimuli that might serve as reminder of sexual arousal (e.g., a certain fragrance) is more likely to promote sexual arousal and may decrease distraction.

Psychoeducation

People, especially men, often hold clear misconceptions about what is "normal" and what sex "should" be like. They are often misinformed about the basic mechanisms and processes of erectile function and the causes of sexual dysfunction (e.g., the effects of an illness, medication, or old age). Male sexual performance is often seen as the foundation and necessary condition of every sexual experience (Zilbergeld, 1992). Therefore, it is important to provide the patient with factually correct information about sex. Both the website for the Kinsey Institute and the report by Laumann *et al.* (1994) are useful resources for this purpose. A number of important facts are listed below.

Clinical Example: Ten Facts about Sex

1. *Frequency of sex:* The majority of people (90% of men and 86% of women) have had sex in the past year. The frequency of sex varies greatly by age and marital status, with younger and married people having more often sex than older and nonmarried people. Among married couples, 45% reported having sex a few times per month, 34% reported it two to three times per week, 13% a few times per year, and 7% reported it four or more times per week.

2. *Infidelity and Promiscuity:* More than 80% of women and 85% of men report that they had no partners other than their spouses. More than half (56%) of men and 30% of women have had five or more sex partners in their lifetime, whereas 20% of men and 31% of American women have had only one sex partner in their lifetime.

3. *Masturbation:* Almost 85% of men and 45% of women who were living with a sexual partner reported masturbating in the past year; only 5% of men and 11% of women have never masturbated. Among men aged 18–39, more than a third (37%) masturbate "sometimes," 28% one or more times per week and 35% do not masturbate.

4. *Orgasm during sex:* Men are more likely to consistently have an orgasm with intercourse than women (75% vs. 29%).

5. *Orgasm in women:* Usually, adequate stimulation of the clitoris is necessary for a woman to reach an orgasm. However, stimulation of other areas of the female genitalia can also produce intense feelings of pleasure. It is controversial weather women can experience two different kinds of orgasms—a clitoral and a vaginal orgasm. Some women experience orgasmic expulsion of fluid that may come from the bladder or the female prostate.

6. *The G-spot:* The G-spot is named after the German physician Ernst Gräfenberg and is believed to be an erogenous area located behind the pubic bone. The existence of the so-called G-spot in women is still controversial. Stimulation of this area is believed to be associated with a vaginal orgasm and female ejaculation.

7. *Penis Size:* The average size of an erect penis is between 5 to 6 inches. The flaccid penis averages 1 to 4 inches.

8. *Multiple orgasms in men:* Multiple orgasms in men, especially multiple orgasms with ejaculations in succession within minutes, are rare. The recovery time after ejaculation for men is normally at least 30 minutes. After an orgasm and ejaculation, the time for a complete erection and time until orgasm is then delayed. Multiple orgasms in women happen more frequently.

9. *Time until ejaculation:* Most sexually functional men ejaculate within 4–10 minutes after intromission, but there are considerable interindividual variations. Premature ejaculation typically happens within minutes after vaginal penetration. Latencies that take more than 20 minutes are rare (representing two standard deviations above the mean) and may meet criteria for delayed ejaculation. However, the important criterion of whether the ejaculation is too early or too late is the degree of voluntary control the man has over ejaculation and the degree of satisfaction or dissatisfaction experienced by both partners.

10. *Anal and oral sex:* Only 10% of men and 9% of women have had anal sex in the past year. Oral sex is slightly more common, but not frequently practiced; 27% of men and 19% of women had oral sex in the past year of the survey.

Cognitive restructuring

Psychological factors that contribute to sexual dysfunction, such as erectile dysfunction, include immediate and remote causes (Laumann *et al.*, 1999). Examples of the immediate causes include fear of failure, performance anxiety, response anxiety (i.e., anxiety about lack of arousal), lack of adequate stimulation, and relationship problems. In order to target the remote causes, therapy needs to address the role of sexual trauma, sexual identity or orientation issues, unresolved partner or parental attachments, religious, societal, and cultural aspects. These issues should be explored early on in treatment to develop specific treatment strategies.

In David's case, it quickly became apparent that he holds very traditional views of gender roles. He strongly identifies himself with the male gender and sex role. As part of this role, he sees himself as being in charge of situations, including sexual intercourse. Similar to other males with such strong gender identification, he believes that a "real" man has to be able to perform at any time. Conversely, if a man cannot perform at any time, he is not a real man. Therefore, being able to perform was proof for him that he was still a real man, and not being able to perform severely challenges the view he holds of himself as a real man. This core belief gives rise to the specific thought that something must be seriously wrong with him if he cannot perform. The following is an example of exploring David's core belief:

Clinical Example: Exploring the Core Belief

Therapist: Why were you so upset last night about not being able to maintain an erection?
David: It feels horrible. It is very embarrassing.
Therapist: I see. But why exactly is it embarrassing? Who is the audience? Your wife?
David: I don't know. My wife is actually quite supportive. I just feel like such a loser.
Therapist: Because you should be able to perform?
David: Of course.
Therapist: Because you are a man and real men have to perform?
David: Sure.
Therapist: What if a man cannot perform?
David: Then he is not a real man, I guess.

Therapist: So if I understand you correctly, if you can't maintain an erection, you feel upset because real men have to be able to perform all the time. And if you can't perform, then you are not a real man. Is that right?

David: Yes, that's right.

Therapist: It seems to me that you have very clear ideas about what men should and should not do. He should always be able to get and maintain an erection, no matter what. And if this does not happen, something has to be seriously wrong. Those "shoulds" and "shouldn'ts" can cause a lot of problems. I would like to take a close look at some of those "shoulds" and "shouldn'ts," if you don't mind. Can you identify your shoulds and shouldn'ts when it comes to sex?

Adequate Stimulation

David's maladaptive belief that men have to be able to perform at any time under any conditions kept him from trying out different strategies that might enhance his own pleasure experience when engaging in sexual activities with his wife. Furthermore, David thought sexual activity was synonymous with sexual intercourse. This further limited his options as well as the possibilities he considered. In the following exchange with David, Karen, and the therapist, the limitations of his thinking are illustrated and they explore other ways to stimulate David. This interchange also exemplifies ways to discuss sex with a couple that is uncomfortable by using the appropriate words. It is important that the therapist is comfortable using words such as anus, breasts, clitoris, climax, erection, foreskin, glans, nipples, oral stimulation, orgasm, penis, scrotum, semen, shaft, testicles, vagina, vulva, and vibrator, to name only a few.

Clinical Example: Exploring Adequate Stimulation Strategies

Therapist: David, could you please describe to me a bit more the last time you and Karen were intimate and tried to have sex.

David: It was just two nights ago. We tried it, but I gave up. It didn't work.

Therapist: You mean you tried to have sex but you couldn't have intercourse?

David: It didn't even get hard enough, so I gave up. It was pretty bad.

Karen: Stop it, Dave. It wasn't that bad.

Therapist: So you got upset because you did not get an erection. Correct?

David: Yes.

Therapist: I understand. Let's see if there is anything you could have done differently in that situation. Let's microanalyze this moments leading up to it. Tell me in as much detail as possible what happened. Who made the first move, what happened then?

David: Well, we went to bed, watched a little TV, turned off the lights and kissed good night. We then started hugging. I then touched her and we tried it. But it didn't go anywhere.

Therapist: Where did you touch Karen?

David: I touched her breasts and down there.

Therapist: Her vagina?

David: Yes.

Therapist: And you stimulated her clitoris?

David: Yes.

Therapist: Did you enjoy this, Karen?

Karen: But of course I did.

Therapist: Great. And what did you do, Karen?

Karen: I touched him also.

Therapist: You touched his penis?

Karen: Yes.

Therapist: Did you enjoy it, David?

David: As I said, it didn't work.

Therapist: I understand that it is very frustrating for you. But I know that there are relatively easy things we can do to make your experience enjoyable again. Let's use this dildo to illustrate some ways to stimulate your penis. I also brought this bottle of baby oil that can greatly enhance this experience. First please show me how you stimulated him using this dildo, Karen . . .

Relaxation

Enjoyable sexual activity and stress are incompatible. Sex can relieve stress, and stress interferes with sex. In contrast, being in a relaxed state promotes sex. It enhances sexual motivation and pleasure. General relaxation practices that were discussed earlier can be helpful to relieve stress, such as progressive muscle relaxation and relaxation with imagery. Obviously, it can be very useful to use a sexual scene as an image. However, if the image induces feelings of fear, shame, or ambiguous feelings, it is not recommended to use imagery strategies. The guiding principle for the therapist is to provide a pleasant environment and to deal with the patient's sexual problems in an open and nonjudgmental way.

Sensate focus

This term, which was introduced by Masters and Johnson (1970), refers to specific exercises to encourage people (usually couples) to focus on pleasant experiences rather than focusing on orgasm or intercourse as the only goal of sex. The sensate focus exercises consist of different stages. In the initial stage, the couple takes turns touching each other's body, except for the breasts and genitals. The goal of nonsexual touching is to heighten awareness of the texture and other qualities of the partner's skin. The person who is doing the touching is instructed to concentrate on what he/she finds interesting in the skin of the other, not on what their partner may or may not like. The couple is further instructed not to proceed to intercourse or other genital stimulation, even if sexual arousal does occur. This initial session is typically done silently because talking can detract from the awareness of the sensations.

In the second stage, the touch option is gradually expanded to include the breasts and genitals. Intercourse and orgasm are still prohibited and the emphasis is on awareness of physical sensations, not on expectation of a sexual response. To communicate, the person who is being touched places his/her hand over their partner's hand in order to show what he/she finds pleasurable in terms of location, pace, and pressure. Further stages include the gradual increased stimulation of the partner's genitals and then full intercourse while focusing on the pleasurable aspects of this activity. Orgasm should not be the focus.

Other strategies

A number of medical treatments exist for treating sexual dysfunctions. For erectile dysfunction, for example, some of the techniques include surgical prostheses, penile implants, intracorporeal injection of vasoactive drugs (i.e., injection of a substance, such as papaverine hydrochloride, that relaxes the muscle cells in the arterial wall, causing dilation and increased blood flow to the penis), construction of rings and vacuum pump devices, and, of course, oral medications, such as sildenafil (Viagra).

In addition to the psychological strategies mentioned earlier, a number of other specific psychological techniques have been developed to treat other male and female sexual dysfunctions. More recently, yoga and mindfulness strategies have been applied to various sexual dysfunctions. Insufficient empirical support exists on these strategies. However, some of the most common and supported strategies are the following:

Specific therapeutic strategies for sexual dysfunctions

Techniques for treating female anorgasmia

- Masturbation training and guided masturbation
- *Kegel exercise:* Exercising the pubococcygeus (pelvic floor) muscle to treat female sexual desire disorder
- *Bridge maneuver:* Clitoral stimulation by the male partner's hand during coitus
- *Coital alignment:* The male partner is on top of the woman in a "high riding" position while aligning the genitalia in order to provide maximum stimulation of the woman

Techniques for treating premature ejaculation

- *Stop-start technique:* The man is instructed to start masturbating by stroking his penis up and down. As he gets close to ejaculation, he is instructed to pay close attention to the tingling sensation just before ejaculation and when it is still possible to stop ejaculation. The man is then asked to stop manipulating the penis for at least 15 seconds for the erection to decrease and then to begin masturbating again until he experiences the tingling sensation again.
- *Squeeze technique:* After the penis is fully erect, the woman presses the erected penis hard with her forefingers and thumb, just below the glans, so that the man loses the erection, and then stimulates the penis again.

Empirical Support

Medication trials by and large have dominated the field, despite the evidence from studies supporting the psychological strategies described in this chapter. An overview of these studies is provided by Rosen and Leiblum (1995). For example, a recent meta-analysis of erectile dysfunction (Melnik *et al.*, 2007), the disorder David is suffering form, identified nine randomized controlled trials comparing psychotherapy with other treatments (sildenafil, vacuum devices, injection) and control groups (no treatment or waitlist). The results showed that people who underwent any of these treatments had a 95% response rate as compared to 0% of individuals in the control group at post-treatment. A comparison between psychotherapy (administered in a group format) plus sildenafil versus sildenafil alone showed that the combination treatment was associated with significantly greater improvement of success-ful intercourse and less dropout than sildenafil alone. No clear difference was found between the various active treatments when administered as monotherapy.

Recommended Further Readings

Therapist guide

Kaplan, H. S. (1987). *The illustrated manual of sex therapy*, 2nd edition. New York: Brunner/Mazel.

Patient guide

Heiman, J., and LoPiccolo, J. (1992). *Becoming orgasmic*. New York: Fireside.

11   Managing Pain

Peter's Pain

Peter is a 49-year-old bus driver who is married to a woman named Jane. They have two adult children who live in a different state. Peter has been suffering for years from chronic pain, primarily in his lower back and more recently in his shoulders, neck, and arms. Peter's pain began 10 years ago when he was rear-ended by another car while he was stopped at a red light. The x-rays and other physical examinations showed only minor bruises on his back, and the physical injury resolved within one month of the accident. However, since this incident, Peter's pain has persisted and even worsened. He has become increasingly distressed about his pain because it impacts on nearly every aspect of his life, including his job, hobbies, and romantic life. He used to enjoy bowling and working on his motorcycle, which he sometimes took for tours. However, the pain severely limited his ability to do these and other tasks and so he stopped going bowling and on motorcycle trips 7 years ago. Peter's pain also significantly interferes with his romantic life. He rarely has any sexual contact with Jane because of the pain and he is afraid that she might leave him or have an affair. Jane is very supportive of Peter and there is no indication that she would have an extramarital affair; however, she is frustrated with Peter's pain problems because they also interfere with her life. Peter often feels sad, frustrated, and hopeless because none of the many doctors he has consulted have been able to really help him. He feels that his life is torturous and unlivable. He wants nothing more than to get rid of his pain, but has not yet found any effective strategies. Peter has tried 11 daily prescription drugs (analgesic, psychotropic, and other medications), none of which provided much pain relief. In addition to consulting numerous physicians, he saw a chiropractor for over a year without much success. In fact, the "readjustments" of his back worsened his pain to the extent that it became debilitating. He was forced to take a leave of absence from his job as a bus driver, and couldn't work for more than 2 months. Three years ago,

An Introduction to Modern CBT: Psychological Solutions to Mental Health Problems, First Edition.
S. G. Hofmann. © 2012 S. G. Hofmann. Published 2012 by John Wiley & Sons, Ltd.

one of his doctors suggested that he had fibromyalgia. Eventually Peter was able to resume his job as a bus driver, but decided to do this on a part time basis. This has put enormous financial strain on the family. As a result, Peter is in a desperate situation and recently consulted a psychologist who specializes in treating chronic pain.

Definition of the Disorder

Everybody is familiar with the experience of pain. Pain is adaptive, as it facilitates the ability to identify, respond to, and resolve physical injury. However, for approximately 10% of adults, pain persists long after any identifiable organic pathology has healed, suggesting that there are other factors that may maintain the pain experience (Waddell, 1987). The traditional medical model considers pain to be a sensory experience arising from physical injury or other pathology. Other, more modern, perspectives have integrated psychological factors to better conceptualize the pain experience (Fordyce, 1976; Gamsa, 1994a, 1994b; Melzack and Wall, 1982). According to these models, pain is a complex perceptual phenomenon which involves a number of psychological factors. Peter's pain started with a minor car accident. Although the physical injury was negligible, his pain problems did not resolve after his injury had healed. Instead, the pain became more debilitating and spread from his neck and back to other parts of his body, including his arm and shoulder areas. He has visited numerous doctors and been treated by a chiropractor, which seems to have worsened the problem even further. He eventually received the diagnosis of fibromyalgia.

Fibromyalgia is a chronic pain syndrome defined by widespread pain across several areas of the body without any identifiable organic basis. Patients with this condition typically report other symptoms, such as sleep problems, fatigue, and feelings of depression. This disorder affects 2%-7% of the general population and is associated with high socioeconomic burden (Bennett *et al.*, 2007; Spaeth, 2009).

The Treatment Model

Peter is suffering from chronic pain in various parts of his body, in particular in his lower back, shoulders, neck, and arms. Similar to that of many people with chronic pain, Peter's pain started with a particular event, but persisted even after he recovered from the physical injuries. In Peter's case, the event that marked the beginning of his problem was a car accident 10 years ago. Since then, pain has greatly affected his life, interfering with his work, hobbies, and even romantic life. As a result, Peter has become depressed and hopeless. His job as a bus driver, which forces him to sit in one particular position for hours at a time, further contributes to his pain problem. In short, Peter's pain has become a main focus of his life. He wants nothing more than to be rid of it. He has already spent a huge sum of money on his pain treatments. However, none of the treatments he has received seem to help. Some of these interventions, especially the treatment with the chiropractor, even made the pain worse.

Clearly, Peter's pain now plays a central and defining role in his life. While the injury was the initial trigger, other factors have maintained the problem. He sees his life with pain as a torturous experience and his existence as unlivable. His pain is ever-present and constantly on his mind. He feels a strong urge to eliminate the pain and free himself from it. However, he can't. The constant frequent experience of his pain makes Peter feel stressed, which manifests in high physiological arousal and feelings of anger and frustration. Peter also tries to avoid pain-inducing tasks, like working, going bowling and riding his motorbike, and sexual contact with his wife. The consequences of these actions reinforce Peter's view that life is not worth living and further strengthen his desire to eliminate the pain. Peter is desperate. Figure 11.1. shows the factors that contribute to Peter's pain problems.

Treatment Strategies

Peter's pain is real. He wishes for nothing more than to get relief from his chronic pain problems. The constant struggle with his pain creates a substantial amount of stress for Peter. Research suggests that the stress associated with pain strengthens catastrophic beliefs about the pain and contributes both to pain severity and interference of pain in daily activities (Sullivan *et al.,* 2001), establishing a vicious cycle between pain, pain-related stress, and stress-related pain.

As is the case for many other pain sufferers, Peter's pain is related to a physical injury. After the initial trigger resolved and his injury due to the accident healed, his pain became chronic, largely as a result of factors that maintain the problem. Some of the most important maintaining factors are Peter's catastrophic beliefs about the pain experience. Similar to other pain

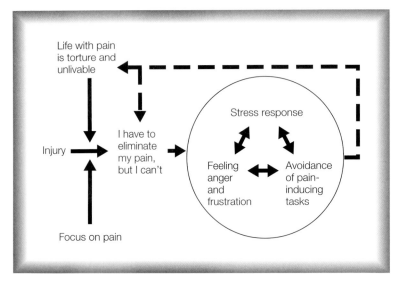

Figure 11.1   Peter's pain problem.

patients, Peter's cognitions about pain amplify his experience. For example, he feels that pain turns his existence into torture and makes life not worth living. As a result, he focuses on the pain experience and the limitations pain places onto his life. He ruminates about his pain, which has become the central focus of his existence. As was discussed earlier (in Chapter 7), ruminating and worrying about pain maintains the problem because it leads to the vicious cycle illustrated in Figure 11.2. Peter's many failed attempts to eliminate the pain have led him to feel frustrated and depressed. In addition, his catastrophic beliefs about pain contribute to stress, heightened physiological arousal, and feelings of anger and frustration. Peter has attempted to avoid the pain using pain medication and other strategies, but these attempts have not been successful and further reinforce his negative beliefs and cognitions. A number of effective intervention strategies can interrupt Peter's vicious cycle of pain. These strategies are summarized below and depicted in Figure 11.2.

Psychoeducation

A critical aspect of treatment, especially at the beginning of therapy, is to discuss with the patient the connection between stress and pain as a contributing factor to the maintenance of the problem. As outlined in Chapter

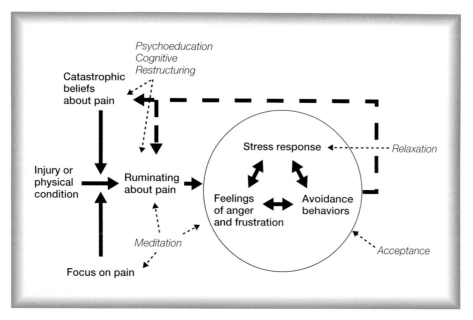

Figure 11.2   Strategies to target pain.

1, there is an important difference between *initiating factors*, which are responsible for why the problem began in the first place (i.e., Peter's car accident that resulted in a back injury) and *maintaining factors*, which are the reasons why the problem persists.

Maintenance factors usually differ from the factors that caused the initial injury. A problem often comes into existence for one reason, but is maintained for a number of other reasons. One very important maintaining factor is the link between stress responses and pain. The fact that stress contributes to pain does not mean that the pain is not real. It simply means that stress exacerbates the pain experience, and that, in turn, pain can trigger stress. Stress can also be made better or worse depending on how one thinks about the pain. In other words, stress can worsen pain, and experiencing pain can create stress. This vicious cycle is often maintained by catastrophic and maladaptive beliefs and cognitive processes. This is typically associated with negative emotional responses and attempts to avoid the pain.

In summary, although pain is real and caused by physical injuries, psychological factors are important. Stress and negative thoughts contribute to the maintenance of the pain experience. Identifying and modifying these maladaptive processes can significantly reduce the pain problem.

Clinical Example: Psychoeducation about Pain

In order to understand the pain experience, we must look not only at the physical and biological issues that are related to the pain, but also consider psychological factors. I would like to spend a few minutes discussing these factors, because they might be important for the maintenance of your pain. As you have noticed, pain causes a significant degree of stress in your life. For example, you used to enjoy bowling and working on your motorcycle. Now, you have basically stopped bowling and going on motorcycle trips. You also mentioned that the pain has had a negative influence on your romantic life. It is completely understandable that this has caused you to become quite depressed.

It is important to note that pain and stress are two closely related things. The pain causes you to be distressed and depressed, and you mentioned that the pain occurs more often and is stronger when you feel stressed. So we are dealing here with a vicious cycle of pain, stress, and pain.

Cognitive restructuring

Peter believes that his life with pain is torture and not worth living. This is a catastrophic belief. However, no matter what he tries, he is unable to eliminate his pain, which triggers a stress response, feelings of anger and frustration. In response, Peter tries hard to avoid the pain-inducing tasks, which means that Peter's pain interferes with his life to a significant degree. In addition, pain occupies a dominant role in his life. This further strengthens his maladaptive beliefs about the effects of pain and the need to avoid anything that might cause pain, leading to even greater distress.

Pain cannot be reasoned away. However, it is certainly possible to highlight the connection between catastrophic thinking and negative feeling. An example of such a discussion is provided below.

Clinical Example: Catastrophic Beliefs about Pain

Therapist: You are saying that your life is torture and that the pain makes your life unlivable. This is a strong statement.
Peter: It is. But it is true.

Therapist: This may sound like a strange question. But if your life with pain is unlivable, then why are you still alive? My intention is not to ridicule you, but I am trying to understand what it is that keeps you going.

Peter: I guess hope that it will change.

Therapist: What if you knew for certain that it will not change. What if the pain will never go away?

Peter: I would kill myself.

Therapist: Let's think about this for a second. So if you knew that the pain would never go away, you think you would kill yourself. Why?

Peter: Because the pain is unbearable.

Therapist: I completely understand it that the pain is a horrific experience. But you are saying that there is no reason to live if the pain persisted. Is this correct?

Peter: Yes, I guess.

Therapist: What would be the advantage of killing yourself?

Peter: The pain would be gone.

Therapist: Right! And what would be the disadvantage of it?

Peter: What do you mean? I would be dead, if course.

Therapist: Yes, but let's think about the people you love, the things you like to do in life, the things you would miss out on.

Peter: I guess there are things I would miss and my friends and family would be sad. But it would be a relief.

Therapist: Yes, but the pain would essentially not only interfere with your current life, it would also take away all of your future because you would be dead because of the pain. The point here is: the pain you are experiencing is a horrific experience. However, your response to the pain gives it enormous power over you. You would even kill yourself over it. We can't effectively control your pain. However, we can stop the pain from controlling you! Does this make sense? Can you tell me what I mean by this?

Relaxation and meditation

One effective set of strategies to target the stress response associated with pain is relaxation and meditation techniques. Meditation practices (e.g., yoga breathing as discussed in Chapter 7 and LKM in Chapter 8) can be a powerful stress-reduction technique for chronic pain patients. In addition, a particularly beneficial relaxation practice for pain patients can be progressive muscle relaxation. This practice is not only a generally effective stress-reduction technique, but it can also effectively target pain directly by relaxing certain muscle groups. An example of a progressive muscle relaxation exercise is given below.

Clinical Example: Progressive Muscle Relaxation

Assume a comfortable position in a comfortable chair in a peaceful environment. Take off your shoes and restrictive clothes. Close your eyes. Tense and relax each muscle group as follows:

1. *Forehead:* Wrinkle your forehead by moving your eyebrows toward your hairline for five seconds. Relax. Notice the difference between tension and relaxation.
2. *Eyes and nose:* Close your eyes as tightly as you can. Hold this position for five seconds, then relax. Notice the difference between tension and relaxation.
3. *Lips, cheeks, and jaw:* Draw the corners of your mouth back as if you are grimacing. Hold this position for five seconds, then relax. Notice the difference between tension and relaxation and feel the warmth and calmness in your face.
4. *Hands:* Stretch your arms horizontally. Make a tight fist with both hands for five seconds, then relax. Notice the difference between tension and relaxation.
5. *Upper arms:* Bend your elbows. Tense your biceps for five seconds, then relax. Notice the difference between tension and relaxation.
6. *Shoulders:* Move your shoulders up and hold them there for five seconds, then relax.
7. *Back:* Push your back and neck against the seat. Hold the tension for 5 seconds, and then relax. Notice the difference between tension and relaxation.
8. *Stomach:* Tighten your stomach muscles for five seconds, then relax. Notice the difference between tension and relaxation.
9. *Hips and buttocks:* Tighten your hip and buttock muscles for five seconds, then relax. Notice the difference between tension and relaxation.
10. *Thighs:* Tighten the muscles of your thighs by pressing your legs together as tightly as you can. Continue this for five more seconds, and then relax. Notice the difference between tension and relaxation.
11. *Feet:* Bend your ankles toward your body. Continue this for five more seconds, and then relax. Notice the difference between tension and relaxation.

12. *Toes:* Curl your toes for five seconds, and then relax.
13. Scan the muscles of your body to determine if there are any muscles that are still tense. If necessary, tighten and relax any specific muscle groups three or four times.

Acceptance

Traditional interventions for chronic pain are primarily concerned with controlling pain; for example, using surgery, medication, and relaxation techniques. However, for many pain sufferers, the pain experience is not very responsive to these interventions. This situation then becomes problematic if the pain dominates the person's existence and interferes with family, work, and other important aspects of life (McCracken *et al.*, 2004). In addition, excessive avoidance of the pain experience is associated with greater disability and suffering (Asmundson *et al.*, 1999).

Acceptance strategies can be useful to target these maladaptive attempts to gain control over a seemingly uncontrollable situation. Acceptance of chronic pain is defined as "an active willingness to engage in meaningful activities in life regardless of pain-related sensations, thoughts, and other related feelings that might otherwise hinder the engagement" (McCracken *et al.*, 2004, p. 6). Acceptance in this context does not imply that patients should resign themselves to the pain and develop a fatalistic and passive attitude, nor does it suggest that patients should try to reframe the pain as a positive experience. Instead, it encourages patients to apply a new perspective toward their pain experience and its effect it has on their lives. By accepting the pain, the patient is encouraged to make a choice to give up the struggle to control the pain and to instead commit to actions that lead to a valued life while at the same time accepting the pain experience (Hayes, 2004). Acceptance strategies appear to be particularly promising for psychiatric disorders that are partially maintained by attempts to avoid or suppress private experiences (e.g., pain and worrisome and obsessive thoughts), leading to the paradoxical persistence and recurrence of the avoided or suppressed experience. Acceptance strategies help the patient to realize that any attempts to control private events are part of the problem, not the solution. This strategy has a long tradition in traditional Eastern medicine, such as Zen Buddhism and Morita therapy (Hofmann, 2008b).

Clinical Example: Introducing Acceptance Strategies

The following excerpt from Morita therapy (Morita 1998/1874, pp. 8–9) may illustrate the use of acceptance strategies:

> A donkey that is tied to a post by a rope will keep walking around the post in an attempt to free itself, only to become more immobilized and attached to the post. The same applies to people with obsessive thinking who become more trapped in their own sufferings when they try to escape from their fears and discomfort through various manipulative means. Instead, if they would persevere through the pain and treat it as something inevitable, they would not become trapped in this way; this would be similar to a donkey grazing freely around the post without getting bound to it.

This example highlights the general strategy for using acceptance–based techniques to deal with pain. Instead of repeating unsuccessful attempts to control the pain, including psychological (e.g., distraction), physiological (e.g., physical therapy) and medical strategies (e.g., use of medication or surgery), the patient is encouraged to accept the pain experience as it is, without trying to avoid or modify it. By not attempting to control it, the patient paradoxically gains control over the experience.

It should be noted that this approach can be difficult to implement in part because it is obviously counterintuitive and in part because it can interfere with other, effective strategies to control pain, including psychological approaches (relaxation strategies) and medical techniques. Therefore, it is recommended that acceptance strategies only be introduced when it is clear that other usually effective and more conventional pain-control strategies are not working. Acceptance-based strategies can then be implemented at a later stage as viable alternatives to other techniques.

Empirical Support

Treatment of chronic pain is challenging, and the prognosis for recovery is poor (Goldenberg et al., 2004). Research suggests that this disorder can be effectively treated with drug therapies, such as antidepressant medication (Hauser et al., 2009). However, pharmacological interventions often lead to treatment dropouts and adverse side effects (Marcus, 2009). Psychological interventions have been found to be effective for chronic pain (Abeles et al., 2008; Eccleston et al., 2009; Richmond et al., 1996), including chronic lower back pain (Hoffman et al., 2007) and fibromyalgia (Glombiewski et al., 2010). A meta-analytic review of psychological interventions for chronic lower back pain examined 22 randomized controlled trials (Hoffman et al., 2007). Positive effects of psychological interventions, contrasted with the effects noted in various control groups, were observed for pain intensity, pain-related interference, health-related quality of life, and depression. CBT and self-regulatory treatments were particularly efficacious. Positive short-term effects on pain interference and positive long-term effects on return to work were also observed for multidisciplinary approaches that included a psychological component. In sum, the results of this study demonstrated positive effects of psychological interventions for chronic lower back pain. Particularly relevant to the current case was a meta-analysis that specifically examined the short- and long-term efficacy of psychological treatments for fibromyalgia (Glombiewski et al., 2010). This study identified 23 trials encompassing 30 psychological treatment conditions and 1,396 patients. The results showed a significant but relatively small effect size for short-term pain reduction (Hedges' $g = 0.37$) and a small-to-medium effect size for long-term pain reduction over an average follow-up phase of 7.4 months (Hedges' $g = 0.47$) for any psychological intervention. These interventions also proved effective in reducing sleep problems (Hedges' $g = 0.46$), depression (Hedges' $g = 0.33$), and improving functional status (Hedges' $g = 0.42$), with effects remaining stable at the follow-up assessment. Moderator analyses revealed that traditional CBT was superior to other psychological treatments in terms of short-term pain reduction (Hedges' $g = 0.60$), with more treatment sessions being associated with better outcome. Aside from traditional CBT techniques, acceptance strategies offer potentially effective methods for dealing with chronic pain. For example, it has been shown that greater acceptance of pain is associated with lower perceived pain intensity, less pain-related anxiety and avoidance, less depression, less physical and psychosocial disability, and better work status (McCracken, 1998). In sum, the efficacy of psychological treatment for fibromyalgia is relatively small but robust and comparable to those reported for other pain and drug treatments used for this disorder. Furthermore, traditional CBT was associated with the greatest effect sizes. Strategies that encourage the patient to accept chronic pain, rather than avoid it, can further enhance the efficacy of treatment in some patients with chronic pain.

Recommended Further Readings

Therapist guide

Thorn, B. F. (2004). *Cognitive therapy for chronic pain: A step-by-step guide.* New York: Guilford.

Patient guide

Otis, J. D. (2007). *Managing chronic pain: A cognitive-behavioral therapy approach (workbook).* New York: Oxford University Press.

12 Mastering Sleep

Tony's Sleep Problems

Tony is a 24-year-old Master's student. He studies business administration and lives off-campus by himself. Tony is a disciplined student with average grades. Except for his sleep problems, he is generally healthy and without any unusual episodes of anxiety, depression, or other psychological problems. Tony's sleep is easily disturbed by stress in school or in social situations. However, even without any unusual stress, Tony finds it difficult to fall asleep. Since he started college, his sleep problems became successively worse. He takes a very long time to fall asleep and sometimes wakes up in the middle of the night or in the early morning and is unable to go back to sleep. As a result, he has started to feel worried when it is time to go to bed, in case he can't sleep. He keeps a TV set in his bedroom, which sometimes helps him to ease his anxiety about going to bed. On a typical evening, he has an early dinner at 6, studies until 7 and gets ready for bed, giving himself enough time to go to sleep. He often cooks for himself and has two to three glasses of alcohol to calm himself down. He usually watches TV for about an hour after dinner before starting his attempts to go to sleep at around 8 or 9. He then tosses and turns and it often takes up to 4 hours before he finally falls asleep. Tony usually gets up at around 6. Sometimes, he wakes up in the middle of the night or early morning at 3 or 4, and is unable to go back to sleep. He then watches TV or checks his e-mail. In order to catch up on his sleep, he sleeps in one or two times during the week and takes short naps in the afternoon around 3 days a week. He also sleeps in and takes long daytime naps on weekends to catch up on his sleep. He often spends Friday and Saturday nights out with his friends going to pubs and sporting events. Tony is slightly overweight. He enjoys cooking and following sports. He does not do any regular exercise, except for the occasional baseball game with his friends. He has tried various medications for his sleep problems, but did not like the side effects.

An Introduction to Modern CBT: Psychological Solutions to Mental Health Problems, First Edition.
S. G. Hofmann. © 2012 S. G. Hofmann. Published 2012 by John Wiley & Sons, Ltd.

Definition of the Disorder

Sleep problems, also known as insomnia, are common. Epidemiological studies suggest that at least three of 10 people have some sleep problems in any 1-year interval, and approximately 7% meet criteria for insomnia (LeBlanc *et al.*, 2006). In general, insomnia is defined as difficulty initiating, sustaining, or obtaining satisfying sleep. These sleep problems cause significant distress or interference in the person's life and occur despite the person's having adequate opportunity to sleep. Insomnia is frequently associated with a number of different psychological problems, including depression, anxiety, substance use problems, and several medical conditions. Approximately 1–2% of the population experience primary insomnia, which is defined as significant sleep problems that persist independent of any comorbid conditions. General insomnia can develop at any age, whereas primary insomnia tends to be more common in younger people like Tony.

The DSM-IV criteria for primary insomnia are as follows: (1) the primary problem is difficulty initiating or maintaining sleep for at least 1 month; (2) the problem causes significant distress and impairment; (3) the problem does not occur exclusively as a result of another sleep or mental disorder, or as a result of the effects of substance use or a medical illness. As previously discussed, Tony had difficulty initiating and maintaining sleep, and is very distressed about this. As his sleep problems were unrelated to any other psychiatric or medical problems, Tony is likely to meet the diagnostic criteria for primary insomnia.

We sleep during the night because our body follows an internal (circadian) clock that is aligned with day and night cycles. This internal clock regulates the sleep-wake cycle as well as digestion and body temperature, among other things. If we are jetlagged or have to work late night shifts, this natural cycle becomes disturbed. In addition, this natural cycle can be disrupted by certain unhealthy habits. These can include sleeping during the day, going to bed too early, not allowing enough time to unwind, engaging in mental tasks right before bed time, watching TV or performing other sleep-incompatible tasks in bed, trying hard to go to sleep, worrying about not being able to sleep, and worrying about the consequences of lack of sleep.

Paradoxically, the harder we trying to fall asleep, the more difficult it becomes. This is most likely related to added cognitive load when trying to fall asleep. This effect has been convincingly illustrated in a study by Ansfield and colleagues (1996). In this study, good sleepers were instructed to either fall asleep as quickly as they could or to fall asleep whenever they wished under conditions of high cognitive load (listening to marching music) or low cognitive load (listening to new age music). Individuals who were told to fall asleep as quickly as possible while listening to marching music had the most difficulty falling asleep, suggesting that cognitive load plays a key role in sleep disturbance.

The Treatment Model

Tony displays a number of the typical behaviors that often contribute to insomnia. He worries a lot about getting enough sleep and believes that he won't be able to function normally unless he gets at least 6 hours of sleep every night. He is concerned that the lack of sleep will negatively impact on his ability to concentrate on his studies, and he will get bad grades and even fail important exams as a result of it. Therefore, he tries to go to bed very early. In addition, Tony does other things that contribute to poor sleep hygiene; he cooks heavy meals before he goes to bed, drinks alcohol shortly before bed time, and watches TV in bed before he turns off his lights. He also does not exercise during the day. Tony's predisposition to sleep problems, the stress he experiences in school, and his poor sleep hygiene, combined with maladaptive cognitive beliefs about sleep, are setting him up for primary insomnia. Figure 12.1 shows the cycle of one Tony's sleep problems.

Treatment Strategies

A prominent cognitive model of primary insomnia was formulated by Harvey (2002). This model exhibits many similarities to Clark's (1986) model of panic (see Chapter 4). This model proposes that people with insomnia are preoccupied with getting to sleep quickly and getting as much sleep as possible. As a result, they worry about not getting enough sleep and the harmful effects of too little sleep on general health and professional functioning. This excessive, negatively valenced cognitive activity is proposed to lead to heightened physiological arousal and subjective distress. As a result, people with insomnia selectively attend to and monitor sleep-related cues, such as any bodily signs that are consistent or inconsistent with falling asleep, as well as keep track of the time they have stayed awake. These

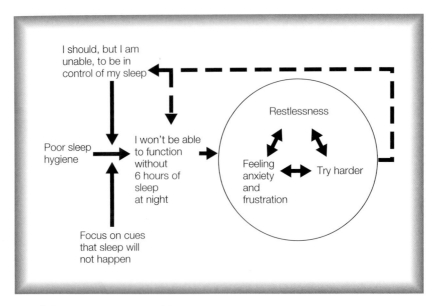

Figure 12.1 Tony's sleep problem.

selective attention and monitoring processes, in conjunction with distorted perception of sleep and daytime deficits, maladaptive beliefs and counterproductive attempts to gain enough sleep are assumed to cause an escalation of excessive worrying associated with physiological arousal and subjective distress.

Effective strategies to interrupt Tony's vicious cycle include (1) correcting his maladaptive cognitions and educating him about the nature of sleep and sleep problems, (2) stimulus control instructions (i.e., eliminating naps during the daytime and avoiding oversleeping during the weekend), and (3) reducing the amount of time he spends in bed trying to fall asleep. Another potentially useful, but as yet untested, strategy may be mindfulness-based meditation. As discussed earlier, worrying about sleep is a major contributor to sleep problems, and, as outlined in Chapter 7, mindfulness-based intervention is an effective strategy to combat worrying and rumination. A summary of useful strategies is depicted in Figure 12.2, with each strategy being discussed in more detail below.

Psychoeducation

Perpetuating mechanisms (e.g., poor sleep hygiene), precipitating events (e.g., stress), and predisposing factors all contribute to the development of

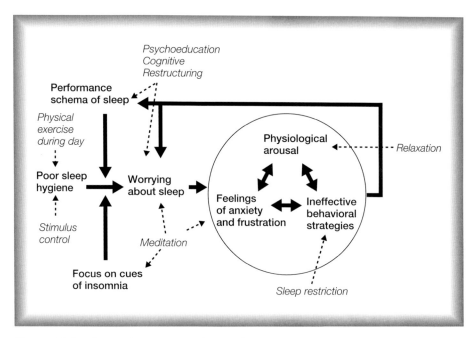

Figure 12.2   Strategies to target insomnia.

insomnia. People with sleep problems often have misconceptions about the typical amount of sleep that is needed, the biological mechanisms underlying sleep, the possible effects of too little sleep, and strategies that are helpful in providing the body with enough sleep. Psychoeducation about these issues is a very effective initial therapeutic strategy. The tendency of patients to overestimate the possible danger of getting too little sleep often perpetuates sleep problems. Sleep is a natural biological process. In the case of primary insomnia, patients paradoxically engage in maladaptive sleep strategies as an attempt to control their sleep. The following is an example of psychoeducation about sleep. It further explains the function of sleep and introduces the idea that many of Tony's attempts to increase his sleep actually exacerbate the problem.

Clinical Example: Psychoeducation about Sleep

Based on our assessment, you meet the diagnostic criteria for primary insomnia. It is called "primary" because there is no other clear reason for your sleep problems, such as depression. The good news is that I believe that your insomnia will likely respond very well to the treatment that we will do. Before we discuss the specific strategies, I would like to take a moment to clarify the function of sleep and discuss with you the strategies that you typically use to control your sleep.

Sleeping is a natural process. If our body requires food, we get hungry and have an urge to eat; if our body requires liquid, we become thirsty, and if our body requires rest, we get tired and have an urge to sleep. These are primary motivations that are guided by lower cortical centers, especially the hypothalamus, which controls the autonomic nervous system. As is implied by the name, the autonomic nervous system works autonomously, without voluntary control and conscious awareness. It controls breathing and body temperature. It also determines if we feel hunger or thirst and controls our sleep. Although these processes are unconscious, they can be disturbed by higher cortical processes, which are under our voluntary control. For example you can deprive yourself of food or water even though you are hungry or thirsty. Similarly, you can disturb your sleep by doing certain things and avoiding others. These are often specific ways of thinking and behaving that you use to help your ability to sleep, but that inadvertently maintain or potentiate your sleep problem.

Before we discuss the behaviors and thoughts that contribute to your sleep problems, I would like to give you some basic information about sleep. Please tell me what you know about sleep. How much sleep do you think people need? What are the consequences of poor sleep? What do you think effective strategies are to overcome sleep problems? (Explore and discuss patient's beliefs about sleep.)

I hope this discussion was helpful. So to summarize, let me make a few points: (1) sleep is a natural process that happens without our voluntary and conscious control; (2) there is no specific minimum amount of sleep that people need; many people need 7–8 hours. Some people need only 5 hours or less, whereas others need 9 or more hours of sleep a night; (3) the amount of sleep that you need is based on your internal (circadian) clock; (4) this circadian clock can be temporarily disturbed by moving to a different time zone (known as jetlag), stress, medications, alcohol, drugs, or your sleep hygiene.

Cognitive restructuring

Psychoeducation about sleep can effectively correct a number of long-held but inaccurate beliefs about sleep. For example, people are often surprised when they learn about the natural occurrence of sleep, the average sleeping time, and the short-term and long-term consequences of sleep deprivation.

Many maladaptive cognitions held by people with insomnia are misconceptions due to errors associated with catastrophic thinking (exaggerating the negative outcomes of an event of situation or blowing things out of proportion). Similar to the cognitive techniques used for other psychiatric problems, the therapist asks guided questions in order to identify and challenge maladaptive thoughts with the goal of encouraging the patient to critically evaluate his/her maladaptive beliefs and assumptions (Socratic dialogue). Worrying about going to sleep is a particularly problematic process because it maintains the problem. The following dialogue illustrates use of the Socratic method to target insomnia.

Clinical Example: Role of Worrying

Therapist: You told me that you worry a lot when you are in bed. Can you tell me what you typically worry about?

Tony: I always worry about not getting enough sleep. I also worry about other things, often related to my studies.

Therapist: When you worry about not getting enough sleep, what are you afraid would happen if you don't get enough sleep?

Tony: It depends. When I have an important project to do the next day, then I worry that I won't be able to do it, or I worry that I would be too tired during the day to do well on an exam.

Therapist: What would happen if you don't do well on the exam or if you can't do the project?

Tony: I guess that I will fail the exam.

Therapist: And then what?

Tony: I will not be able to get my degree.

Therapist: And then what?

Tony: That would be horrible. My parents would be furious.

Therapist: I bet they would be. You see, based on the information about sleep we discussed earlier, this scenario is not very likely. We talked about how, even when you don't feel like you are getting enough sleep, you are usually able to carry out important tasks the next day. However, in order to understand why you think it is so important to get a good night sleep, we need to figure out what you are afraid would happen if you don't get enough sleep. To do this, I would like to explore the worst possible scenario and outcome. So let's assume that you drop out of college and your parents are furious. Then what?

Tony: I don't know. I have not thought things through. I suppose I would have to look for another job.

Therapist: What kind of job?

Tony: I'm not really sure. I would have to think about it. I guess I could work in a restaurant—I used to do this when I started college.

Therapist: I understand that it is not a desirable situation to drop out of college and to disappoint your parents. However, it sounds like even if this did happen, you would find a way to deal with it. Plus, we both know that this is a very unlikely scenario. Would you agree?

Tony: I think so.

Therapist: So, there is a very low probability that this is going to happen, and even if it did, you would manage. The ironic thing is that worrying actually makes it more likely to happen than if you did not worry about it. Worrying about not being able to get enough sleep is the very reason why you don't get enough sleep. So what we need to do is to convince your mind that worrying is not helping. In fact, it makes things worse because worrying interferes with your natural urge to fall asleep.

Tony: So how can I stop worrying?

Therapist: Good question. We will discuss a number of strategies that will reduce your worries. The first important step is to realize that worrying is a big part of the problem. It is also important that you understand that not getting enough sleep is not going to lead to the catastrophic events that you predict. Instead of trying to force your body to sleep, I want to encourage you to start listening to your body and to gently retrain your body to sleep at night.

Stimulus control

Stimulus control strategies address the inhibitory mechanisms that arise due to the conditioned arousal that is associated with insomnia. For example, the situational cues of the bed and bedroom can be associated with sleep problems and the feelings associated with these problems (e.g., anxiety or worries) when the person struggles many nights with sleep problems in the same situation. Stimulus control strategies are based on the assumption that timing and sleep setting (i.e., bedtime and bedroom) are associated with repeated unsuccessful attempts to go to sleep. Over time, these stimuli become conditioned cues for the arousal that maintains insomnia. The goal of stimulus control is to reassociate the bed, bedtime, and bedroom with successful sleep attempts. Stimulus control is a basic and effective behavioral principle to re-establish sleep. There are a number of relatively simple, but very effective strategies to associate sleep and sleepiness with bed and bedroom. The following are effective methods of stimulus control.

Clinical Example: Stimulus Control

1. Go to bed only when you are sleepy.
2. Use your bed for sleeping and sex but nothing else (e.g., reading or watching TV).
3. If you can't sleep for more than 30 minutes, get out of bed, go to a different room and do something that makes you sleepy (e.g., listen to music or read something enjoyable).
4. Get up at the same time every morning.
5. Do not take daytime naps.

Sleep restriction

Sleep restriction strategies target the excessive amount of time that a person spends in bed, attempting to sleep. The goal of sleep restriction is to align the total amount of time spent in bed with the actual needed sleep time. In order to determine the needed sleep time, it is necessary to keep a sleep log for about 2 weeks that lists at the minimum the time the person goes to bed, the time the person went to sleep, and the time the person woke up. Based on this sleep log, the average sleep time is then calculated. The time spent in bed should be restricted to the average sleep time plus 30 minutes. For example, if Tony's sleep log suggests that his average sleep time is 6.5 hours, his time in bed should be 7 hours. Because he decided to set his alarm in the morning to 6 am, he should go to bed every night at 11 pm. Although people vary considerably in the amount of sleep they need, the time in bed should rarely be set below 5 hours. However, the therapist should use a considerable degree of flexibility in determining this time and the time in bed should be adjusted, depending on the success of this method.

Relaxation and meditation

A number of techniques can be helpful to lower physiological arousal associated with anxiety about sleeping. Contrary to folk wisdom, counting sheep is not helpful, because the activity, despite being boring, requires a considerable amount of cognitive activity. Instead, body-focused relaxation strategies appear to be more successful. It should be noted, however, that some relaxation practices, such as progressive muscle relaxation, are most effective when listing to a recorded script (e.g., via an audio track), which is cognitively demanding. Typically, these are not ideal relaxation methods to encourage sleep as they do not lower cognitive arousal. Some alternative methods include toe tensing, imagery, and breathing strategies (see below). These exercises can be done for as long as is desired, but it is generally recommended that they be practiced for approximately 15 minutes before attempting to fall asleep. Depending on the needs of the patient, these practices can easily be combined (i.e., toe tensing while breathing and imagining a pleasant scene). Finally, many of the meditation practices that were discussed in earlier chapters can also be used either as alternatives to or in conjunction with these relaxation practices. Some of the effective strategies are described below.

Clinical Example: Toe Tensing

1. Lie on your back and close your eyes.
2. Pull your 10 toes back toward your face.
3. Slowly count to 10. Relax your toes.
4. Slowly count to 10 again.
5. Repeat the cycle.

Clinical Example: Breathing Exercise

1. Lie on your back and close your eyes.
2. Put one hand on your belly and one hand on your chest. Notice how your belly and your chest moves up and down as you inhale and exhale.
3. Concentrate on your breathing. If other thoughts enter your mind, let them come and go and gently refocus on your breathing.
4. Slow down your breathing by waiting for about two seconds to inhale after your completed the exhalation cycle.

Clinical Example: Imagery

1. Lie on your back with your eyes closed.
2. Imagine yourself in a peaceful place (e.g., a beach, forest, mountain, or meadow).
3. Imagine the sounds, smell, and sights at this place (e.g., the waves of the ocean, the rustling of the leaves in the forest, the cool breeze on the mountain).
4. This experience can be enhanced by listening to an audiotape that includes nature sounds (there are many websites that allow the visitor to freely download nature sounds).

Improving sleep hygiene

Poor sleep hygiene refers to habits that contribute to disturbed sleep. These habits include many of the factors that have already been discussed earlier. Additional factors are described below.

Clinical Example: Improving Your Sleep Hygiene

1. Avoid drinking alcohol and caffeine (including soda and tea) and eating chocolate. If you can't avoid these altogether, don't consume them within 4 to 6 hours before you go to bed. Chocolate and caffeine are psychostimulants. Alcohol initially produces sleepiness, however, there is a stimulant effect a few hours later, when the level of blood alcohol level drops.
2. Avoid sugary, spicy, and heavy foods. If you can't avoid these altogether, don't eat those foods within 4 to 6 hours before you go to bed. Instead, eat light meals that are easy to digest (e.g., chicken, white rice, white bread, cooked vegetables, chicken soup, plain pasta).
3. Give yourself some time to unwind before bed and avoid doing strenuous mental activities right before bedtime.
4. Avoid dealing with emotionally arousing situations, including emotional movies, right before bedtime.
5. Make sure your bedroom is a pleasant environment. Your bed should feel comfortable. The bedroom should have a pleasant (cool) temperature, the right humidity, and it should be well ventilated (i.e., should not be stuffy or smelly).
6. The bedroom should be dark and quiet. If there is a lot of distracting noise, try using earplugs or choose a different room.
7. Establish a sleeping ritual to be implemented before you go to bed. This can include a number of things. You may try any of the following: listen to a particular song or album (e.g., listen to relaxing classical music or jazz), listen to the radio, or take a warm bath. Try not to watch TV because it can be too stimulating. Also, be careful with drinking liquid right before bedtime (such as a warm milk or tea) because this could interrupt your sleep later on if you need to get up in the middle of the night to go to the bathroom. For those who find that drinking liquid immediately before bed does not disturb their sleep, try warm milk and honey.

> **8.** Monitor which sleeping position works best for you. Some people find it easier to lie on their back; others prefer to lie on the right side. When lying on the left side, the heart beat is more noticeable, which can be distracting to some people.

Physical exercise during the day

A surprising and under-researched strategy for insomnia is physical exercise. The general recommendation is to do some physical exercise (such as walking) during the day, but to avoid any heavy exercise too close to bed time. Given the restorative function of sleep, it is very likely that strenuous exercise (e.g., at least thirty minutes on the treadmill or jogging) in the morning or during the day is beneficial for treating insomnia. The simple effect of being physically exhausted combined with performing an activity that supports the body's circadian rhythm is likely to result in shorter sleep onset and improved sleep maintenance.

Empirical Support

The most common treatment for primary insomnia has been pharmaco-therapy, such as hypnotics and antidepressant drugs (Walsh and Schweitzer, 1999). A cost-effective, healthy, and enduring alternative to pharmacother-apy is CBT, as shown in numerous studies (e.g., Morin et al., 2006; for review, see Lacks and Morin, 1992; Edinger and Means, 2005). These studies suggest that psychological and behavioral therapies lead to reliable changes in several sleep parameters of people with primary insomnia or insomnia associated with medical and psychiatric disorders. Furthermore, the sleep improve-ments achieved with these treatments were well maintained over time. For example, a double-blind placebo controlled trial compared CBT (which included psychoeducation, stimulus control, and bedtime restriction) with progressive muscle relaxation and a psychological placebo intervention, con-sisting of a quasi-desensitization treatment designed to eliminate conditioned arousal (Edinger et al., 2001). Seventy-five patients were randomly assigned to one of three treatments that lasted for 6 weeks. Assessments occurred at pretest, post-test, and at the 6-month follow-up. CBT produced greater improvements than the other two groups immediately after the treatment and also at the 6-month follow-up assessment. These improvements were evident in the patient's sleep logs, self-report questionnaires, and recordings by polysomnography.

Recommended Further Readings

Therapist guide

Edinger, J. D., and Carney, C. E (2008). *Overcoming insomnia: A cognitive-behavioral therapy approach. Therapist guide.* New York: Oxford University Press.

Patient guide

Silberman, S., and Morin, C. M. (2009). *The insomnia workbook: A comprehensive guide to getting the sleep you need.* Oakland, CA: New Harbinger.

References

Abeles, M., Solitar, B. M., Pillinger, M. H., and Abeles, A. M. (2008). Update on fibromyalgia therapy. *American Journal of Medicine, 121,* 555–561.

Abramowitz, J. S. (2009). *Getting over OCD: A 10-step workbook for taking back your life.* New York: NYL Guilford Press.

Abramson, L. Y., and Seligman, M. E., (1978). Learned helplessness in humans: Critique and reformulation. *Journal of Abnormal Psychology, 87,* 49–74.

Allen, J. P., Mattson, M. E., Miller, W. R., Tonigan, J. S., Connors, G. J., Rychtarik, R. G., Randall, C. L., Anton, R. F., Kadden, R. M., Litt, M., Cooney, N. L., DiClemente, C. C., Carbonari, J., Zweben, A., Longabaugh, R. H., Stout, R. L., Donovan, D., Babor, T. F., Del Boca, F. K., Rounsaville, B. J., Carroll, K. M., Wirtz, P. W., Bailey, S., Brady, K., Cisler, R., Hester, R. K., Kiylahan, D. R., Nirenberg, T. D., Pate, L. A., and Sturgis, F. (1997). Matching alcoholism treatments to client heterogeneity. Project MATCH post-treatment drinking outcomes. *Journal of Studies on Alcohol, 58,* 7–29.

Allen, J. P., Anton, R. F., Babor, T. F., Carbonari, J., Carroll, K. M., Carroll, K. M., Connors, G. J., Cooney, N. L., Del Boca, F. K., DiClemente, C. C., Donovan, D., Kadden, R. M., Litt, M., Longabaugh, R., Mattson, M., Miller, W. R., Randall, C. L., Rounsaville, B. J., Rychtarik, R. G., Stout, R. L., Tonigan, J. S., Wirtz, P. W., and Zweben, A. (1998). Matching alcoholism treatments to client heterogeneity: Project MATCH three-year drinking outcomes. *Alcoholism: Clinical and Experimental Research, 22,* 1300–1311.

Alloy, L. B., and Clements, C. M. (1992). Illusion of control: Invulnerability to negative affect and depressive symptoms after laboratory and natural stressors. *Journal of Abnormal Psychology, 101,* 234–245.

Altman, L. K. (2006, September 17). Psychiatrist is among five chosen for medical award. *New York Times,* http://www.nytimes.com/2006/09/17/health/17lasker.html.

Ansfield, M. E., Wegner, D. M., and Bowser, R. (1996). Ironic effects of sleep urgency. *Behaviour Research and Therapy, 34,* 523–531.

Antony, M. M., Orsillo, S. M., and Roemer, L. (2001). *Practitioner's guide to empirically based measures of anxiety.* New York: Kluwer Academic/Plenum Publishers.

Antony, M. M., Craske, M. G., and Barlow, D. H. (2006). *Mastering your fears and phobias: Treatments that work*, 2nd edition, workbook. New York: Oxford University Press.

Asmundson, G. J. G., Norton, P. J., and Norton, G. R. (1999). Beyond pain: The role of fear and avoidance in chronicity. *Clinical Psychology Review*, 19, 97–119.

Astin, J. A., Berman, B. M., Bausell, B., Lee, W. L., Hochberg, M., and Forys, K. L. (2003). The efficacy of mindfulness meditation plus Qigong movement therapy in the treatment of fibromyalgia: A randomized controlled trial. *Journal of Rheumatology*, 30, 2257–2262.

Baer, R. (2003). Mindfulness training as a clinical intervention: A conceptual and empirical review. *Clinical Psychology: Science and Practice*, 10, 125–143.

Baker, S. L., Heinrichs, N., Kim, H.-J., and Hofmann, S. G. (2002). The Liebowitz Social Anxiety Scale as a self-report instrument: A preliminary psychometric analysis. *Behaviour Research and Therapy*, 40, 701–715.

Bandura, A. (1977). Self-efficacy: Toward a unifying theory of behavioral change. *Psychological Review*, 84, 191–215.

Barlow, D. H. (1986). Causes of sexual dysfunction: The role of anxiety and cognitive interference. *Journal of Consulting and Clinical Psychology*, 54, 140–148.

Barlow, D. H. (2002). *Anxiety and its disorders: The nature and treatment of anxiety and panic*, 2nd edition. New York: Guilford Press.

Barlow, D. H., and Craske, M. G. (2006). *Mastery of your anxiety and panic*, 3rd edition, workbook. New York: Oxford University Press.

Barlow, D. H., Gorman. J. M., Shear, M. K., and Woods, S. W. (2000). Cognitive-behavioral therapy, imipramine, or their combination for panic disorder: A randomized control trial. *Journal of the American Medical Association*, 283, 2529–2536.

Beck, A. T. (1970). Cognitive therapy: Nature and relation to behavior therapy. *Behavior Therapy*, 1, 184–200.

Beck, A. T. (1979). *Cognitive therapy and the emotional disorders*. New York: New American Library/Meridian.

Beck, A. T., and Alford, B. A. (2009). *Depression: Causes and treatment*, 2nd edition. Philadelphia: University of Pennsylvania Press.

Beck, A. T., Rush, A. J., Shaw, B. F., and Emery, G. (1979). *Cognitive therapy of depression*. New York: Guilford Press.

Bem, D. J. (1967). Self-perception: An alternative interpretation of cognitive dissonance phenomena. *Psychological Review*, 74, 183–200.

Bennett, R. M., Jones, J., Turk, D. C., Russell, I. J., and Matallana, L. (2007). An Internet survey of 2,596 people with fibromyalgia. *BMC Musculoskelettal Disorder*, 8, 27.

Bishop, M., Lau, S., Shapiro, L., Carlson, N. D., Anderson, J., Carmody Segal, Z. V., Abbey, S., Speca, M., Velting, D., and Devins, G. (2004). Mindfulness: A proposed operational definition. *Clinical Psychology: Science and Practice*, 11, 230–241.

Borkovec, T. D., and Hu, S. (1990). The effect of worry on cardiovascular response to phobic imagery. *Behaviour Research and Therapy, 28,* 69–73.

Borkovec, T. D., and Ruscio, A. M. (2001). Psychotherapy for generalized anxiety disorder. *Journal of Clinical Psychiatry, 62,* 37–42.

Borkovec, T. D., and Sharpless, B. (2004). Generalized anxiety disorder: Bringing cognitive behavioral therapy into the valued present. In S. Hayes, V. Follette, and M. Linehan (Eds.), *New directions in behavior therapy* (pp. 209–242). New York: Guilford Press.

Borkovec, T. D., Ray, W. J., and Stöber, J. (1998). Worry: A cognitive phenomenon intimately linked to affective, physiological, and interpersonal behavioral processes. *Cognitive Therapy and Research, 22,* 561–576.

Breslin, F. C., Borsoi, D., Cunningham, J. A., and Koski-Jannes, A. (2001). Help-seeking timeline followback for problem drinkers: Preliminary comparison with agency records of treatment contacts. *Journal of Studies on Alcohol, 62,* 262–267.

Burns, D. D. (1980). *Feeling good: The new mood therapy.* New York: HarperCollins.

Butler, A. C., Chapman, J. E., Forman, E. M., and Beck, A. T. (2006). The empirical status of cognitive-behavioral therapy: A review of meta-analyses. *Clinical Psychology Review, 26,* 17–31.

Campbell-Sills, L., Barlow, D. H., Brown, T. A., and Hofmann, S. G. (2006). Effects of suppression and acceptance on emotional responses of individuals with anxiety and mood disorders. *Behaviour Research and Therapy, 44,* 1251–1263.

Carver, C. S., Scheier, M. F., and Weintraub, K. J. (1989). Assessing coping strategies: A theoretical based approach. *Journal of Personality and Social Psychology, 56,* 267–283.

Chalmers, L. (2007). *Buddha's teachings: Being the sutta nipata, or discourse collection.* London, UK: Oxford University Press.

Chambless, D. L., Caputo, G. C., Jassin, S. E., Gracely, E. J., and Williams, S. (1985). The mobility inventory for agoraphobia. *Behaviour Research and Therapy, 23,* 35–44.

Choy, Y., Fyer, A. J., and Lipsitz, J. D. (2007). Treatment of specific phobia in adults. *Clinical Psychology Review, 27,* 266–286.

Cioffi, D., and Holloway, J. (1993). Delayed costs of suppressed pain. *Journal of Personality and Social Psychology, 64,* 274–282.

Clark, D. M. (1986). A cognitive approach to panic. *Behaviour Research and Therapy, 24,* 461–470.

Clark, D. M., and Wells, A. (1995). A cognitive model of social phobia. In R. G. Heimberg, M. R. Liebowitz, D. A. Hope, and F. R. Schneier (Eds.), *Social phobia: Diagnosis, assessment, and treatment* (pp. 69–93). New York: Guilford Press.

Clark, D. M., Ehlers, A., McManus, F., Hackman, A., Fennell, M., Campbell, H., Flower, T., Davenport, C., and Louis, B. (2003). Cognitive therapy versus fluoxetine in generalized social phobia: A randomized placebo-controlled trial. *Journal of Consulting and Clinical Psychology, 71,* 1058–1067.

Compton, S. N., March, J. S., Brent, D., Albano, A. M., Weersing, V. R., and Curry, J. (2004). Cognitive-behavioral psychotherapy for anxiety and depressive disorders in children and adolescents: An evidence-based medicine review. *Journal of the American Academy of Child and Adolescent Psychiatry, 43,* 930–959.

Cook, M., and Mineka, S. (1989). Observational conditioning of fear to fear-relevant versus fear-irrelevant stimuli in rhesus monkeys. *Journal of Abnormal Psychology, 98,* 448–459.

Coyne, J. C., Pepper, C. M., and Flynn, H. (1999). Significance of prior episodes of depression in two patient populations. *Journal of Consulting and Clinical Psychology, 67,* 76–81.

Craske, M. G., and Barlow, D. H. (2006). *Mastery of your anxiety and panic: Therapist guide.* New York: Oxford University Press.

Craske, M. G., Antony, M. M., and Barlow, D. H. (2006). *Mastering your fears and phobias: Treatments that work,* 2nd edition. New York: Oxford University Press.

Cuijpers, P., Dekker, J., Hollon, S. D., and Andersson, G. (2009). Adding psychotherapy to phamacotherapy in the treatment of depressive disorders in adults: A meta-analysis. *Journal of Clinical Psychiatry, 70,* 1219–1229.

Dalai Lama, and Cutler, H. C. (1998). *The art of happiness: A handbook for living.* New York: Riverhead Books.

Darymple, K. L., and Herbert, J. D. (2007). Acceptance and commitment therapy for generalized social anxiety disorder: A pilot study. *Behavior Modification, 31,* 543–568.

Davey, G. C. L. (2002). "Nonspecific" rather than "nonassociative" pathways to phobias: A commentary on Poulton and Menzies. *Behaviour Research and Therapy, 40,* 151–158.

Davidson, J. R. T., Foa, E. B., Huppert, J. D., Keefe, F., Franklin, M., Compton, J., Zhao, N., Connor, K., Lynch, T. R., and Kishore, G. (2004). Fluoxetine, comprehensive cognitive behavioral therapy, and placebo in generalized social phobia. *Archives of General Psychiatry, 61,* 1005–1013.

DeRubeis, R. J., Hollon, S. D., Amsterdam, J. D., Shelton, R. C., Young, P. R., Salomon, R. M., O'Reardon, J. P., Lovett, M. L., Gladis, M. M., Brown, L. L., and Gallop, R. (2005). Cognitive therapy vs. medications in the treatment of moderate to severe depression. *Archives of General Psychiatry, 62,* 409–416.

Dobson, K. S. (1989). A meta-analysis of the efficacy of cognitive therapy for depression. *Journal of Consulting and Clinical Psychology, 57,* 414–419.

Dobson, K. S., Hollon, S. D., Dimidjian, S., Schmaling, K. B., Kohlenberg, R. J., Gallop, R. J., Rizvi, S. L., Gollan, J. K., Dunner, D. L., and Jacobson, N. S. (2008). Randomized trial of behavioral activation, cognitive therapy, and antidepressant medication in the prevention of relapse and recurrence in major depression. *Journal of Consulting and Clinical Psychology, 76,* 468–477.

Eccleston, C., Williams, A. C. D., and Morley, S. (2009). Psychological therapies for the management of chronic pain (excluding headache) in adults. *Cochrane Database Systematic Review, 108.*

Edinger, J. D., and Carney, C. E. (2008). *Overcoming insomnia: A cognitive-behavioral therapy approach (workbook)*. New York: Oxford University Press.

Edinger, J. D., and Means, M. K. (2005). Cognitive-behavioral therapy for primary insomnia. *Clinical Psychology Review, 25*, 539–558.

Edinger, J. D., Wohlgemuth, W. K., Radtke, R. A., Marsh, G. R., and Quillian, R. E. (2001). Cognitive behavioral therapy for treatment of chronic primary insomnia. A randomized controlled trial. *Journal of the American Medical Association, 285*, 1865–1864.

Ehlers, A., Hofmann, S. G., Herda, C. A., and Roth, W. T. (1994). Clinical characteristics of driving phobia. *Journal of Anxiety Disorders, 8*, 323–339.

Elkin, I., Gibbons, R. D., Shea, M. T., Sotzky, S. M., Watklins, J. T., Pilkonis, P. A., and Hedeker, D. (1995). Initial severity and differential treatment outcome in the National Institute of Mental Health Treatment of Depression Collaborative Research Program. *Journal of Consulting and Clinical Psychology, 63*, 841–847.

Ellis, A. (1962). *Reason and emotion in psychotherapy*. New York: Lyle Stuart.

Epstein, E. E., and McCrady, B. S. (2009). *Overcoming alcohol use problems: A cognitive-behavioral treatment program workbook*. New York: Oxford University Press.

Festinger, L. (1957). *A theory of cognitive dissonance*. Stanford, CA: Stanford University Press.

Festinger, L., and Carlsmith, J. M. (1959). Cognitive consequences of forced compliance. *Journal of Abnormal and Social Psychology, 58*, 203–210.

Field, A. P. (2006). Is conditioning a useful framework for understanding the development and treatment of phobias? *Clinical Psychology Review, 26*, 857–875.

First, M. B., Spitzer, R. L., Gibbon, M., and Williams, J. B. W. (1995). *Structured Clinical Interview for DSM-IV Axis I Disorder—Patient Edition (SCID-IV)*. New York: Biometrics Research Department, New York State Psychiatric Institute.

Foa, E. B., and Kozak, M. J. (1986). Emotional processing of fear: Exposure to corrective information. *Psychological Bulletin, 99*, 20–35.

Foa, E. B., and Kozak, M. J. (2004). *Mastery of obsessive-compulsive disorder: A cognitive-behavioral therapist guide. Treatments that work*. New York: Oxford University Press.

Fordyce, W. E. (1976). *Behavioral methods for chronic pain and illness*. St. Louis, MO: Mosby.

Fordyce, W. E., Shelton, J. L., and Dundore, D. E. (1982). The modification of avoidance learning in pain behaviors. *Journal of Behavioral Medicine, 5*, 405–414.

Freeston, M. H., Rhéaume, J., and Ladouceur, R. (1996). Correcting faulty appraisals of obsessional thoughts. *Behaviour Research and Therapy, 34*, 433–446.

Gamsa, A. (1994a). The role of psychological factors in chronic pain: I. A half century of study. *Pain, 57*, 5–15.

Gamsa, A. (1994b). The role of psychological factors in chronic pain: II. A critical appraisal. *Pain, 57*, 17–29.

Garfield, E. (1992). A citationist perspective of psychology. Part 1: Most cited papers, 1986–1990. *APS Observer, 5*, 8–9.

Gilbert, D. (2006). *Stumbling on happiness.* New York: Alfred Knopf.

Gloaguen, V., Cottraux, J., Cucherat, M., and Blackburn, I. (1998). A meta-analysis of the effects of cognitive therapy in depressed patients. *Journal of Affective Disorders, 49,* 59–72.

Glombiewski, J. A., Sawyer, A. T., Gutermann, J., Koenig, K., Rief, W., and Hofmann, S. G. (2010). Psychological treatments for fibromyalgia: A meta-analysis. *Pain, 151,* 280–295.

Goldenberg, D. L., Burckhardt, C., and Crofford, L. (2004). Management of fibromyalgia syndrome. *Journal of the American Medical Association, 292,* 2388–2395.

Gotlib, I. H., and Hammen, C. L. (2009). *Handbook of depression,* 2nd edition. New York: Guilford Press.

Greenberger, D., and Padesky, C. A. (1995). *Mind over mood: Change how you feel by changing the way you think.* New York: Guilford.

Gross, J. J. (2002). Emotion regulation: Affective, cognitive, and social consequences. *Psychophysiology, 39,* 281–291.

Gross, J. J., and John, O. P. (2003). Individual differences in two emotion regulation processes: Implications for affect, relationships, and well-being. *Journal of Personality and Social Psychology, 85,* 348–362.

Gross, J. J., and Levenson, R. W. (1997). Hiding feelings: The acute effects of inhibiting negative and positive emotion. *Journal of Abnormal Psychology, 106,* 95–103.

Guastella, A. J., Richardson, R., Lovibond, P. F., Rapee, R. M., Gaston, J. E., Mitchell, P., and Dadds, M. R. (2008). A randomized controlled trial of d-cycloserine enhancement of exposure therapy for social anxiety disorder. *Biological Psychiatry, 63,* 544–549.

Harvey, A. G. (2002). A cognitive model of insomnia. *Behaviour Research and Therapy, 40,* 860–893.

Hauser, W., Bernardy, K., Uceyler, N., and Sommer, C. (2009). Treatment of fibromyalgia syndrome with antidepressants: A meta-analysis. *Journal of the American Medical Association, 301,* 198–209.

Hayes, S. C. (2004). Acceptance and commitment therapy, relational frame theory, and the third wave of behavior therapy. *Behavior Therapy, 35,* 639–665.

Heiman, J., and LoPiccolo, J. (1992). *Becoming orgasmic.* New York: Fireside.

Higgins, S. T., and Silverman, K. (Eds.) (1999). *Motivating behavior change among illicit-drug abusers: Research on contingency-management interventions.* Washington, DC: American Psychological Association.

Hodgson, R. J., and Rachman, S. (1977). Obsessive compulsive complaints. *Behaviour Research and Therapy, 15,* 389–395.

Hoffman, B. M., Papas, R. K., Chatkoff, D. K., and Kerns, R. D. (2007). Meta-analysis of psychological interventions for chronic low back pain. *Health Psychology, 26,* 1–9.

Hofmann, S. G. (2007a). Cognitive factors that maintain social anxiety disorder: A comprehensive model and its treatment implications. *Cognitive Behaviour Therapy, 36,* 195–209.

Hofmann, S. G. (2007b). Enhancing exposure-based therapy from a translational research perspective. *Behaviour Research and Therapy, 45,* 1987–2001.

Hofmann, S. G. (2008a). Cognitive processes during fear acquisition and extinction in animals and humans: Implications for exposure therapy of anxiety disorders. *Clinical Psychology Review, 28,* 200–211.

Hofmann, S. G. (2008b). ACT: New wave or Morita Therapy? *Clinical Psychology: Science and Practice, 15,* 280–285.

Hofmann, S. G., and Asmundson, G. J. (2008). Acceptance and mindfulness-based therapy: New wave or old hat? *Clinical Psychology Review, 28,* 1–16.

Hofmann, S. G., and DiBartolo, P. M. (2010). *Social anxiety: Clinical, developmental, and social perspectives,* 2nd edition. New York: Elsevier/Academic Press.

Hofmann S. G., and Otto, M. W. (2008). *Cognitive-behavior therapy of social anxiety disorder: Evidence-based and disorder specific treatment techniques.* New York: Routledge.

Hofmann, S. G., and Smits, J. A. J. (2008). Cognitive-behavioral therapy for adult anxiety disorders: A meta-analysis of randomized placebo-controlled trials. *Journal of Clinical Psychiatry, 69,* 621–632.

Hofmann, S. G., Ehlers, A., and Roth, W. T. (1995). Conditioning theory: A model for the etiology of public speaking anxiety? *Behaviour Research and Therapy, 33,* 567–571.

Hofmann, S. G., Barlow, D. H., Papp, L. A., Detweiler, M., Ray, S., Shear, M. K., Woods, S. W., and Gorman, J. M. (1998). Pretreatment attrition in a comparative treatment outcome study on panic disorder. *American Journal of Psychiatry, 155,* 43–47.

Hofmann, S. G., Heinrichs, N., and Moscovitch, D. A. (2004). The nature and expression of social phobia: Toward a new classification. *Clinical Psychology Review, 24,* 769–797.

Hofmann, S. G., Moscovitch, D. A., Litz, B. T., Kim, H.-J., Davis, L., and Pizzagalli, D. A. (2005). The worried mind: Autonomic and prefrontal activation during worrying. *Emotion, 5,* 464–475.

Hofmann S. G., Meuret, A. E., Smits, J. A. J., Simon, N. M., Pollack, M. H., Eisenmenger, K., Shiekh, M., and Otto, M. W. (2006). Augmentation of exposure therapy for social anxiety disorder with d-cycloserine. *Archives of General Psychiatry, 63,* 298–304.

Hofmann, S. G., Sawyer, A. T., Korte, K. J., and Smits, J. A. J. (2009). Is it beneficial to add pharmacotherapy to cognitive-behavioral therapy when treating anxiety disorders? A meta-analytic review. *International Journal of Cognitive Therapy, 2,* 160–175.

Hofmann, S. G., Sawyer, A. T., Witt, A., and Oh, D. (2010). The effect of mindfulness-based therapy on anxiety and depression: A meta-analytic review. *Journal of Consulting and Clinical Psychology, 78,* 169–183.

Hollon, S. D., DeRubeis, R. J., Shelton, R. C., Amsterdam, J. D., Salomon, R. M., O'Reardon, J. P., Lovett, M. L., Young, P. R., Haman, K. L., Freeman, B. B., and Gallop, R. (2005). Prevention of relapse following cognitive therapy vs.

medications in moderate to severe depression. *Archives of General Psychiatry*, 62, 417–422.

Hope, D. A., Heimberg, R. G., and Turk, C. L. (2010). *Managing social anxiety: A cognitive-behavioral therapy approach*, 2nd edition, workbook. New York: Oxford University Press.

Horwitz, A. V., Wakefield, J. C., and Spitzer, R. L. (2007). *The loss of sadness: How psychiatry transformed normal sorrow into depressive disorder*. New York: Oxford University Press.

Joiner, E., Van Orden, K. A., Witte, T. K., and Rudd, D. (2009). *The interpersonal theory of suicide: Guidance for working with suicidal clients*. Washington, DC: American Psychological Association.

Kabat-Zinn, J. (1994). *Wherever you go there you are*. New York: Hyperion.

Kabat-Zinn, J. (2003). Mindfulness-based interventions in context: Past, present, and future. *Clinical Psychology: Science and Practice, 10*, 144–156.

Kaplan, H. S. (1987). *The illustrated manual of sex therapy*, 2nd edition. New York: Brunner/Mazel.

Kaplan, H. S. (1979). *Disorders of sexual desire*. New York: Brunner/Mazel.

Kessler, R. C., Berglund, P., Demler, O., Jin, R., Koretz, D., Merikangas, K. R., Rush, A. J., Walters, E. E., and Wang, P. S. (2003). The epidemiology of major depressive disorder: Results from the National Comorbidity Survey Replication (NCS-R). *Journal of the American Medical Association, 289*, 3095–3105.

Kessler, R. C., Berglund, P., Demler, O., Jin, R., Merikangas, K. R., and Walters, E. E. (2005). Lifetime prevalence and age-of-onset distribution of DSM-IV disorders in the National Comorbidity Survey Replication. *Archives of General Psychiatry, 62*, 593–602.

Klein, D. F. (1964). Delineation of two drug-responsive anxiety syndromes. *Psychopharmacologia, 5*, 397–408.

Klein, D. F., and Klein, H. M. (1989). The definition and psychopharmacology of spontaneous panic and phobia. In P. Tyrer (Ed.), *Psychopharmacology of anxiety* (pp. 135–162). New York: Oxford University Press.

Klein, D. F. (1993). False suffocation alarms, spontaneous panics, and related conditions. An integrative hypothesis. *Archives of General Psychiatry, 50*, 306–317.

Koerner, N., Rogojanski, J., and Antony, M. M. (2010). Specific phobias. In S. G. Hofmann and M. Reineck (Eds.), *Cognitive-behavioral therapy with adults* (pp. 60–77). Cambridge, UK: Cambridge University Press.

Kushner, M. G., Kim, S. W., Donahue, C., Thurus, P., Adson, D., Kotlyar, M., McCabe, J., Peterson, J., and Foa, E. B. (2007). D-cycloserine augmented exposure therapy for obsessive-compulsive disorder. *Biological Psychiatry, 62*, 835–858.

Lacks, P., and Morin, C. (1992). Recent advances in the assessment and treatment of insomnia. *Journal of Consulting and Clinical Psychology, 60*, 586–594.

Ladouceur, R., Gosslin, P., and Dugas, M. J. (2000). Experimental manipulation of intolerance of uncertainty: A study of a theoretical model of worry. *Behaviour Research and Therapy, 38*, 933–941.

Laumann, E. O., Gagnon, J. H., Michael, R. T., and Michaels, S. (1994). *The social organization of sexuality: Sexual practices in the United States*. Chicago: University of Chicago Press.

Laumann, E. O., Paik, A., and Rosen, R. C. (1999). Sexual dysfunction in the United States. Prevalence and Predictors. *Journal of the American Medical Association, 281*, 537–544.

Lazarus, R. S. (1993). Coping theory and research: Past, present, and future. *Psychosomatic Medicine, 55*, 234–247.

Leahy, R. L. (2005). *The worry cure: Seven steps to stop worry from stopping you*. New York: Harmony Books.

Leahy, R. L. (2010). *Beat the blues before they beat you: How to overcome depression*. Carlsbad, CA: Hay House.

LeBlanc, M., Merette, C., Savard, J., Ivers, H., Baillargeon, L., and Morin, C. M. (2006). Incidence and risk factors of insomnia in a population-based sample. *Sleep, 32*, 1027–1037.

LeDoux, J. (1996). *The emotional brain: The mysterious underpinnings of emotional life*. New York: Touchstone.

Ley, R. A. (1985). Blood, breath and fears: A hyperventilation theory of panic attacks and agoraphobia. *Clinical Psychology Review, 5*, 271–285.

Liebowitz, M. R. (1987). Social phobia. *Modern Problems in Pharmacopsychiatry, 22*, 141–173.

Lovibond, P. F. (2004). Cognitive processes in extinction. *Learning and Memory, 11*, 495–500.

MacLeod, A. K., and Cropley, M. L. (1996). Anxiety, depression, and the anticipation of future positive and negative experiences. *Journal of Abnormal Psychology, 105*, 286–289.

MacLeod, C., Rutherford, E., Campbell, L., Ebsworthy, G., and Holker, L. (2002). Selective attention and emotional vulnerability: Assessing the causal basis of their association through the experimental manipulation of attentional bias. *Journal of Abnormal Psychology, 111*, 107–123.

March, J. S. (2004). Fluoxetine, cognitive-behavioral therapy, and their combination for adolescents with depression: Treatment for Adolescents with Depression Study (TADS) randomized controlled trial. *Journal of the American Medical Association, 292*, 807–820.

Marcus, D. A. (2009). Fibromyalgia: Diagnosis and treatment options. *Gender Medicine, 6 (Suppl. 2)*, 139–151.

Masters, W. H., and Johnson, V. E. (1970). *Human sexual inadequacy*. Boston: Little, Brown.

McCracken, L. M. (1998). Learning to live with the pain: Acceptance of pain predicts adjustment in persons with chronic pain. *Pain, 74*, 21–27.

McCracken, L. M., Carson, J. W., Eccleton, C., and Keefe, F. J. (2004). Acceptance and change in the context of chronic pain. *Pain, 109*, 4–7.

McNally, R. J. (1994). *Panic disorder: A critical analysis*. New York: Guilford Press.

McNally, R. J. (2011). *What is mental illness?* Cambridge, MA: Belknap Press of Harvard University Press.

Melbourne Academic Mindfulness Interest Group (2006). Mindfulness-based psychotherapies: A review of conceptual foundations, empirical evidence and practical considerations. *Australian and New Zealand Journal of Psychiatry, 40,* 285–294.

Melnik, T., Soares, B., and Nasello, A. G. (2007). Psychosocial interventions for erectile dysfunction. *Cochrane Database of Systematic Reviews, 3,* DOI: 10.1002/14651858.

Melzack, R., and Wall, P. (1982). *The challenge of pain.* London: Penguin.

Menzulis, A., H., Abramson, L. Y., Hyde, J. S., and Hankin, B. L. (2004). Is there a universal positive bias in attributions? A meta-analytic review of individual, developmental, and cultural difference in the self-serving attributional bias. *Psychological Bulletin, 130,* 711–747.

ret, A. M., Rosenfield, D., Seidel, A., Bhaskara, L., and Hofmann, S. G. (2010). Respiratory and cognitive mediators of treatment change in panic disorder: evidence for intervention specificity. *Journal of Consulting and Clinical Psychology, 78,* 691–704.

Meyer, T. J., Miller, M. L., Metzger, R. L., and Borkovec, T. D. (1990). Development and validation of the Penn State Worry Questionnaire. *Behaviour Research and Therapy, 28,* 487–495.

Miller, W. R., and Rollnick, S. (1991). *Motivational interviewing: Preparing people to change addictive behaviors.* New York: Guilford Press.

Mineka, S., and Öhman, A. (2002). Born to fear: Non-associative versus associative factors in the etiology of phobias. *Behaviour Research and Therapy, 40,* 173–184.

Mischel, W. (1979). On the interface of cognition and personality beyond the person-situation debate. *American Psychologist, 34,* 740–754.

Mogg, K., and Bradley, B. P. (1998). A cognitive-motivational analysis of anxiety. *Behavior Research and Therapy, 36,* 809–848.

Mogg, K., and Bradley, B. P. (2006). Time course of attentional bias for fear-relevant pictures in spider-fearful individuals. *Behaviour Research and Therapy, 44,* 1241–1250.

Morin, C. M., Bootzin, R. R., Buysse, D. J., Edinger, J. D., Espie, C. A., and Lichtenstein, K. L. (2006). Psychological and behavioral treatment of insomnia: update of the recent evidence (1998–2004). *Sleep, 29,* 1396–1414.

Morita, S. (1998/1874). *Morita therapy and the true nature of anxiety-based disorders (Shinkeishitsu).* Albany: State University of New York.

Mowrer, O. H. (1939). Stimulus response theory of anxiety. *Psychological Review, 46,* 553–565.

Myers, K. M., and Davis, M. (2002). Behavioral and neural analysis of extinction. *Neuron, 36,* 567–684.

National Institute on Alcohol Abuse and Alcoholism (2011). What is a standard drink? Available at http://pubs.niaaa.nih.gov/publications/practitioner/pocketguide/pocket_guide2.htm.

Nolen-Hoeksema, S., and Morrow, J. (1993). Effects of rumination and distraction on naturally occurring depressed mood. *Cognition and Emotion, 7*, 561–570.

Norberg, M. M., Krystal, J. H., and Tolin, D. F. (2008). A meta-analysis of d-cycloserine and the facilitation of fear extinction and exposure therapy. *Biological Psychiatry, 63*, 1118–1126.

Nowinski, J., and Baker, S. (1998). *The twelve-step facilitation handbook: A systematic approach to early recovery from alcohol and addiction.* San Francisco, CA: Josey-Bass.

Ochsner, K. N., Bungem, S. A., Gross, J. J., and Gabrieli, J. D. (2002). Rethinking feelings: An fMRI study of the cognitive regulation of emotion. *Journal of Cognitive Neuroscience, 14*, 1215–1229.

Öhman, A., Flykt, A., and Esteves, F. (2001). Emotion drives attention: Detecting the snake in the grass. *Journal of Experimental Psychology, 130*, 466–478.

O'Leary, K. D., and Beach, S. R. H. (1999). Marital therapy: A viable treatm for depression and marital discord. *American Journal of Psychiatry,* 183–186.

Öst, L. G., Fellenius, J., and Sterner, U. (1991). Applied tension, exposure ir iv and tension-only in the treatment of blood phobia. *Behaviour Research a Therapy, 29*, 561–574.

Otis, J. D. (2007). *Managing chronic pain: A cognitive-behavioral therapy approach, workbook.* New York: Oxford University Press.

Otto, M. W., Tolin, D. F., Simon, N. M., Pearlson, G. D., Basden, S., Meunier, S. A., Hofmann, S. G., Eisenmenger, K., Krystal, J. H., and Pollack, M. H. (2010). Efficacy of d-cycloserine for enhancing response to cognitive-behavior therapy for panic disorder. *Biological Psychiatry, 67*, 365–370.

Poulton, R., and Menzies, R. G. (2002a). Non-associative fear acquisitions: A review of the evidence from retrospective and longitudinal research. *Behaviour Research and Therapy, 40*, 127–149.

Poulton, R., and Menzies, R. G. (2002b). Fears born and bred: Toward a more inclusive theory of fear acquisition. *Behaviour Research and Therapy, 40*, 197–208.

Prochaska, J. O., DiClemente, C. C., and Norcross, J. C. (1992). In search of how people change: Applications to addictive behaviors. *American Psychologist, 47*, 1102–1114.

Rachman, S. (1991). Neoconditioning and the classical theory of fear acquisition. *Clinical Psychology Review, 11*, 155–173.

Rachman, S. (1993). Obsessions, responsibility, and guilt. *Behaviour Research and Therapy, 31*, 149–154.

Rachman, S. (1998). A cognitive theory of obsessions: Elaborations. *Behaviour Research and Therapy, 36*, 385–401.

Rapee, R. N., and Heimberg, R. G. (1997). A cognitive-behavioral model of anxiety in social phobia. *Behaviour Research and Therapy, 35*, 741–756.

Rassin, E., and Koster, E. (2003). The correlation between thought–action fusion and religiousity in a normal sample. *Behaviour Research and Therapy, 41*, 361–368.

Reiss, S. (1991). Expectancy model of fear, anxiety and panic. *Clinical Psychology Review, 11*, 141–153.

Ressler, K. J., Rothbaum, B. O., Tannenbaum, L., Anderson, P., Graap, K., Zimand, E., Hodges, L., and Davis, M. (2004). Cognitive enhancers as adjuncts to psychotherapy: Use of d-cycloserine in phobic individuals to facilitate extinction of fear. *Archives of General Psychiatry, 61*, 1136–1144.

Reynolds, C. F., Dew, M. A., Pollock, B. G., Mulsant, B. H., Miller, F. E., Houck, P. R., Mazumdar, S., Butters, M. A., Stack, J. A., Schlernitzauer, M. A., Whyte, E. M., Gildengers, A., Karp, J., Lenze, E., Szanto, K., Bensasi, S., and Kupfer, D.J. (2006). Maintenance treatment of major depression in old age. *New England Journal of Medicine, 354*, 1130–1138.

Richmond, J., Berman, B. M., Docherty, J. P., Goldstein, L. B., Kaplan, G., Keil, J. E., Krippner, S., Lyne, S., Mosteller, F., Oconnor, B. B., Rudy, E. B., Schatzberg, A. F., Friedman, R., Altman, F., Benson, H., Elliott, J. M., Ferguson, J. H., Gracely, R., Greene, A., Haddox, J. D., Hall, W. H., Hauri, P. J., Helzner, E. C., Kaufmann, P. G., Kiley, J. P., Leveck, M. D., McCutchen, C. B., Monjan, A. A., Pillemer, S. R., MacArthur, J. D., Sherman, C., Spencer, J., and Varricchio, C. G. (1996). Integration of behavioral and relaxation approaches into the treatment of chronic pain and insomnia. *Journal of the American Medical Association, 276*, 313–318.

Rosen, R. C., and Leiblum, S. R. (1995). Treatment of sexual disorders in the 1990s: An integrated approach. *Journal of Consulting and Clinical Psychology, 63*, 877–890.

Rosen, R. C., Ryley, A., Wagner, G., Oserlow, I. H., Kirpatik, J., and Mishra, A. (1997). The international index of erectile function (IIEF): A multidimensional scale for the assessment of erective dysfunction. *Urology, 49*, 822–830.

Roth, W. T., Wilhelm, F. H., and Pettit, D. (2005). Are current theories of panic falsifieable? *Psychological Bulletin, 131*, 173–192.

Rothbaum, B. O., Hodges, L. F., Smith, S., Lee, J. H., and Price, L. (2000) A controlled study of virtual reality exposure therapy for the fear of flying. *Journal of Consulting and Clinical Psychology, 68*, 1020–1026.

Rusting, C. L., and Nolen-Hoeksema, S. (1998). Regulating responses to anger: Effects of rumination and distraction on angry mood. *Journal of Personality and Social Psychology, 74*, 790–803.

Salkovskis, P. M. (1985). Obsessional-compulsive problems: A cognitive-behavioural analysis. *Behaviour Research and Therapy, 23*, 571–583.

Salkovskis, P. M., and Harrison, J. (1984). Abnormal and normal obsessions: A replication. *Behaviour Research and Therapy, 22*, 549–552.

Schachter, S., and Singer, J. E. (1962). Cognitive, social, and physiological determinants of emotional state. *Psychological Review, 69*, 379–399.

Segal, Z. V., Williams, J. M. G., and Teasdale, J. D. (2002). *Mindfulness-based cognitive therapy for depression: A new approach to preventing relapse.* New York: Guilford Press.

Segal, Z. V., Kennedy, S., Gemar, M., Hood, K., Pedersen, R., and Buis, T. (2006). Cognitive reactivity to sad mood provocation and the prediction of depressive relapse. *Archives of General Psychiatry, 63*, 749–755.

Seligman, M. E. P. (1971). Phobias and preparedness. *Behavior Therapy, 2,* 307–320.

Shafran, R., Thordarson, D., and Rachman, S. (1996). Thought–action fusion in obsessive compulsive disorder. *Journal of Anxiety Disorders, 10*, 379–391.

Shear, M. K., Brown, T. A., Barlow, D. H., Money, R., Sholomksas, D. E., Woods, S. W., Gorman, J. M., and Papp, L. A. (1997). Multicenter collaborative panic disorder severity scale. *American Journal of Psychiatry, 154*, 1571–1575.

Silberman, S., and Morin, C. M. (2009). *The insomnia workbook: A comprehensive guide to getting the sleep you need.* Oakland, CA: New Harbinger.

Smits, A. J., and Hofmann (2009). A meta-analytic review of the effects of psycho-therapy control conditions for anxiety disorders. *Psychological Medicine, 39*, 229–239.

Solomon, D. A., Keller, M. B., Leon, A. C., Mueller, T. I., Lavori, P. W., Shea, M. T., et al. (2000). Multiple recurrences of major depressive disorder. *American Journal of Psychiatry, 157*, 229–233.

Spaeth, M. (2009). Epidemiology, costs, and the economic burden of fibromyalgia. *Arthritis Research and Therapy, 11*, 117.

Stinson, F. S., Dawson, D. A., Chou, S. P., Smith, S., Goldstein, R. B., June Ruan, W., and Grant, B. F. (2007). The epidemiology of DSM-IV specific phobia in the USA: Results from the national epidemiologic survey on alcohol and related conditions. *Psychological Medicine, 37*, 1047–1059.

Sullivan, M. J. L., Thorn, B. E., Haythornthwaite, J. A., Keefe, F., Martin, M., Bradley, L., and Lefebvre, J. C. (2001). Theoretical perspectives on the relation between catastrophizing and pain. *Clinical Journal of Pain, 17*, 52–64.

Szasz, T. (1961). *The myth of mental illness: Foundations of a theory of personal conduct.* New York: Hoeber-Harper.

Thorn, B. F. (2004). *Cognitive therapy for chronic pain: A step-by-step guide.* New York: Guilford.

van Oppen, P., and Arntz, A. (1994). Cognitive therapy for obsessive-compulsive disorder. *Behaviour Research and Therapy, 32*, 79–88.

Waddell, G. (1987). A new clinical model for the treatment of low back pain. *Spine, 12*, 632–644.

Walsh, J. K., and Schweitzer, P. K. (1999). Ten-year trends in the pharmacologic treatment of insomnia. *Sleep, 22*, 371–375.

Watson, J. B., and Rayner, R. (1920). Conditioned emotional reactions. *Journal of Experimental Psychology, 3*, 1–34.

Wegner, D. M. (1994). *White bears and other unwanted thoughts: Suppression, obses-sion, and the psychology of mental control.* New York: Guilford Press.

Wakefield, J. C. (1992). The concept of mental disorder: On the boundary between biological facts and social values. *American Psychologist, 47*, 373–388.

Weissman, M., Markowitz, J., and Klerman, G. L. (2007). *Clinician's quick guide to interpersonal psychotherapy*. New York: Oxford University Press.

Wells, A. (2009). *Metacognitive therapy for anxiety and depression*. New York: Guilford Press.

Whisman, M. A., and Bruce, M. L. (1999). Marital dissatisfaction and incidence of major depressive episode in a community sample. *Journal of Abnormal Psychology, 108*, 674–678.

Whittal, M. L., Thordarson, D. S., and McLean, P. D. (2005). Treatment of obsessive-compulsive disorder: Cognitive behavior therapy vs. exposure and response prevention. *Behaviour Research and Therapy, 43*, 1559–1576.

Wilhelm, S., Buhlmann, U., Tolin, D.F , Meunier, S. A., Pearlson, G. D., Reese, H. E , Cannistraro, P., Jenike, M. A., and Rauch, S. L. (2008). Augmentation of behavior therapy with d-cycloserine for obsessive-compulsive disorder. *American Journal of Psychiatry, 165*, 335–341.

Wolitzky-Taylor, K. B., Horowitz, J. D., Powers, M., and Telch, M. J. (2008). Psychological approaches in the treatment of specific phobias: A meta-analysis. *Clinical Psychology Review, 28*, 1021–1037.

Wolpe, J., and Lang, P. J. (1964). A fear survey schedule for use in behaviour therapy. *Behavioural Research and Therapy, 2*, 27–30.

Zilbergeld, B. (1992). *The new male sexuality*. New York: Bantam Books.

Index

An Introduction to Modern CBT: Psychological Solutions to Mental Health Problems, First Edition.
Stefan G. Hofmann. © 2011 Stefan G. Hofmann. Published 2011 by Blackwell Publishing Ltd.